BUSINESS LAW

BUSINESS LAW

S.P. Sharma

Associate Professor
Department of Commerce
VVN Degree College, VV Puram
Bangalore

I.K. International Publishing House Pvt. Ltd.

NEW DELHI • BANGALORE

Published by
I.K. International Publishing House Pvt. Ltd.
S-25, Green Park Extension
Uphaar Cinema Market
New Delhi – 110 016 (India)
E-mail: info@ikinternational.com
Website: www.ikbooks.com

ISBN 978-93-81141-82-3

10 9 8 7 6 5 4 3 2 1

Published by Krishan Makhijani for I.K. International Publishing House Pvt. Ltd., S-25, Green Park Extension, Uphaar Cinema Market, New Delhi – 110 016 and Printed by Rekha Printers Pvt. Ltd., Okhla Industrial Area, Phase II, New Delhi – 110 020.

I dedicate this work of mine to

Sri Sai Baba of Shirdi

and seek his blessings for my future prospects.

—S.P. Sharma

Preface

The basic knowledge of commercial law is very essential for a businessman. One should be familiar with the changing scenario in the field of business law. As the corporate sector and other business establishments have increased not only in numbers but also in their area of operations they are showing tremendous growth, this has essentially made necessary for everybody to have the knowledge of business law. The present book deals with Contract Act in a very lucid manner and it will help the beginner to understand the basics of contract in business clearly.

The book is specially meant for the students of sixth semester B.Com. stream. The latest additions are made wherever required particularly in case of Cyber Laws and Competition Laws.

The main sources of the material are from the institutional websites and the publications, I deeply place my indebtedness to the scholars and earlier authors in the field of mercantile law. I also express my gratitude to all of them.

S.P. Sharma

Acknowledgements

This project could not have succeeded without the help and support of many people who truly care about nurturing the effective needs of students.

My special thanks to all my friends, students and colleagues and my sincere thanks to the members of VVN Trust, the Principal, my senior colleague of my department. I sincerely place my gratitude and respect to Dr. Janardhan - Dean and Chairman, Canara Bank School of Management, Bangalore University, Bangalore for his support in my academic works.

I wish to place my sincere regards to Dr. M. Ramachandra Gowda, Dean and Chairman of Department of Commerce, P.G. Studies in Commerce, Bangalore University, Bangalore, and Dr. K. Eresi, Senior Professor in Department of Commerce, P.G. Studies in Commerce, Bangalore University, Bangalore, who have always supported me in my academic works. I wish to acknowledge my sincere regards to my friend Prof. K.M. Nagaraj, Department of Commerce, BES College, Jayanagar, Bangalore for his continuous support in all my academic pursuits.

I wish to place on record my sincere thanks to my wife Smt. Manju Sharma, my son Pavan Pal Sharma and my daughter Poonam Pal Sharma for all the support provided while completing the present work. I would also like to place my regards and respects to my parents and Sai Baba of Shirdi for all the blessings throughout.

I would be failing if the acknowledgements are not extended to Mr. Srinivas for his neat and flawless typeset work.

Suggestions from the learned faculty are most welcome to improvise the present work in future.

S.P. Sharma

SYLLABUS

Objective:

To familiarise the students with Business Law and its interpretations.

UNIT-I **4 hours**

Introduction: Meaning and Scope of Business Law - Sources of Indian Business Law.

UNIT-II **30 hours**

Indian Contract Act of 1872: Definition - types of contract - essentials - offer, acceptance, consideration, capacity of parties - free consent (meaning only) - legality of object and consideration - various modes of discharge of a contract- remedies for breach of contract.

UNIT-III **5 hours**

Intellectual Property Legislations: Meaning and scope of intellectual properties - Patent Act of 1970 and amendments as per WTO agreements: Background - objects - definitions - inventions - patentee - true and first inventor - procedure for grant of process and product patents, WTO rules as to patents (in brief), rights to patentee - infringement - remedies.

UNIT-IV **4 hours**

The Environment Protection Act, 1986: Background - definition of (1) Environment, (2) Environmental pollutant, (3) Environment pollution, (4) Hazardous substances, and (5) Occupier - Power of Central Government in relation to protection of environment and prevention of environmental pollution.

UNIT-V **4 hours**

Consumer Protection Act [COPRA], 1986: Background - definitions of (1) Consumer, (2) Consumer dispute, (3) Complaint, (4) Deficiency, (5) Service- Consumer Protection Council, Consumer redressal agencies - District Forum, State Commission and National Commission.

UNIT-VI **4 hours**

Foreign Exchange Management Act, 1999: Objectives, scope and salient features - offences under the Act.

UNIT-VII **5 hours**

Cyber Laws, 1999: Objectives, definitions and sailent features, provisions pertaining to piracy and related offences and penalties.

UNIT-VIII **4 hours**

Competition Laws, 2003: Meaning and scope, sailent features, offence, and penalties under the Act.

Contents

Preface vii

Acknowledgements ix

Syllabus xi

1. Introduction 1

1.1 Introduction 1
1.2 Meaning and scope of Business Law 2
1.2.1 Definitions 2
1.2.2 Essentials of Law 3
1.2.3 Business Law 3
1.2.4 Scope of Business Law 4
1.3 Source of Indian Business Law 4

2. Indian Contract Act, 1872 7

2.1 Introduction 7
2.1.1 The Indian Contract Act, 1872 7
2.1.2 Meaning and Definition of Contract 8
2.1.3 Agreement = Offer + Acceptance 9
2.1.4 Consensus ad idem 9
2.1.5 Essential Elements of a valid contract 9
2.1.6 Classification of contracts 11
2.2 Offer 14
2.2.1 Meaning and Definition 14
2.2.2 Types 15
2.2.3 Legal Rules 16
2.2.4 Tenders 18
2.2.5 Cross offers 19
2.2.6 Counter offers 19
2.3 Acceptance 19

2.3.1 Meaning and Definition 19
2.3.2 Legal Rules 20
2.4 Communication of Offer, Acceptance and Revocation 22
2.4.1 How communication is effected? 22
2.4.2 When is communication complete (Sec 4) 23
2.4.3 Communication of Acceptance 23
2.4.4 Revocation 23
2.4.5 Communication of Revocation 24
2.4.6 When docs an offer come to an end? (Sec.6) 24
2.5 Consideration 25
2.5.1 Meaning and Definition 25
2.5.2 Need for Consideration 26
2.5.3 Legal Rules 26
2.6 Stranger to Contract 30
2.6.1 Exceptions 31
2.7 No Consideration No Contract 32
2.8 Capacity to Contract 34
2.9 Minors 34
2.9.1 Legal Rules 35
2.9.2 Liability for Necessaries 37
2.10 Persons of Unsound Mind 37
2.10.1 Types of persons of unsound mind 38
2.11 Persons Disqualified by Law 38
2.11.1 Alien 39
2.11.2 Corporation 39
2.11.3 Insolvent 39
2.11.4 Convict 39
2.12 Free Consent 40
2.12.1 Meaning and Definition 40
2.12.2 Free consent 40
2.13 COERCION 41
2.13.1 Essentials 42
2.13.2 Threat to commit suicide: Does it amount to coercion? 42
2.13.3 Effects 43
2.13.4 Duress 43
2.14 Undue Influence 43
2.14.1 Essentials 44
2.14.2 Burden of Proof [Sec 16 (3)] 45

2.14.3 Effects 45

2.15 Fraud 46

2.15.1 Essentials 47

2.15.2 Exceptions 47

2.15.3 Mere silence is not Fraud 48

2.15.4 Effects 49

2.16 Misrepresentation 49

2.16.1 Essentials 50

2.16.2 Effects 50

2.17 Mistake 51

2.17.1 Mistake of law 51

2.17.2 Mistake of fact 52

2.18 Legality of Object 54

2.18.1 When consideration or object is unlawful? 54

2.18.2 What is public policy? 56

2.18.3 Agreements opposed to public policy 57

2.18.4 Exceptions 60

2.19 Performance of Contract 62

2.19.1 Rules Relating To Performance 62

2.19.2 Who can demand performance? 65

2.19.3 Reciprocal promises 66

2.20 Discharge of Contract 69

2.20.1 Types of Discharge 70

2.21 Remedies for Breach of Contract 75

2.21.1 Remedies 76

2.22 Rescission 76

2.23 Suit for Damages 77

2.23.1 Rules 78

2.23.2 Damages and Penalty 79

2.24 Quantum Meruit 80

2.25 Specific Performance of Contract 81

2.26 Injunction 82

2.27 Contingent Contracts 82

2.27.1 Essential characteristics 83

2.27.2 Rules 83

2.28 Wagering Agreements 85

2.28.1 Essentials 86

2.28.2 Exceptions 88

2.29 Quasi Contracts 89

2.29.1 Types of Quasi Contracts 89

3. Intellectual Property Legislations **99**

3.1 Intellectual Property Legislations 99

3.1.1 Background 99

3.1.2 Meaning 99

3.1.3 Objectives 100

3.1.4 Salient features 100

3.1.5 Definitions 100

3.1.6 Specifications 101

3.1.7 Application and Procedure to obtain patents 102

3.2 Term of patents (Section 53) 103

3.3 Opposition to grant of Patent 103

3.4 Lapse of Patent and its Renewal 104

3.5 Surrender of Patent 104

3.6 Revocation of Patents 105

3.7 Infringement and Remedies 105

3.8 Intellectual Property Rights 106

3.9 Conclusion 106

4. Environment Protection Act, 1986 **107**

4.1 Introduction and Background 109

4.2 Definitions 109

4.2.1 Environment 109

4.2.2 Environment Pollutant [See 2(b)] 110

4.2.3 Environment Pollution [See 2(e)] 110

4.2.4 Handling [See 2 (d)] 110

4.2.5 Hazardous substance [See 2(e)] 110

4.2.6 Occupier (See 2(f)] 110

4.3 Objectives 110

4.4 Powers of Central Government 111

4.5 Protection and Prevention of Environment Pollution 112

4.6 Powers of Entry and Inspection [Section 10] 112

4.7 Hazardous Substance 113

4.8 Prevention of Environment Pollution 114

4.9 Conclusion 115

5. Consumer Protection Act (COPRA), 1986 117

5.1 Introduction and Background 117
5.2 Emergency of the Consumer Rights 117
5.3 Objectives of the Act 119
5.4 Definitions 120
5.5 Consumer Protection Council 123
5.6 The State Consumer Protection Council-[Sections 7 & 8] 125
5.7 The District Consumer Protection Council-[Sections 8A and 8B] 126
5.8 Consumer Disputes Redressal Agencies 127
5.9 District Forum 128
5.9.1 Admission of Complaint 131
5.10 State Commission 136
5.11 National Commission 141
5.11.1 Special Powers 144
5.12 Enforcement of Orders of the District Forum, the State Commission or the National Commission-(Section 25) 146

6. Foreign Exchange Management Act, 1999 151

6.1 Introduction 151
6.2 Background 151
6.3 Objects and Reasons for Enactment of FEMA 152
6.4 Salient Features of FEMA 152
6.4.1 Suspension of Operation of FEMA (Sec. 40) 153
6.4.2 Bar of Legal Proceedings (Sec 44) 153
6.5 Repeal, Savings and Cognizance of Offences (Sec. 49) 154
6.6 Regulation and Management of Foreign Exchange 154
6.6.1 Capital Account Transaction [Sec. 2(e)(ze) 86] 154
6.6.2 Foreign Exchange [Sec 2 (n) 2(m)] 157
6.6.3 Indian Currency [Sec 2 (g)(h)(i)] 157
6.6.4 Security [Sec 2 (za)] 157
6.6.5 Foreign Security [Sec 2 (0)] 157
6.7 Restrictions of Dealings in Foreign Exchange [Sec 3 and 4] 158
6.7.1 Realisation and Repariation of Foreign Exchange [Sec, 2 (7, 8 and 9)] 159
6.7.2 Exemption from Realisation and Repatriation of Foreign Exchange 160
6.7.3 Person Sec. 2 (4) 161
6.7.4 Person Resident in India [Sec. 2 (v)] 161
6.7.5 Person Resident outside India [Sec. 2 (w)] 162
6.7.6 Export of Goods and Services [Sec. 2 (1) (zb) & 7] 162

6.7.7 Foreign Trade Development 164
6.7.8 Objectives 164
6.7.9 Procedure in Brief 165
6.8 Conditions of Licence 165
6.8.1 Deemed Conditions of Licence for Import 166
6.8.2 Authorised Person (Sees. 2 (e) 10, 11 & 12) 167
6.8.3 Reserve Bank Powers to Issue Directions to Authorised Persons 168
6.8.4 Power of the Reserve Bank to Inspect Authorised Person 168

7. Cyber Laws and the Information Technology Act, 2000 **171**

7.1 Background and Introduction 171
7.2 Need and Scope of Cyber Law 172
7.3 Electronic Governance (Sections 4-10) 180
7.4 Information Technology Act, 2000 181
7.5 Attribution, Receipt and Despatch of Electronic Records (Sections 11-13) 184
7.6 Secure Electronic Records and Secure Digital Signatures (Section 14-16) 185
7.7 Regulation of Certifying Authorities (Sections 17-34) 185
7.8 Digital Signature Certification (Sections 35-39) 187
7.9 Duties of Subscribers (Sections 40-42) 188
7.10 Penalties and Adjudication (Sections 43-47) 188
7.11 Offences 192
7.12 Network Service Providers not to be Liable in Certain Cases 194

8. The Competition Act, 2002 **199**

8.1 Introduction 199
8.2 Definitions 200
8.3 Prohibition of Certain Agreements 203
8.3.1 Analysis 204
8.4 Prohibition of Abuse of dominant position (Section 4) 205
8.4.1 Analysis 205
8.4.2 Comments 206
8.5 Competition Commission of India (CCI) 209
8.6 Duties, Powers and Functions of Commission (Sections 18 to 40) 212
8.7 Competition Advocacy 221

Model Question and Answers of Business Law *223*

Index *239*

CHAPTER 1

INTRODUCTION

1.1 INTRODUCTION

An organised activity of commerce can be understood as business, though generally business activities which result in profit, but these business activities must be in an organised manner. A little knowledge of law is necessary for every human being living in the society, as one has to come across many events whether social or business, they have to be responded in a right way. Life of an individual must be controlled by a set of natural rules and regulations, even without our knowledge we may be following certain rules and regulations in our daily life. Indeed, every person is confronted daily with situations that demand legal information for a systematic and correct behaviour of persons. Just as a game of cricket cannot be played satisfactorily without proper rules to govern the players, so also life in general and the business worlds in particular cannot continue without Law to regulate the conduct of people and to protect their property and rights. Thus, without law, life and business would soon become a matter of survival not only of the fittest but also of the most ruthless. In fact it is the Law which assures us a safe and secured life in the society. As Anson rightly puts it "Law is body of principles which are framed by the state in the administration of Justice". As a social being man comes in contract with people in different capacities, with landlord as a tenant, with government as a tax-payer, with a trader as customer and so on. In all these capacities he is expected to observe a code of conduct or a set of rules. This set of rules is called Law. Further as opined by Blackstone: "Law in its most general and comprehensive sense signifies a rule of action and it is applied indiscriminately to all kinds of actions whether animate or inanimate, rational or irrational". In simple terms law means rules and in legal sense law means those different sets of rules regulating external human actions and conduct of individuals in their dealings with other individuals and the government. It operates to regulate the actions of persons in respect to one another and in respect to entire group or society. In short, the term law denotes rules of conduct enforced by the state. As rightly observed by Woodrow Wilson law is: the established habits and thoughts of mankind which have gained distinct and formal recognition in the shape of uniformity of rules and regulations backed by authority and power of the government.

1.2 MEANING AND SCOPE OF BUSINESS LAW

Meaning of Law: Generally, law means all those rules and regulations which are normally followed by people when they come across others in their day-to-day life. E.g., for a person riding a two-wheeler on the road law means following traffic rules, for a person watching a play in theatre is maintaining silence, and for a normal citizen law means conducting himself with others in an orderly manner, in a manner which will not unnecessarily trouble others. Thus law has different meanings for different meanings for different people for different situations.

1.2.1 Definitions

It is very difficult to define law, because it contains various aspects which cannot be incorporated in one definition. Hence to understand the various meanings of law for different situations, better it is for us to go through the important definitions of law, which are as follows.

According to Austin

"Law is rule of conduct imposed and enforced by the sovereign."

According to Anson

"The object of law is order, and the result of order is that men are able to look ahead with some sort of security as to the future. Although human actions cannot be reduced to uniformities of nature, men have now endeavoured to reproduce by law something approaching to the uniformity."

According to Blackstone

"Law in its most general and comprehensive sense signifies a rule of action and is applied indiscriminately to all kinds of actions whether animate or inanimate, rational or irrational".

According to Prof. Ihering

"Law is a form of guarantee of the conditions of life of society, assured by the state's power of constraint."

According to Holland

"Law is a form of guarantee of the conditions of life of society, assured by the state's power of constraint."

According to Oxford English Dictionary

"Law is referred as the body of rules, whether proceeding from formal enactment or from custom, which a particular state or community recognises as binding on its subjects or members.

According to Woodrow Wilson

"Law is that portion of established habits and thought of mankind which has gained distinct and formal recognition in the shape of uniformities rules backed by the authority and power of the government."

From the above definitions it is clear that the term law means rules of conducting which are recognised and enforced by the state or authority on its people.

1.2.2 Essentials of Law

A rule in order to become law must have the following essential characteristics:

- It is set of rules.
- It is recognised and enforced by the state.
- It pre-assumes a state as a territorial division in which people live subject to uniformities systematic of law administered by the authority.
- It is for the guidance of human conduct.
- It attempts to achieve some sort of security and uniformity in its application.
- It is a living thing. It is not static. As such circumstances and conditions in a society change, laws are changed to fit the requirements of the society.

1.2.3 Business Law

The terms 'business law, 'commercial law' and 'mercantile law' are synonymous. In other words they represent the same meaning. However, the term 'business' means any economic activity carried on in order to earn profits. It includes trade, industry and commerce on the other hand, Law refers to a set of rules to be observed in dealing with others. Business law is a branch of general law which deals with the rights and obligations arising out of mercantile or business transactions among business people. It is used to denote the aggregate body of those legal rules which are connected with trade, industry and commerce.

1.2.4 Scope of Business Law

Law is a wider subject which touches all the walks of our life. In modern situations due to alarming increase in the business activities, the scope and area of law also has widened, no doubt it includes almost all the traditional laws like civil laws to regulate the transactions, like Sale of Goods Act, Contract Activities- I and II, Partnership Act, Companies Act, provisions relating to Insurance Act, Intellectual Property Act, Environment Protection Act, Foreign Exchange Management Act, Information Technology Act (Cyber Laws), Competition Activities etc.,

1.3 SOURCE OF INDIAN BUSINESS LAW

The important sources of Indian Business Law are as follows.

I. English Business Law: Most of the Indian business laws are largely based on English business law. Though in the Indian law the contexts relate to Indian conditions but the judgements of English Law have always influenced the Indian business law. In the absence of any specific law, usage or custom on a particular point arising before a court, rules of English Law are applied. However, English Law originates from the following sources, so also the Indian business law has been influenced.

(a) Common Law: It refers to a systematic of law based upon English customs, usages and traditions which were developed over centuries by the English courts. It is unwritten. Its principles are applied whenever subsequent disputes of similar nature arise. The Common law was found to be inadequate as it can be applied only in similar disputes. But in practical life we may come across varieties of disputes to understand different circumstances.

(b) Principles of Equity: Wherever the common law was harsh and oppressive, judges applied rules of equity i.e. fair or say justice. It refers to a body of legal rules emanating from the administration of justice developed to enlarge, supplement or override a narrow rigid system. Equity principles were accepted by everyone with a common concern. It grew as a systematic of law supplementary to Common law. It enforced new remedies for the enforcement of Common law.

(c) English statute law: It refers to the laws which are enacted by the British parliament. Statutory law has the power to override the earlier laws i.e., common law, equity, principles etc. Salmoud infact called statutory law as an enacted law, according to him 'Law that has its sources in Legislation may be most accurately termed as enacted law, all other forms being distinguished as un-enacted law.

(d)Law Merchant: The law merchant or Lex Mercatoria was the forerunner of the English law relating to mercantile transactions. This source of law was based on the usage, customs prevailing among traders. As the trade activities progressed so also the book of Law merchant, progressed.

II. Customs and Usages: In primitive society, customs used to be the only law that governed the conduct of the people. They developed out of necessity or convenience. Customs means usage or practice common to many or to a particular place. A particular act, usage or conduct practised by a group of people for a long period becomes a custom. So, when a particular practice was repeatedly followed it becomes a custom. Customs and usages should be ancient, reasonable and constant. Customs when accepted by the court and incorporated in a judicial decision becomes legal custom.

III. Case Laws: Case laws are also called judicial decisions or precedents. It is a judgement of a superior court including a point of law or principle and which necessitates its adoption and adherence in a subsequent case involving the same point. Interpretation of statutes by judges and their application depending on the facts of each case, meting out justice to the aggrieved parties has today formed a very important source of law. Wherever Indian statute, customs or usages are silent, courts apply law based on English judgements which came to be recognised as an important basis of the law in our country.

Thus, case law is useful as it helps courts render uniformity with regard to the interpretation of statutes or formulation of principles.

IV. Legislations: Legislations are the common source of law. The term 'Legislation' is used in different senses. In a broad sense it includes all methods of law making and therefore, would include laws made by judges also. In the strict sense, it may be defined as the promulgation of legal rules by competent authority like the parliament or state assemblies. Both the parliament and state assemblies have enacted a number of legislations that cover various aspects of business activities, for example, Indian Contract Act, 1872, Indian Sale of Goods Act, 1930, Indian Partnership Act, 1932, Indian Companies Act, 1956, Indian Negotiable Instruments Act, 1881 and Indian Majority Act, 1875 etc.

QUESTIONS FOR PRACTICE

Section - A (Two Marks Questions)

1. What is law?
2. What is business law?
3. What is common law?
4. What is the objective of law?

5. What are customs and usages in law?
6. What are judicial precedents?
7. What is equity?

Section - B (Five Marks Questions)

1. State the objectives of business law.
2. State the essential features of business law.
3. State the limitations of business law.
4. What is the need for law?
5. What are the characteristic features of law?
6. What is the significance of law?

Section - C (Fifteen Marks Questions)

1. Explain the sources of Indian business law.
2. Explain the sources of English Mercantile Law.

Chapter 2

Indian Contract Act, 1872

2.1 INTRODUCTION

In commercial life promises are made. Sometimes, promises are honoured but sometimes breach is also committed. In case of breach, it is obvious to determine the remedies that are available in a court of law against a person who fails to honour his promise and the conditions under which the remedies are available. The law of contract is that branch of business law which determines the circumstances in which promises made by the parties to a contract shall be legally binding on them. It affects all of us in one way or the other. It is, however, more applicable to people engaged in trade, commerce and industry because bulk of their transactions are based on contracts.

2.1.1 The Indian Contract Act, 1872

Prior to the enactment of the Indian Contract Act, 1872 English common law was applied indiscriminately to Indian natives which led to many inconveniences. Therefore, separate statutes were enacted to supersede English law and to regulate the contracts where parties were Hindus and Mohammedans. If both the parties were Hindu, they were regulated by the Hindu law and where both parties were Mohammedans, Mohammedan law applied. Where, however, one party was a Hindu and the other Mohammedan, then law of defendant applied. Only where laws and usuages of Hindus or Mohammedans were silent on any point, English law was applied. Gradually importance of the enactment of general law regulating the contracts and to define and amend certain parts of law relating to contracts common to all was felt and this gave birth to the Indian Contract Act, 1872.

The Indian Contract Act came into force on 1st September 1872. The Act applies to the whole of India except the state of Jammu and Kashmir.

The Indian Contract Act does not profess to be a complete and exhaustive code. It deals with the general principles of the law of contract and with some special contracts only viz., indemnity and guarantee, bailment, and pledge and agency. Some of the contracts not dealt with by the Act are those relating to partnership, sale of goods, negotiable instruments, insurance, bill of lading etc. There are separate Acts which deal with these contracts.

In this chapter, unless otherwise stated, sections referred to are those of the Indian Contract Act, 1872.

The law of contract differs from other branches of law in an important aspect. It does not lay down a number of rights and duties which the law will enforce; it consists rather of a number of limiting principles, subject to which the parties may create rights and duties for themselves which the law will uphold. In other words, the parties to a contract make the law for themselves, So long as they do not infringe some legal protection, they can make rules they like in respect of the subject-matter of their agreement and the law will give effect to their decisions.

2.1.2 Meaning and Definition of Contract

In a broad sense, a contract is an exchange of promises by two or more persons resulting in an obligation, which is recognised and enforced by the law. In creating a legal obligation a contract gives the right to one person and casts a corresponding duty on another person. On account of the presence of rights and obligations, the law gives a remedy for the breach of promises and recognises its due performance as a duty. Thus, a contract refers to an agreement creating an obligation which means a binding agreement.

A contract may be defined as "legally binding agreement between two or more persons by which rights are acquired by one or more to act or forbearance on the part of the others".

According to Salmond, a contract is "an agreement creating and defining obligations between the parties".

In the words of Pollock "Every agreement and promise enforceable at law is a contract".

Section 2(h) of the Act defines a contract as "an agreement enforceable by law".

If we analyse the above definitions we find a contract essentially consists of two elements, viz. (1) an agreement and (2) its enforceability by law.

Section 2(e) defines agreement as "every promise and every set of promises, forming consideration for each other".

Section 2(b) defines promise as "When the person to whom the proposal is made signifies his asset thereto, the proposal is said to be accepted. A proposal, when accepted, becomes a promise".

Thus, in order to form an agreement, there must be a proposal or an offer by one party and its acceptance by the other.

2.1.3 Agreement = Offer + Acceptance

The term obligation is defined as a "legal tie which imposes upon a definite person or persons the necessity of doing or abstaining from doing a definite act or acts". So, an agreement must give rise to a legal obligation or duty in order to become a contract.

An agreement is a wider term which includes contract. It may relate to social or legal matters. An agreement which gives rise to a social obligation is not a contract. It must give rise to a legal obligation in order to become a contract.

Examples

- ☞ A invitees his friend B to attend a dinner at his home and B accepts it. Now when B comes to A's house, A has not arranged dinner as his wife had died the day before. It is a social agreement and is not enforceable in a court of law.
- ☞ A agrees to sell his car to B for ₹1,00,000. Now there is an obligation on the part of A to deliver the car to B and on the part of B to pay ₹1,00,000 to A. It is a legal agreement and results in contract.

2.1.4 Consensus ad idem

The essence of an agreement in order to become a contract is consensus ad idem. It means that the parties to the agreement must have agreed on the subject-matter of the agreement in the same sense and at the same time. In other words, it means the meeting of the minds of the parties in full and agreement.

Examples

- ☞ A owns two horses named Raja and Boja and agrees to sell Raja to B. B is under the impression that he is purchasing Boja. There is no consensus ad idem and consequently no contract.
- ☞ A tells B, "will you purchase my car for ₹1,00,000? and B says 'Yes' to it. There is consensus ad idem and an agreement comes into existence.

2.1.5 Essential Elements of a Valid Contract

According to section 10, all agreements are contracts if they are made by the free consent of parties to contract, for a lawful consideration and with a lawful object and are not expressly declared to be void. So, all agreements are not contracts. The law of contract is the law of those agreements which create legal obligations. An agreement, which creates legal obligation, in order to be valid and binding must possess certain essentials. These essentials are the essential elements of a contract. The following are the essentials or characteristics or features of a valid contract.

1. Offer and Acceptance

There must be two parties to an agreement i.e. one party making the offer and the other party accepting it. The terms of the offer must be definite and the acceptance of the offer must be absolute and unconditional. In other words, offer and acceptance must be both lawful i.e. it must conform to the rules laid down in the Indian Contract Act.

2. Consideration

An agreement to be enforceable by law must be supported by consideration. Consideration means an advantage or benefit moving from one party to the other. In short, it means 'something in return'. An agreement is legally enforceable only when both the parties give something and get something in return. A promise to do something, getting nothing in return, is usually not enforceable by law.

3. Capacity of Contract

The parties to the agreement must be competent of entering into a valid contract. A person is said to be competent if he is (a) of age of majority (b) of sound mind and (c) not disqualified from contracting by law to which he is subject.

4. Free Consent

Any agreement must be based on free consent of the parties in order to become a valid contract. The consent of the parties is said to be free when they are of the same mind on all the material terms of the contract. The parties are said to be of the same mind when they agree about the subject-matter of the contract in the same sense and at the same time. Free consent does not exist when it is obtained by coercion, undue influence, fraud, mistake or misrepresentation.

5. Lawful Object

The object of the agreement must be lawful. It is unlawful if the object is forbidden by law, illegal, immoral or opposed to public policy. Any agreement with an unlawful object cannot be enforced by law.

6. Legal Relationship

The intention of the parties to the agreement must create legal relationship between them i.e. an agreement in the nature of a commercial bargain. In the absence of such intention, the agreement cannot be enforced by law.

7. Not Expressly Declared Void

The agreement must not have been expressly declared to be void under any law. Void agreements cannot be enforced by law.

8. Certainty

The terms of the agreement must be certain and clear. In other words, the agreement must not be vague, uncertain or ambiguous. Vague or uncertain terms make the agreement unenforceable.

9. Possibility of Performance

The act contemplated in the agreement should be capable of performance. Agreement to perform an impossible act cannot be enforced. For example, A promises to share with B 50% of treasure if B creates a treasure by magic. Such agreements are incapable of performance and therefore void.

10. Legal Formalities

There are some legal formalities which have to be complied with in order to make an agreement legally enforceable. One of the such legal formalities is that the agreement may be in writing or oral. But it is in the interest of the parties that the agreement must be in writing. Registration is another aspect of legal formalities. It is also again optional, though it is compulsory in case of gifts and mortgages. Similarly, in some cases, the documents containing agreements need to be stamped.

Thus, the above essential elements must be present in an agreement in order to become a contract. That is why it is said that "All contracts are agreements but all agreements are not necessarily contracts".

2.1.6 Classification of Contracts

Contracts may be classified on different basis as shown in the following chart.

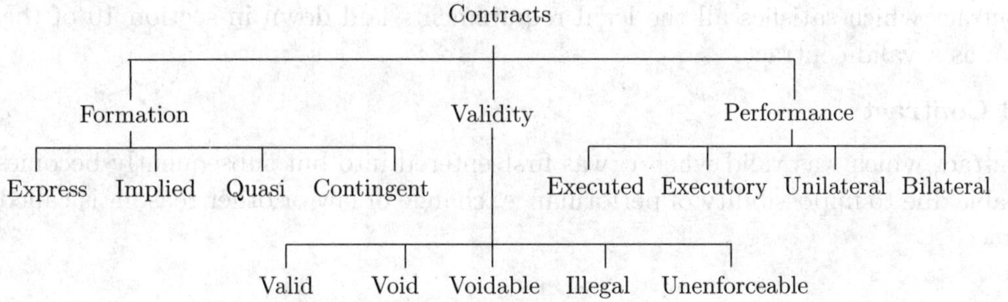

Express contracts

When the terms of a contract are expressly agreed upon (whether by words spoken or written) at the time of the formation of the contract, the contract is said to be an express contract.

Example: A writes a letter to B, his offer to sell scooter for ₹20,000. B accepts it and replied in a letter.

Implied Contracts

An implied contract is one which is inferred from the acts or conduct of the parties or course of dealings between them.

In other words, the proposal or acceptance of any promise is made otherwise than in words, the promise is said to be implied.

Example: A boards a KSRTC bus. It is implied from his conduct that he has entered into a contract with KSRTC to travel in the bus by purchasing a ticket.

Quasi Contract

Quasi contract is a legal obligation that has a number of similarities to a contract but is not exactly the same. A quasi contract arises not from an agreement, but from a mere relationship that comes about between individuals. It is a relationship based on action without searching of an agreement. It simply means that the actions of one person have conferred a benefit on other.

Example: A leaves goods at C's house by mistake. C treats the goods as his own. C is bound to pay for the goods.

Contingent Contract

A contingent contract is one in which a promise is conditional and the contract shall be performed only on the happening of some future uncertain event.

Example: A contracts to pay B ₹10,000 if B's house is burnt.

Valid Contract

A contract which satisfies all the legal requirements laid down in section 10 of the Act is known as a valid contract.

Void Contract

A contract which was valid when it was first entered into but subsequently becomes unenforceable due to impossibility of performance, change of law or other reason, is called a void contract.

Example: A of India agrees to import goods from B of Pakistan. If war breaks out between the two countries; it becomes impossible to import goods.

Voidable Contract

An agreement which is enforceable by law at the option of one or more of the parties thereto but not at the option of the other or others is a voidable contract. It happens when the essential element of a free consent is missing.

Example: A agrees to sell his car to B for ₹50,000. His consent is obtained by use of force. The contract is voidable at the option of A. He may avoid the contract or elect to be bound by it.

Illegal Contracts

The terms 'illegal' and 'contract' cannot go together. What is illegal or against the law cannot be enforced. Therefore, more appropriate expression would be illegal agreement.

An illegal agreement is an agreement, the consideration or object of which (i) is forbidden by law (ii) defeats the provisions of any law (iii) is fraudulent (iv) involves injures to the person or property of another (v) is immoral or (vi) opposed to public policy.

All illegal agreements are void but all void agreements or contracts are not necessarily illegal. It is because illegal agreement is forbidden by law but not void agreement. An illegal agreement is not only void as between the immediate parties but has this further effect that even the collateral transactions to it become tainted with illegally.

Example: A borrows ₹10,000 from B to import prohibited goods. B knows the purpose of the loan. The transaction between A and B is collateral to the main agreement.

Unenforceable Contract

An unenforceable contract is one which is valid but is not enforceable in a court of law because of some technical defects such as lack of proof, expiry of the period within which it was enforceable, insufficiency of stamp duty etc.

Executed Contract

An executed contract is one in which both the parties have performed their respective obligations.

Example: A agrees to paint the house of B for ₹1,000. When A paints the house and B pays the amount i.e. when both the parties perform their obligations, the contract is said to be an executed contract.

Executory Contract

An executory contract is one in which both the parties are yet to perform their obligations.

Example: A agrees to engage B as his servant from the next month, the contract is executory.

Unilateral Contract

A unilateral or one-sided contract is one in which only one party has to fulfil his obligation at the time of formation of the contract, the other party having fulfilled his obligation at the time of the contract or before the contract comes into existence. Such contracts are also known as contracts with executed consideration.

Example: Mr. X permits a coolie to carry his luggage and keep it in the car. A contract comes into existence as soon as the luggage is kept in the car. But by that time the coolie has already performed his obligation. Now only Mr. X has to fulfil his obligation i.e. payment of reasonable charges.

Bilateral Contract

A bilateral contract is one in which the obligations on the part of both the parties to the contract are outstanding at the time of the formation of the contract. In this sense, bilateral contracts are similar to executory contracts and are also known as contracts with executory consideration.

2.2 OFFER

Offer is the first and foremost essential element of a valid contract. It is the first step in the process of making a contract. For the formation of a contract, there must be a definite offer by one person to another and its unqualified acceptance by the person to whom it is made. The word 'proposal' used in section 2(a) of the Indian Contract Act is synonymous in English use with 'offer'.

2.2.1 Meaning and Definition

An offer is a statement by one person of what he will give in return for some act or promise of another. In other words, an offer is a proposal by one person whereby he expresses his willingness to enter into a contractual obligation in return for a promise, or act or forbearance. In short, an offer is a proposal by one party to another to enter into a legally binding agreement with him.

Section 2(a) of the Act defines offer as "A person is said to have made a proposal when he signifies his willingness to do or to abstain from doing anything with a view to obtaining the assent of that other to such act or abstinence."

Example: A says to B "will you purchase my car for ₹50,000? In this case, A is making an offer to B as he signifies to B his willingness to sell his car to B with a view to obtaining B's assent to purchase the car.

The person making the offer is known as the offeror or proposer or promisor and the person to whom it is made is called the offeree or proposee. When the offeree accepts the offer, he is called the acceptor or promisee. In the above example A is an offeror and B is an offeree.

2.2.2 Types of Offer

An offer is of the following types.

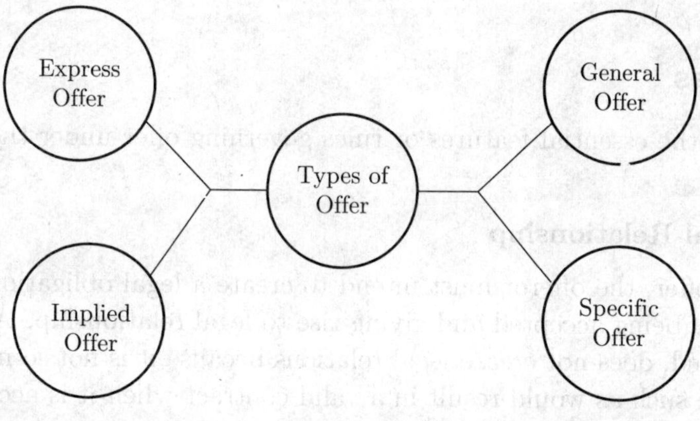

Express offer

An offer is said to be express, when it is made either by spoken words or in writing.

Example: A says to B, will you purchase my house at Bangalore for ₹5,00,000? There is an express offer.

Implied offer

An offer is said to be implied when it is gathered from the conduct of the parties or the circumstances of the case.

Example: A transport company runs a bus on a particular route. There is an implied offer by the transport company to carry passengers for a certain fare.

General offer

When an offer is made to the world at large, it is called a general offer. Such an offer, with the notice of it, may be accepted by any person and when a certain person accepts it, it results in a contract.

Carlill Vs Carholic Co. (1893)

A company advertised in newspapers that a reward of ₹100 would be given to any person who contracted influenza after using the smoke balls of the company according to its printed directions. One Mrs. Carlill used the smoke balls according to the directions of the company but contracted influenza. Held, she could recover the amount as by using the smoke balls she had accepted the offer.

Specific Offer

When an offer is made to a definite person, it is called a specific offer. It can be accepted only by the person to whom it is made.

2.2.3 Legal Rules

The following are the essential features or rules governing offer under the Indian Contract Act.

1. Creating legal Relationship

To constitute an offer, the offeror must intend to create a legal obligation. Hence, an offer must be capable of being accepted and giving rise to legal relationship. A social invitation, even if it is accepted, does not create legal relations because it is not so intended. An offer, therefore, must be such as would result in a valid contract when it is accepted.

Balfour Vs Balfour (1919)

The husband promised to pay ₹30 to his wife every month. On his failure to pay, the wife sued him for the recovery of the amount. Held, she could not recover as the agreement did not create any legal relationship.

2. Terms must be definite and certain

The terms of offer must be definite and certain. Vague and ambiguous terms make the offer invalid. If, therefore, the terms of an offer are vague or indefinite, its acceptance cannot create any contractual relationship.

Examples

a) A offered to take a house on lease for 3 years at ₹285 per annum, if the house was put into through repair and drawing rooms handsomely decorated according to the present style. Held, the offer was too vague to result in a contractual relation (Taylor Vs Postington, (1985) ALL ER 128).

b) A says to B "I will sell you a horse". A owns three different horses. The offer is indefinite.

c) A husband on leaving his wife promised to pay her ₹15 a week so long as I can manage it". Held, although the husband and wife who lived apart because of break-up of their marriage, could enter into a legally binding agreement, the vague or discretionary terms of the arrangement indicated an intention not to create legal relations.

3. Offer must be made to obtain the assent

The offer to do or not to do something must be made with a view to obtaining the assent of the other party addressed and not merely with a view to disclosing the intention of making an offer. When the person invites offers through price lists, catalogues, advertisements, window displays, tenders etc., it is an invitation to an offer by which he reserves his right to accept or to do some further act to be bound by it. He proposes certain terms on which he is willing to negotiate. He invites others to make an offer. So if the person making the statements intends to be bound by it no sooner it is accepted. It is an instance of an offer. On the other hand if he intends to do so some further act before he becomes bound by it, it is an instance of an invitation to an offer.

Harvey Vs Facey and Spencer

A advertises to sell his house. B, C and D offer to purchase the house at a certain price. A refuses to accept all the offers. A can't do so, as the advertisement issued by A is not an offer but an invitation to an offer. It is B,C and D who actually offer and it is for A to accept the same or not.

4. Offer must be communicated

An offer, to be complete, must be communicated to the person to whom it is made. Unless an offer is communicated to the offeree by the offeror or by his duly authorised agent, there can be no acceptance of it. Even if an offer is accepted in ignorance of the offer, is no acceptance and does not confer any right on the acceptor.

Lalman Vs Gouri Dutt

S sent his servant, L to trace his missing nephew. He then announced that anybody who traced his nephew would be entitled to a certain reward. L traced the boy in ignorance of this announcement. Subsequently when he came to know of the reward he claimed it. Held, he was not entitled to the reward because he had no knowledge of the existence of an offer when he found the boy.

5. Offer with special conditions

If there are special terms or conditions in an offer, these must be brought to the notice of the offeree at the time of making a proposal. A conditional offer lapses when the condition is not accepted by the offeree.

Thomson Vs L MS Railway Co.

A traveller takes a ticket for a railway journey containing on its face the usual reference to the conditions under which it is issued. Held, that he is bound by its contents, whether he reads the document or otherwise informs himself of its contents or not.

6. Offer should not contain a term the non-compliance of which may be assumed to amount to acceptance.

Thus, a man cannot say that if the acceptance is not communicated by a certain time, the offer would be considered as accepted. For example, A writes to B, "I will sell you my car for ₹50,000 and if you do not reply, I shall assume you have accepted the offer," there is no contract if B does not reply.

7. A statement of price is not an offer

A mere statement of price is not construed as an offer to sell. For example, A is riding his scooter by mentioning the price of scooter ₹10,000 on the number plate of it. It does not mean he is offering to sell it to somebody else.

2.2.4 Tenders

A tender (in response to an invitation to offer) is an offer and may be either definite offer or standing offer.

1. Tender as a definite offer

When tenders are invited for the supply of specified goods or services, each tender submitted is an offer. The party inviting tenders may accept any tender he chooses and thus form a binding contract.

Example: A invites tenders for the supply of a printing machine. P, Q, R and S submit the tenders. A accepts Q's tender. There is binding contract between A and Q.

2. Tender as a standing offer

Where goods or services are required over a certain period, a person may invite tenders as a standing offer which is continuing offer. The acceptance of such offer has the effect that as and when the goods or services are required, an order is placed with the person who submitted the tender and each time a distinct contract is made.

Example: A railway company invited tenders for certain iron articles which it might require over a year. W's tender was accepted. He supplied goods to the company for sometime under its orders. He refused to execute an order on one day during the currency of the tender. Held, W could not refuse to supply goods within the terms of the tender (Great Northern Rail Vs. Witham (1873) LRGCP 16).

2.2.5 Cross Offers

When the parties make identical offers to each other in ignorance of each other's offer, the offers are said to be cross offers. In such a case, the court will not construe one offer as the offer and the other as the acceptance and as such there can be no concluded contract.

Example: A writes a letter to B offering to sell his scooter for ₹25,000. B without the knowledge of A's letters, offers to buy it for ₹25,000.

2.2.6 Counter Offers

A counter offer is a rejection of the original offer. It is a new offer which needs acceptance by the original promisor before a contract is made. In other words, it is a fresh offer made in place of acceptance of the original offer.

Example: A offers to sell his house to B for ₹25,000 and B writes to A that he is ready to buy for ₹20,000. It is a counter proposal by B which must be accepted by the original proposer i.e. A, in order to be binding on A.

2.3 ACCEPTANCE

Acceptance is yet another requirement of a valid contract. If an offer is the starting point of forming an agreement, acceptance represents the end point of the process. In between there are certain formalities to be fulfilled. Hence, a contract emerges from the acceptance of an offer.

2.3.1 Meaning and Definition

Acceptance means the act of assenting by the offeree to an offer. In other words, it is the manifestation by the offeree of his willingness to be bound by the terms of the offer. It is to an offer what a lighted match is to a train of gunpowder. It produces something which cannot be recalled or undone." It means once the offeree gives his assent to the offer he cannot go back.

Section 2(b) of the Act defines acceptance as "when the person to whom the proposal is made signifies his assent thereto, the proposal is said to be accepted. A proposal, when accepted becomes a promise".

Example: A offers to sell his house to B at the price of ₹2,00,000. This is a proposal by A. B agrees to buy the house at the prescribed price. This is an acceptance by B. Now there is a contract between A and B.

Acceptance may be express or implied. It is express when it is communicated by words spoken or written or by doing some required act. It is implied when it is to be gathered from the surrounding circumstances or conduct of the parties.

Examples

a) A offers to sell his horse to B for ₹10,000. B says 'yes, I will buy it' to A. This is an express acceptance.
b) At an auction sale, S is the highest bidder. The auctioneer accepts the offer by striking the hammer on the table. This is an implied acceptance.

Who can accept?

When an offer is made to a particular person, it can be accepted by him alone. If it is accepted by any other person, there is no valid acceptance. On other hand, when an offer is made to world at large, any person, with the knowledge of it, can accept it.

2.3.2 Legal Rules

As the acceptance of an offer is the very essence of a contract, it shall satisfy the following conditions to become legally effective.

1. Absolute and unqualified

An acceptance, in order to be binding, must be absolute and unqualified in respect of all terms of the offer, whether material or immaterial, major or minor. If acceptance is given to a proposal with some conditions, variations and reservations, there is no acceptance at all. Acceptance with variations is a counter proposal and there is no contract unless this counter proposal is accepted by the original proposer.

Example: A offers to sell his watch to B for ₹500. B accepts it on a condition that A should bear repair expenses in future for 6 months. It is not a valid acceptance and hence, there is no contract between A and B unless A accepts it.

2. Communicated

The acceptance must be communicated in some perceptible form in order to constitute a contract. A mere resolve or mental determination on the part of the offeree to accept an offer when there is no external manifestation of the intention to do so, is not sufficient. In other words mental acceptance is no acceptance at all.

Example: A tells B that he intends to marry C but tells C nothing of his intention. There is no contract even if C is willing to marry A.

Felthous Vs Bindley [(1862) II CB (NS) 869J]

F offered to buy his nephew's horse for £30 saying: "If I hear no more about it I shall consider the horse is mine at £30. The nephew did not write to F at all, but he told his auctioneer who was selling his horses not to sell that particular horse because it had been sold to his uncle. The auctioneer inadvertently sold the horse. Held, F had no right of action against the auctioneer as the horse had not been sold to F, his offer of £30 not having been accepted.

3. Prescribed or Reasonable Mode

If the acceptance is not according to the mode prescribed or some usual and reasonable mode (where no mode is prescribed) the offeror may intimate to the offeree within a reasonable time that the acceptance is not according to the mode prescribed and may insist that the offer must be accepted in the prescribed mode only. If the offeror fails to do he is said to have accepted the acceptance.

Example: A makes an offer to B and says: If you accept the offer, reply by telephone, there is a valid acceptance if A does not raise objection. If he objects, there is no valid acceptance.

4. Acceptance when offer is in force

Acceptance must be made before the offer lapses. If any time limit is prescribed, the offer must be accepted before the expiry of the time. If no time is prescribed, the offer must be accepted within reasonable time.

Ramagate Victoria Hotel Com. Vs Moantefoire [(1886)LR 1 Ex 109]

M offered to take shares in a company on 8th June and received acceptance on 23rd November. M refused to take the shares. As the reasonable period of acceptance had elapsed, he was entitled to refuse to take the shares.

5. Acceptance must be preceded by offer

An offer must precede acceptance. Acceptance without offer is no acceptance. In other words, there must be an offer by one person in order to accept it by another person. For example, allotment of shares previous to the application is not valid.

6. Mere Mental Acceptance is no Acceptance

No contract is formed if the offeree remains silent and does nothing to show that he has accepted the offer. A mere mental determination to accept unaccompanied by an external indication will not be sufficient. In other words, mental acceptance is no acceptance at all. In the words of Shah J in the case of Bhagavandas Vs Giridhariial (1966) "An agreement does not result from a mere state of mind; intent of accept an offer or even a mental resolve to accept an offer does not give rise to contract. There must be... some external manifestation of the intent by speech, writing or other act". Thus, an acceptance to be complete must be communicated by words or conduct by an offeree to the offeror. Example: A wrote to B, "I offer you my car for ₹25,000. If I don't hear from you in 7 days, I shall assume that you accept". B did not reply at all. There is no contract.

7. Acceptance by a definite person

When an offer is made to a particular person, he alone must accept the proposal. Acceptance by anybody else invalidates the offer. On the other hand, when the offer is made to world at large, one must accept the offer. It is closed as soon as it is accepted by a definite person. **Example:** A offers to sell his car to B for ₹50,000. C, who stands by the side of them, cannot accept it.

8. Acceptance of the proposal

Acceptance of the proposal indicates the acceptance of all the terms and conditions of the offer, even though the offeree is ignorant of some of the terms, except where the terms and conditions are not apparent on the face and no reasonable caution is taken to draw attention of the acceptor.

Henderson Vs Sternson (1875)

The plaintiff sued the defendant company for damages for loss of his luggage on account of the negligence of the servants of the company. The company's defence was that it was protected by the conditions of the contract which were printed in small types on the back of the ticket that the company was not liable for the loss of passengers due to the negligence of the servants of the company and it was not liable.

2.4 COMMUNICATION OF OFFER, ACCEPTANCE AND REVOCATION

As it was discussed already an offer, its acceptance and its revocation to be completed must be communicated. There can be no valid offer unless it is communicated to the offeree. Similarly, the offeree must communicate his acceptance of the offer to the offeror. Acceptance cannot be valid unless it is communicated to the offeror. Again where proposal or acceptance is revoked, the same should be communicated to the concerned party. Thus, communication constitutes an important aspect of a contract. It is, therefore, proposed to discuss in detail the role of communication in effecting an agreement.

2.4.1 How communication is effected?

Communication is effected in any of the following two methods (Section 3)

1. By any act

Act includes - by conduct, by words, written or oral. Communication can, therefore, be by a letter, telegram, telex or by telephone. Any act by a person by which he intends to communicate or has the effect of communication, will constitute communication, for instance, entering into a bus by a person is communication of acceptance by act or conduct.

2. By Omission

Omission includes conduct or forbearance. An abstinence or forbearance on the part of one person which has the effect of communicating will constitute communication. A mere mental act is not communication.

2.4.2 When is communication complete (Sec 4)

Communication of offer

The communication of an offer is complete when it comes to the knowledge of the person to whom it is made.

Example: A offers, by a letter, to sell a house to B for ₹2,00,000. The letter is posted on 5th March. It reaches B on 10th March. The communication of the offer is complete when B receives the letter.

2.4.3 Communication of Acceptance

Communication of an acceptance is complete:

- ☞ as against the offeror when it is put into a course of transmission to him, so as to be out of the power of the acceptor.
- ☞ as against the acceptor when it comes to the knowledge of the offeror

Example: In the above case, B accepts A's proposal by a letter sent by post on 12th instant. The letter reaches A on 15th instant. The communication of the acceptance is complete, as against A, when the letter is by posted i.e. 12th, as against B, when the letter is received by A i.e. on 15th.

2.4.4 Revocation

Revocation means 'withdrawing' or 'taking back' or 'recalling'. It may be revocation of offer or acceptance. After a transaction has ripened into a contract it requires the consent of both the parties to revoke or modify it.

Revocation of offer (Sec. 5 Para 1)

An offer may be revoked at any time before the communication of its acceptance is complete as against the offeror but not afterwards.

Revocation of Acceptance (Sec. 5 Para 2)

An acceptance may be revoked at any time before the communication of the acceptance is complete as against the acceptor, but not afterwards.

Example: A proposes by a letter sent by post to sell his house to B. The letter is posted on 1st March. B accepts the proposal by a letter sent by post on 4th March. The letter reaches A on 6th.

A may revoke his proposal at any time before B posts his letter of acceptance i.e. 4th but not afterwards.

B may revoke his acceptance at any time before the letter or acceptance reaches A i.e. 6th but not afterwards.

2.4.5 Communication of Revocation

Communication of revocation is complete

(i) as against the person who makes it when it is put into a course of transmission to the person to whom it is made so as to be out of power of the person who makes it.

(ii) as against the person to whom it is made, when it comes to his knowledge.

Example A proposes by letter to sell a house to B at a certain price. A revokes his proposal by telegram.

The revocation is complete as against A when the telegram is despatched. It is complete as against B when he receives it.

B revokes his acceptance by telegram. B's revocation is complete as against B when the telegram is despatched and as against A when it reaches him.

2.4.6 When docs an offer come to an end? (Sec.6)

An offer may come to an end by revocation or lapse or rejection. Section 6 of the Act deals with various modes of revocation of an offer. They are as follows.

I. Notice of Revocation

An offer is revoked once the offeror gives notice of revocation to the offeree. Notice must be given by the offeror at any time before its acceptance as against him.

Example: At an auction sale, A makes the highest bid for B's goods. He withdraws the bid before the fall of the hammer.

2. Lapse of time

Offer lapses if it is not accepted within prescribed time when the definite time is stipulated. If, however, no time is prescribed, it lapses by the expiry of a reasonable time.

Example: A offered to sell wool to B on Thursday and agreed to give him 3 days time to accept. B accepted the offer on Monday, but by that time A had sold the wool.

3. Failure to fulfil conditions

Where the offer is subject to a condition precedent thereto, it lapses on failure to accept it without fulfilling the condition.

Example: A agrees to sell certain goods to B subject to the condition that B pays the agreed price before a certain date. If B fails to pay the price by that date the offer stands revoked.

5. Death or insanity of the offeror

An offer lapses on the death or insanity of the offeror provided that the fact comes to the knowledge of the offeree before he makes his acceptance. If he accepts an offer in ignorance of the death or insanity of the offeror, the acceptance is valid.

6. Change of law

An offer comes to an end if the law is changed so as to make the contract contemplated by the offer illegal or incapable of performance.

2.5 CONSIDERATION

Consideration is one of the essential elements to support a valid contract. In addition to a valid offer and acceptance the question of whether there is a binding contract frequently turns on whether there is a consideration to the agreement. Subject to certain exceptions, an agreement made without consideration is *nudum pactum* (a nude contract) and is void.

2.5.1 Meaning and Definition

In simple terms, consideration means the element of exchange in a bargain. In technical sense consideration means *quid proquo* (i.e. something in return). When a party to an agreement promises to do something, he must get "something" in return. This something is known as consideration.

Example: A agrees to sell his car to B for ₹1,00,000. Now the car is the consideration for B and price is the consideration for A.

Consideration may be defined as "something which is of value in the eyes of law, moving from the plaintiff to the defendant".

In the words of Pollock "consideration is the price for which a promise of other is bought".

According to Lush. J "Consideration is some right, interest, profit or benefit accruing to one party for some forbearance, detriment, loss or responsibility given, suffered, or undertaken by the other".

Section 2(d) of the Act defines consideration as "when at the desire of the promisor, the promisee or any other person has done or obtained from doing or does or abstains from doing, or promises to do or to abstain from doing something, such act or abstinence or promise is called a consideration for the promise".

2.5.2 Need for Consideration

Contracts result only when one promise is made in exchange for something in return. This something in return means consideration. The requirement of consideration stems from the policy of extending the arm of the law to the enforcement of mutual promises of parties. So, a mere promise to make a gilt, although presumably creating a moral obligation, is not enforceable at law, as the person to whom the promise of a gift is given does not give anything in return. To be enforceable a promise must be purchased, or the consideration be bargained for or given in exchange for the promise.

2.5.3 Legal Rules

The nature of consideration can be easily understood by analysing the various rules or essentials of consideration. The following are the essentials of a valid consideration.

1. Consideration must move at the desire of the promissor

The act or abstinence constituting consideration must be done at the desire of the promisor. If it is done at the instance of a third party or without the desire of the promisor, it is not a consideration. The definition of consideration in section 2(d) clearly emphasises that an act or abstinence which is to be a consideration for the promise must be done or promised to do be done in accordance with the desire of the promisor.

Example: A notices B' house being on hire and rushes voluntarily to B's help, there is no consideration. If, however, A goes to B's help at B's request, there is good consideration.

Durgaprusad Vs Baldleo (1880)

B spent some money on improvement of a market at the desire of the collector of the district. In consideration of this D who was using the market promised to pay some money to B. The act was the result of the collector's order but not of the promisor. Hence, it was held that the agreement was void being without consideration.

However, consideration need not be to the benefit of the promisor. Even if an act done at the promissor's desire is of no personal benefit to him, yet it will form a good consideration. In Kedar Nath Vs Gorie Mohamed (1886), the defendant had subscribed to the fund for constructing a town hall at Howrah but he failed to pay the amount. The plantiff had on the faith of the promise of the defendant entered into a contract with a contractor for building the hall. The defendant was held liable to pay the amount as the act of the plaintiff in entering into a contract was done at the desire of defendant as a promissor so as to constitute consideration. The promissor will be held liable to his promise only when the promisee carries out the act desired by the promissor.

Example: A promises to pay B ₹1000 for giving coaching to C. It forms good consideration even though coaching is not for the benefit of A as it moves at his desire.

2. Consideration may move from the promisee or any other person

Under the English law, consideration must move only from the promisee. But under Indian law consideration may either move from the promisee or any other person i.e. even a stranger. It means that as long as there is consideration for a promissor, it is immaterial who has furnished it. But the stranger to consideration will be able to sue only if he is a party to the contract.

Example: 'H' insures his life with Life Insurance Corporation of India and appoints W, his wife a nominee. Now 'W' is the beneficiary under the policy and, therefore, she can sue the Insurance Corporation to recover the consideration amount mentioned in the policy.

Chinnayya Vs Ramayya (1882. 4, Mad 137)

'A' gifted certain property to her daughter 'D' on a condition that the daughter should pay certain sum of money annually to 'A's sister 'P'. On the same day D entered into an agreement with P to pay her the agreed amount. Later, D refused to pay the amount on the plea that no consideration had moved from P to D. Held, P was entitled to maintain suit as consideration had moved from her sister 'A' to the daughter 'D'.

But according to English law, as pointed out earlier. consideration must come from the promisee only. In Dunlop Pneumatic Tyre Co. Ltd Vs Selfridge and Co. Ltd (1915) case, S bought tyres from the company on the condition that S will not sell below company's sale price falling which S will pay damages. S sold the tyres to B a sub-dealer, in turn, who sold the tyres below the stipulated price. The company sued B for damages. It was held that the company was stranger to the contract and, therefore, could not maintain the suit.

3. Consideration may be past, present or future

The definition of consideration given under section 2(d) reads as "has done or abstained from doing (past) or does or abstains from doing (present), or promises to do or to abstain from doing (future) something ...." It means consideration may be past, present or future.

Past consideration

When consideration by a party for a present promise was given in the past i.e. before the date of the promise, it is said to be past consideration. In other words it represents the value or benefit given prior to the date of promise.

Example: A renders some services to B in January. In March B promises to compensate A for the service rendered. It is past consideration.

Present consideration

When consideration is given simultaneously with promise i.e. at the time of the promise, it is said to be present consideration. In other words, it represents consideration which moves simultaneously with promise. It is also called executed consideration.

Example: A receives ₹500 in return for which he promises to deliver goods to B. The money A receives is present consideration for the promise he makes to deliver the goods. It is present consideration.

Future consideration

When consideration from one party to the other is to pass subsequently to the making of the contract it is said to be future consideration. In other words, it represents consideration which is to move at a future date. It is also called executory consideration.

Example: A promises to deliver certain goods to B after a week. B promises to pay the price after a fortnight. The promise of A is supported by the promise of B. It is future consideration.

4. Consideration need not be adequate

Consideration, as explained earlier, means 'something in return' This something in return need not necessarily be equal in value to something given. So, consideration need not be adequate nor equivalent to promise. What is important is that a contract must he supported by some consideration in order to enforce it in a court of law. The courts, generally, will not assume the role of settling what should be the appropriate consideration for a promise. It is for the parties to decide the adequacy of consideration at the time of making the contract. Hence, consideration must be something to which the law attaches value though it need not be equal in value to the promise made. The courts do not exist to repair bad bargains.

Anson J observed in an English case that "consideration need not be adequate to the promise, but it must be of some value in the eyes of the law. The courts will not make bargains for the parties to a suit and if a man gets what he contracted for, will not inquire whether it was an equivalent to the promise which he gave in return".

Example: A purchased from B, a old motor cycle for ₹1,000. It would be a difficult, though not an impossible task for the court to ascertain whether the price paid was adequate or not or whether the motor cycle was worth the price paid.

The Indian Contract Act, in explanation 2 to section 25, further provides that an agreement to which the consent of the promisor is freely given is not void because the consideration is inadequate. However the inadequacy of the consideration may be taken into account by the court in determining the question whether the consent of the promisor was freely given.

Example: A agrees to sell a house worth ₹1,000 for ₹100 to B. The agreement is a contract notwithstanding the inadequacy of the consideration. But if A says that his consent was not freely given the inadequacy of the consideration is a fact which the court should take account in considering whether or not A's consent was freely given.

5. Consideration must be real and not illusory

Consideration must be real, competent and of some value in the eyes of the law although it need not be adequate. Consideration is not real when it is uncertain, illusory or when it is physically or legally impossible to perform.

(a) Physical impossibility

A promises to put life into the dead body of B's wife and B should pay him ₹500. A's promise is physically impossible to perform.

(b) Legal impossibility

A owes ₹100 to B. He promises to pay ₹20 to C, the servant of B, who in return promises to discharge A from the debt. It is legally impossible because C cannot give discharge for a debt due to B, his master.

(c) Uncertain consideration

A engages B for doing a certain work and promises to pay a "reasonable" sum. The promise is unenforceable as consideration is uncertain.

(d) Illusory consideration

Two of the crew of a ship deserted it half way through a voyage. The captain thereby promised to divide the salary of the deserters among the rest of the crew if they worked the vessel home. They could not recover the amount as the consideration was illusory and they were already under an obligation to bring the vessel home.

6. Consideration may be an act, abstinence or forbearance or a return promise

An act, abstinence or promise is called a consideration for the promise. To do or not do something in return is consideration.

Similarly the party may derive benefit, suffer loss or damage or inconvenience, it will be regarded in law as a consideration for the promise.

Example: A borrows from B ₹1000 at 24% pa and fails to pay the amount. When B is about to file a suit, A agrees to pay a higher rate of interest. B, as a result, does not file the suit. This forbearance on the part of B to file a suit is a sufficient consideration and B can enforce the promise of A to pay the higher rate of interest.

Debi Radha Rani Vs Dass (1941)

D is ready to sue her husband for maintenance allowance on husband's agreeing to pay her a monthly allowance by way of maintenance, she forbears to sue. Held, the wife's forbearance to sue amounts to consideration for the husband's agreement for payment of maintenance allowance.

7. Performance of existing obligation is no consideration

The performance of an act by a person who is already bound to perform the same either as a public duty or under the existing contractual obligation cannot be consideration for a contract.

Example: A promised to pay B, who had received summons to appear at a trial in a civil suit, a certain sum being a compensation for the loss of time during his attendance. The promise was without consideration as B was under a duty imposed by law to appear and give evidence.

Ramachandra Chirithanman Vs Kalu Raja [(1877) 2, B.Com 302]

There was a promise to pay to the vakil an additional sum if the suit was successful. Held, the promise was void for want of consideration. The vakil was under a pre-existing contractual obligation to render the best of his services under the original contract.

8. It must not be illegal, immoral or opposed to public policy

The consideration given for an agreement must not be unlawful, illegal immoral or opposed policy. If it is so, the courts do not allow an action on the agreement.

2.6 STRANGER TO CONTRACT

Stranger to contract is a person who is not a party to the contract. Since a contract is a private relationship between the parties who make it the rights and obligations under such a contract are strictly confined to them. So, a stranger cannot have any right and obligation upon a contract entered into between the other parties. Thus, it is a general rule of law that only parties to a contract may sue and be sued on that contract. This rule is known as the doctrine of privity of contract.

Privity of contract means relationship subsisting between the parties who have entered into contractual obligation. It implies a mutuality of will and creates a legal bond or tie between the parties to a contract.

There are two consequences of the doctrine of privity of contract:

(a) A person who is not a party to contract cannot sue upon even though the contract is for his benefit and he provided consideration.

Example: A and B make a contract, where by B is to pay A, if A does something for C. C cannot sue A if he fails to do what he promised. It makes no difference even if C gives consideration for the promise - he cannot sue unless he is a party to the contract.

(b) A contract cannot confer rights or impose obligations arising under it on any person other than the parties to it.

Example: A and B make a contract. C cannot enforce it.

2.6.1 Exceptions

The following are the exceptions to the rule that a stranger to a contract cannot sue.

1. A trust or charge

A person (called beneficiary) in whose favour a trust or other interest in some specific immovable property has been created can enforce it even though he is not a party to the contract.

Example: A agrees to transfer certain properties to be held by B in trust for the benefit of Core. C can enforce the contract even though he is not a party to the contract.

Gandy Vs Gandy [1884, 30, Ch. D. 57]

A husband who was separated from his wife executed a separation deed by which he promised to pay the trustees all expenses for the maintenance of his wife. Held, the agreement created a trust in favour of the wife could be enforced.

2. Marriage settlement, partition or other family arrangements

When an agreement is made in connection with marriage settlement, partition of property or other family arrangements and a provision is made for the benefit of a person, he may sue although he is not a party to the agreement.

Example: A promised to 'B' to give a gold chain to his daughter-in-law at the time of her marriage. C, though she is not a party to the contract, can enforce it.

Shuppu Ammal Vs Subramaniyan [1910]

Two brothers, on a partition of joint properties, agreed to invest in equal shares a certain sum of money for the maintenance of their mother. Held, she was entitled to require her sons to make the investment.

3. Acknowledgement or Estoppel

Where the promisor, by his conduct, acknowledges or otherwise constitutes himself as an agent of a third party, a binding obligation is thereby incurred by him towards the third party.

Example: A receives some money from B to be paid over to C. A admits of this receipt. C can recover the amount from A who shall be regarded as his agent.

4. Assignment of a contract

The assignee of rights and benefits under a contract not involving personal skill can enforce the contract subject to the equalties between the original parties.

Example: A draws a cheque in favour of B. B, though he is not a party to the contract between A and banker, can make the banker liable to pay and realise the cheque.

5. Contracts entered into through an agent

The principal can enforce the contracts entered into by his agent provided the agent acts within the scope of his authority and in the name of the principal.

2.7 NO CONSIDERATION NO CONTRACT

The general rule is *ex nudo pacto oritur* action. i.e. an agreement made without consid eration is void. It means an agreement cannot be enforceable in the court unless there is some consideration to it. But section 25 lays down certain exceptions to this rule. Under the following circumstances, an agreement made without consideration is valid.

1. Love and affection

Where an agreement is expressed in writing and registered under the law for the time being in force for the registration of documents and is made on account of natural love and affection between parties standing in close relation to each other, it is enforceable even if there is no consideration. In other words, a written and registered agreement based on natural love and affection between close relatives is enforceable even if it is without consideration.

What is natural love and affection?

A man makes an agreement with a prostitute and maintains that he has done so on account of natural love and affection. Even though this agreement is registered, it would be void as there cannot be natural love and affection for a prostitute and the consideration is immoral. Natural love and affection may exist between husband and wife, father and son or daughter, brother and sister etc .... It would include parties related by blood or marriage.

However, when a husband to get rid of his wife promised to give her separate flat for residential purposes and in the agreement stated that on account of frequent quarrels he decided to give his wife the flat, it was held that the promise to make the gift was not made on account of natural love and affection.

2. Compensation for voluntary services

A promise to compensate, wholly or in part, a person who has already voluntarily done something for the promisor, is enforceable, even though without consideration. In simple words, a promise to pay for a voluntary service is binding.

In order to come under this exception, service should have been rendered voluntarily and also for the promisor. Thus, where services were rendered for a company not then in existence, a subsequent promise to pay for them will not make a contract. But I promise made after attaining majority to pay for goods supplied to the promisor during minority is valid.

Examples
(a) A finds B's purse and gives it to him. B promised to pay A ₹l00. This is a contract.
(b) A says to B "At the risk of your life you saved me from a serious accident I promise to pay you ₹10,000." It is a contract.

3. Time-barred debt

A promise by debtor to pay a time-barred debt is enforceable provided it is made in writing and is signed by the debtor or his authorised agent. The promise may be to pay the whole or any part of the debt. The debt must be such "of which the creditor might have enforced payment but for the law for the limitation or suits."

A debt is time-barred by Limitation Act if it retains or unclaimed for a period of 3 years. Such a debt becomes legally irrecoverable.

Example: A owed to B ₹10, 000 but it is time barred by limitation. A gives a letter to B promising to pay ₹6,000 on account of debt. This is a contract.

4. Completed gifts

According to explanation 1, to section 25 "Nothing in this section shall affect the validity, as between the donor and the donee if any gift actually made." Thus, in case of a gift actually made, not being an agreement make a gift, no consideration is necessary.

5. Agency

No consideration is necessary to create an agency.

2.8 CAPACITY TO CONTRACT

One of the essential elements of a valid contract is that the parties who enter into a contract must have the capacity to do so. According to section 10, an agreement becomes a contract if it is entered into between the parties who are competent to contract. Capacity here means competence of the parties to enter into a valid contract. In other words, it refers to the status or attributes necessary for a person to have his or her acts legally allowed and recognised. Every person is presumed to have legal capacity to make a contract until the contrary is proved.

According to section 11, every person is competent to contract (a) who is of the age of majority according to the law to which he is subject (b) who is of sound mind and (c) who is not disqualified from contracting by any law to which he is subject. Thus, section 11 declares the following persons to be incompetent to contract.

1. Minors
2. Persons of unsound mind
3. Persons disqualified by law to which they are subject.

2.9 MINORS

A minor is a person who has not attained the age of majority according to the law to which he is subject. According to section 3 of the Indian Majority Act, 1875 "a minor is a person who has not completed 18 years of age". However, in the following two cases, he attains majority after 21 years of age.

1. When a guardian of a minor's person or property has been appointed under the Guardians and Wards Act 1980.
2. When superintendence of a minor's property is assumed by a court of wards.

Nature of Minor's agreements

Section 10 says that the parties to a contract must be competent and section 11 declares that a minor is not competent. But neither section makes it clear whether minor agreements would be voidable at his option or altogether void. Therefore, these provisions had quite naturally given rise to a controversy about the nature of a minor's agreement. Till some time an agreement with a minor was absolutely void but now the position is changed and if a guardian, on behalf of minor, enters into an agreement it is enforceable. However, the rules governing minor's agreements are based on two fundamental rules.

1. The law protects their (infants) persons, preserves their rights and estates excuseth their laches (negligence or unduly delay in enforcing their rights) and assist them in their pleadings; the judges are their counsellors, the jury their servants and law is their guardian.
2. In pursuing the above object, the law should not cause unnecessary hardships to persons who deal with minors.

2.9.1 Legal Rules

The legal rules relating to minor's agreements are summarised as follows.

1. Minor's contract is absolutely void

An agreement with or by a minor is void and inoperative ab inito. A minor's agreement being absolutely void, neither he nor the other party acquires any right or incurs any liability under the agreement. So a minor neither is liable to perform what he has promised under an agreement nor is he liable to repay money that he has received under it. The principle behind this ruling is, that a minor is incapable of judging what is good for him.

Mohori Bibi Vs Dharmadas Ghose (1903)

A minor mortgaged his house in favour of a moneylender for a sum of ₹20,000 out of which he received ₹8,000. Subsequently, the minor filed a suit for setting aside the mortgage. The moneylender claimed refund of ₹8,000 from the minor. It was held that minor's contract is altogether void and the moneylender, therefore, cannot recover the amount.

2. Specific performance of minor's contracts

As a minor's contract is absolutely void, there can be no specific performance of such a contract. The guardian has no power to bind a minor by a contract for the purchase of immovable property. Even a minor cannot enforce specific performance as there is no mutuality. However, when such a contract is entered into by a guardian on behalf of a minor for his benefit, it can be specifically enforced by or against the minor.

3. Ratification of minor's contracts

Ratification means consenting to a past contract entered into during minority at a future date on attaining majority. It relates back to the date of making contract. Since a minor's contract is absolutely void, there can be no question of ratifying it as the consideration given during the minority is held to be no consideration at all. It cannot be made valid by a subsequent ratification. If it is necessary a minor can enter into a fresh contract on attaining majority with a fresh consideration.

Indian Ramaswamy Vs Anthiappa Chettiar [1906,6 MLJ 422]

M, a minor, borrows ₹5,000 from L and executes a promissory note in favour of L. After attaining majority he executes another promissory note in settlement of the first note. The second promissory note is void for want of consideration.

4. False representation by a minor estoppel

A minor cannot be stopped by a false representation, as there can be no estoppel against a statue. A minor who falsely represents himself to be a major and thereby induces another person to enter into a contract with him, can plead minority as a defence. The infant is not stopped from setting up infancy.

A minor cannot be sued on the ground that he falsely represented that he is of full age and thereby induced other person to enter into a contract, because to allow an injured person to sue a minor person, it would be giving him indirect means of enforcing a void contract.

Example: A, a minor, by fraudulently representing himself to be of full age, induced B to lend him ₹1,000. He refused to repay it and B sued for the money. The contract is void and A is not liable to repay the amount.

5. Doctrine of Restitution

If an infant acquires property or goods by misrepresenting his age, he can be compelled to restore it to the owner, but as long as the same is traceable in his possession. This is known as the equitable doctrine of restitution. It is based on the principle that law gives protection to the minors; it does not give them liberty to "cheat men". However, doctrine of restitution is not applied where the infant has obtained cash instead of property or goods.

6. Liability of a third person-surety for a minor

An agreement by a minor is void but an agreement by a guardian on his behalf is valid. Where a guardian enters into a contract in respect of his property on behalf of the minor, it is valid, provided it is for his benefit or for legal necessity.

7. Insolvency

A minor cannot be adjudicated insolvent, as he is incapable of contracting.

8. Minor's marriage

Minor's marriage contracted by their parents and guardians is valid. It is valid on the ground of the custom of the community. However, the contract of marriage can be enforced against the other party at the instance of the minor, but the same cannot be enforced against the minor.

9. Compromise

A compromise entered into by a minor is void. Thus, a compromise entered into by minor's settling a dispute as regards inheritance between themselves and their father's collaterals is void and not binding on them. Such an agreement cannot be held as a family settlement.

10. Service contracts

A contract for personal service by a minor is void under the Indian law and the mere fact that it is for his benefit would not entitle the minor to sue under the contract. For instance, minor girls entering into a contract of service with a person can leave the service at any time without any actionable wrong.

2.9.2 Liability for Necessaries

A minor is liable for necessaries supplied to him or his minor dependent by another person. It implies that a minor can make valid contract for necessaries. Necessaries mean goods, which are suitable to the infant's condition in life and to his actual requirements at the time of sale and delivery. Even goods of luxurious nature are considered necessaries, provided they have some actual utility and fit the requirements of the infant. Whether an article is necessary or not also depends upon the circumstances in which it is bought and the use for which it is put. Some of the examples of necessaries are food, cloth, shelter, education, funeral expenses of parents, expenses incurred on the protection of property etc.

2.10 PERSONS OF UNSOUND MIND

One of the essential conditions of competency of parties to a contract is that they should be of sound mind. Section 12 of the Act defines that a person is said to be of sound mind for the purpose of making a contract if, at the time when he makes it, he is capable of understanding it and of forming a rational judgment as to its effect upon his interests. So, a person is said to be of unsound mind who is not in a position so understand ordinary matters of life. An agreement with a person of unsound mind, like of minor, is absolutely void. However, a person who is usually of unsound mind but occasionally of sound mind may make a contract when he is of sound mind. On the other hand, a person who is usually of sound mind but occasionally of unsound mind, cannot make a contract when he is of unsound mind.

Examples:

(a) A patient in a lunatic asylum, who is at intervals of sound mind, may contract during those intervals.

(b) A sane man, who is delirious from fever or who is so drunk that he cannot understand the terms of a contract or from a rational judgment as to its effect on his interests, cannot contract while such delirium or drunkenness exists.

Soundness of mind of a person depends on two facts: (1) his capacity to understand the contents of the business concerned and (2) his ability to form a rational judgement as to its effect upon his interests. If a person is incapable of both, he suffers from unsoundness of mind. Whether a person is of sound mind or not is a question of fact to be decided by the court. There is a presumption in favour of sanity. If a person relies on unsoundness of mind, he must prove it sufficiently to satisfy the court.

2.10.1 Types of persons of unsound mind

Lunatic

A lunatic is a person who is mentally deranged due to some mental strain or other personal experience. He suffers from intermittent intervals of sanity and insanity. He can enter into contracts during the period when he is of sound mind.

Idiot

An idiot is a person who has completely lost his mental powers. He does not exhibit understanding of even ordinary matters. Idiocy is permanent whereas lunacy denotes periodical insanity with lucid intervals. An agreement with an idiot is always absolutely void.

Drunkard

A drunkard is an intoxicated person who suffers from temporary incapacity to contract i.e. at the time when he is so drunk or intoxicated that he is incapable of forming a rational judgment. The position of a drunkard is similar to that of a lunatic.

Effects of contracts

A contract entered into by a person, who at that time, was of unsound mind is void. But according to Section 68 an agreement entered into by a person who is of unsound mind, for the supply of necessaries suited either to his condition in life or to anyone whom he is legally so bound to support, the person who has furnished such supplies is entitled to be reimbursed from the property of such an incapable person.

Example: A supplies B, a lunatic, with necessaries suited to his conditions in life. A is entitled to be reimbursed from B's properties.

2.11 PERSONS DISQUALIFIED BY LAW

Certain persons, even though they are not minors or of unsound mind, are disqualified by law to enter into a legally binding contract. They are not qualified for contracting by any law to which they are subject. The following are such categories of persons.

2.11.1 Alien

An alien is a person who is a citizen of a foreign country. He is not a subject of the Republic of India. He may be (i) an alien friend or (ii) an alien enemy.

An alien friend is a foreign citizen whose state is at peace with the Republic of India. Contracts with an alien friend are valid subject to certain restrictions.

An alien enemy is a foreign citizen whose state is at war with the Republic of India. The status of an alien enemy with regard to contractual capacity depends on the timing of the contract in question. While the war is in progress the alien enemy can neither enter into a contract with an Indian subject nor can be sued in an Indian court. Contracts made before the war may be either suspended or dissolved. They will be dissolved if they are against the public policy or if their performance would benefit the enemy. Others are suspended till the war ends and are revived provided they have not become time-barred under the law of limitation.

2.11.2 Corporation

A corporation is an artificial person created by law under the Indian Companies Act, 1956 or formed by special Act of the legislature. Though it is competent to contract, it cannot enter into contracts of strictly personal nature. Its contractual capacity is limited by the statute governing it. Its contractual capacity is regulated by the terms of its memorandum of association and the provisions of the Act applicable. If it exceeds its powers, whether expressly conferred on it or derived by reasonable implication from its objects clause in the memorandum, the contract is ultra vires the company and is void.

2.11.3 Insolvent

Insolvent is a person whose liabilities exceed his assets. In other words he is a person who is not in a position to pay off his liability in full. When a person is adjudged insolvent, his property vests in the Official Receiver or Official Assignee. As such the insolvent is deprived of his power to deal in that property. It is only the Official Receiver or Official Assignee who can enter into contracts relating to his property and sue and be sued on his behalf.

2.11.4 Convict

Convict is a person who is undergoing imprisonment in jail for a crime. He is incapable of entering into contracts while undergoing imprisonment. He can, however, enter into contract if he is lawfully at large under a licence called "Ticket of leave." This disqualification comes to an end once the term of imprisonment expires or when the convict is acquitted. He, however, does not suffer from the rigours of the law of limitation. It is held abeyance during the period of his sentence.

2.12 FREE CONSENT

Free consent is also another essential requirement of a valid contract. It is necessary to the creation of the contract that the parties to it must give consent. Their consent must be free. A contract, which is regular in all other respects, may still fail because there is no free consent to it by one or both the parties. Section 10 also says that "all agreements are contracts if they are made by the free consent of parties."

2.12.1 Meaning and Definition

Consent means acquiescence or act of assenting to an offer. It is said to exist when the parties agree upon the same thing in the same sense.

Section 13 of the Act defines consent as "Two or more persons are said to be consent when they agree upon the same thing in the same sense". When both the parties agree upon the same thing in the same sense, they are said to be 'ad idem'. It means they have the identity of mind. Where the minds of both the parties are directed to different objects, there is no consent.

2.12.2 Free consent

Not only the parties to a contract should have identity of mind but the consent of the parties must also be real and free. Free consent is the consent, which has been obtained by the free will of the parties out of their own accord.

Section 14 of the Act defines free consent as "consent is said to be free when it is not caused by:

1. Coercion
2. Undue influence
3. Fraud
4. Misrepresentation
5. Mistake.

When there is no consent, there is no contract. Salmond describes it as error in consensus. One such circumstance, which interferes with consensus ad idem, is mistake. When consent is caused by mistake, the agreement is void.

Example: An illiterate woman executed a deed of gift in favour of her nephew under the impression that she was executing a deed authorising her nephew to manage her lands. The evidence showed that the woman never intended to execute such a deed of gift nor was the deed ever read or explained to her. Held, the deed was void and inoperative (Bala Debi Vs S. Majumdar AIR (1956) Cal. 575).

When there is consent but no free consent, there is generally a contract voidable at the option of the party whose consent was not free. This is known as error in causa. Such an error results from coercion, undue influence, fraud or misrepresentation.

Example: A is forced to sign an agreement to sell his site to B at the point of pistol. A knows what he is signing but his consent is not free. The contract in this case is voidable at his option.

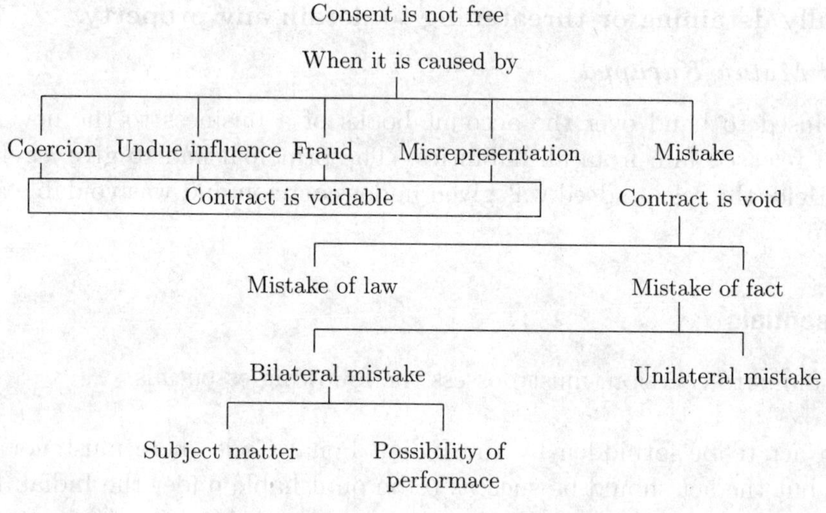

2.13 COERCION

Coercion refers to threat or force used by one party against the other for making him to enter into an agreement. In other words, when a person is compelled to enter into a contract by the use of force by the other party or under a threat, coercion is said to be employed.

Example: A threatens to shoot B if he does not sell his car to him. B sells the car. The threat amounts to coercion.

According to section 15, "coercion is the committing or threatening to commit any act forbidden by the Indian Penal Code 1860 or the unlawful detaining or threatening to detain any property to the prejudice of any person whatever, with the intention of causing any person to enter into an agreement." This section also says that "it is immaterial whether the Indian Penal Code is or is not in force in place where the coercion is employed".

Thus, consent is said to be caused by coercion when it is obtained by pressure extended by either of the following techniques.

1. Committing or threatening to commit any act forbidden by the Indian Penal Code.

Ranganayakamma Vs Alwar Settey (1889)

A young girl of 13 years was forced to adopt a boy to her husband who had just died by the relatives of husband who prevented the removal of his body for cremation until she consented. It was held that the adoption was not binding on her as consent was obtained under coercion within the meaning of section 15 since any person who obstructed a dead body from being removed would be guilty of an offence under section 297 of the IPC. Consequently, the adoption was set aside.

2. Unlawfully detaining or threatening to detain any property.

Muthia Vs Muthu Karuppa

An agent refused to hand over the account books of a business to the new agent unless the principal released him from all liabilities. The principal had to give a release deed as demanded. Held, the release deed was given under coercion and was voidable at the option of the principal.

2.13.1 Essentials

Any act, amounts to coercion, must possess the following essentials.

1. For an act to be forbidden by the Indian Penal Code there must not be merely a threat but the act should be such as to be punishable under the Indian Penal Code.
2. The act must have been done or threatened with the intention of causing any person to enter into an agreement.
3. It includes physical compulsion fear and even menace to goods.
4. It does not matter whether the Indian Penal Code is or is not in force in the place where the coercion is employed.
5. Coercion may proceed from anybody even a person who is not a party to the contract and may be directed against even a member of his household not necessarily the other contracting party.

2.13.2 Threat to commit suicide: Does it amount to coercion?

A person may obtain consent to an agreement by threatening to commit suicide. Thus, the question may arise to whether a threat to commit suicide is an act forbidden by the Indian Penal Code and consequently amounts to coercion.

Amiraju Vs Sheshamma

By threat of suicide, a Hindu husband induced his wife and son to execute a release in favour of his brother in respect of certain properties. The wife and son executed the release deed under the threat. It was held that the threat of suicide amounted to coercion under section 15 and the deed was, therefore, voidable. Further Old-field J observed that one person committing suicide places himself beyond the reach of law and necessarily beyond the reach of any punishment too. But, an attempt to commit suicide is punishable under the Indian Penal Code.

Thus an attempt to commit suicide amounts to coercion.

2.13.3 Effects

The following consequences will arise for an agreement made out of coercion

1. The agreement is a contract voidable at the option of the party whose contract was so caused (Sec 19).
2. A person to whom money had been paid or anything delivered under coercion must repay or return it (Sec 72).
3. He may rescind the contract within a reasonable time under the Specific Relief Act, 1963.

2.13.4 Duress

In English, the near equivalent of the term 'coercion' is 'duress'. Duress involves actual or threatened violence over the contracting party (or his wife, children or parent) with a view to obtaining his consent to the agreement. If the threat is with regard to the goods or property, it is not duress. Thus, the Indian law is much wider than the English law. The threat complained of the under the former relates to persons and property, whereas, under the latter it is confined to persons.

2.14 UNDUE INFLUENCE

Sometimes a person is compelled to enter into an agreement against his will as a result of unfair persuasion by the other party. This happens when a special kind of relationship exists between the parties such that one party is in a position to exercise undue influence over the other [father and son, husband and wife, doctor and patient, advocate and client, debtor and creditor etc.]

Undue influence is said to exist when one of the parties to the contract obtains, through dominance, consent of another party. It is the unconscientious use by one person of power possessed by him over another in order to induce the other party to enter into a contract. It is sometimes called moral coercion.

Example: A husband forcing his wife to sell her necklace to another person against her will, is a case of undue influence and the agreement may be set aside.

Section 16 of the Act defines undue influence as "A contract is said to be induced by undue influence where the relations subsisting between the parties are such that one of the parties is in a position to dominate the will of the other and uses that position to obtain an unfair advantage over the other."

Undue influence is the domination of a weak mind by a strong mind to an extent, which causes the behaviour of the weaker person to assume an unnatural character. It is an influence which compels another person to do something which he would not have done, if he had been a free agent. A friendly advice or persuasion would not constitute undue influence.

2.14.1 Essentials

In order to constitute undue influence the following ingredients are necessary.

1. The relations subsisting between the parties should be such that one of the parties is in a position to dominate the will of the other.
2. The dominant party obtains an unfair advantage over the other.
3. The act of undue influence must range under one or the other heads of 'coercion' or 'fraud'.

However, whether a party was in a position to dominate the will of the other is a question of fact. Section 16(2) says that a person is deemed to be in a position to dominate the will of another:

(a) where he holds real or apparent authority over the other or where he stands in a fiduciary relation to the other.

Example: A having advanced money to his son 'B' during his minority upon B's coming of age obtains, by misuse of parental influence, a bond from B for a greater amount than the sum due in respect of the advance. A employs undue influence.

(b) where he makes a contract with a person whose mental capacity is temporarily or permanently affected by reason of age, illness or mental or bodily distress.

Example: A, man enfeebled by disease or age is induced by B's influence over him as his medical attendant, to agree to pay B an unreasonable sum for his professional services. B employs undue influence.

2.14.2 Burden of Proof [Sec 16 (3)]

Where a person who is in a position to dominate the will of another, enters into a contract with him and the transaction appears, on the face of it or on the evidence induced to be unconscionable, the burden of proving that such a contract was not induced by undue influence shall lie upon the person in a position to dominate the will of the other.

Example: A being in debt to B, a moneylender of his village contracts a fresh loan on terms, which appears to be unconscionable. It lies on B to prove that the contract was not induced by undue influence.

What is an unconscionable transaction?

When a person who is in a dominant position makes an unreasonable use of his superior power over the other and enters into a bargain which is so much to his own advantage that it "shocks the conscience or makes an exorbitant profit of the other's distress, the transaction is said to be unconscionable. The mere fact that the rate of interest is very high in a moneylending transaction will not make unconscionable because it is usual for moneylenders to charge high rate of interest from the needy borrowers. But if the rate of interest is exorbitant and the court regards the transaction unconscionable, the burden of proving that no undue influence was used lies on the lender.

Example: A applies to a banker for a loan at a time when there is stringency in the money market. The banker declines to make the loan except at an unusually high rate of interest. A accepts the loan on these terms. It is a transaction in the ordinary course of business and the contract is not induced by undue influence.

2.14.3 Effects

The following consequences will arise for an agreement resulted on account of undue influence.

1. The agreement is a contract voidable at the opinion of the party whose consent was taken by undue influence.
2. Any such contract may be set aside either absolutely or if the party who was entitled to avoid it has received any benefit thereunder upon such terms and conditions as the court may deem just [Sec 19(A)].
3. Only a party to the contract can avoid or rescind the contract. This right does not lie in the hands of the third party.

Comparison between coercion and undue influence

Coercion	Undue influence
1. Consent is obtained by threat of an offence.	1. Consent is obtained by the dominating will of the other.
2. It is mainly of physical character. It involves mostly use of physical or violent force.	2. It is of moral character. It involves use of moral force or mental force.
3. The contract is voidable at the option of the promisor.	3. The contract is either voidable or the court may set aside or enforce it in a modified form.
4. It attracts the provisions of the Indian Penal Code as the party exercising coercion exposes himself to criminal liability.	4. There is no such criminal liability.

2.15 FRAUD

Fraud is the wilful representation made by a party to a contract with the intent to deceive the other party or to induce such party to enter into a contract. It means a false statement made knowingly or without belief in its truth. In short it is intentional or deliberate misrepresentation of facts. It denotes an absence of honest belief and a wicked mind. Whenever one person obtains any material advantage from another by unfair and wrongful means, it is said that he has committed fraud.

Fraud may be defined as "an untrue statement made knowingly, or without belief in its truth, or recklessly, careless whether it be true or false with intent to deceive".

Section 17 defines fraud as "Fraud means and includes any of the following acts done with 'intend to deceive' or to induce a person to enter into a contract".

1. The suggestion that a fact is true when it is not true and the person making the suggestion does not believe it to be true.
2. The active concealment of a fact by a person who has knowledge or belief of the fact.
3. Promise made without any intention of performing it.
4. Any other fact fitted to deceive.
5. Any such act or omission as the law specifically declares to be fraudulent.

Examples

(a) A sells a horse by auction to B that A knows to be unsound. A says nothing to B about horse's unsoundness. This is not fraud in A.

(b) B is A's daughter and has just come of age. Here the relation between the parties would make it A's duty to tell B if the horse is unsound.

(c) B says to A "if you do not deny it, I shall assume that the horse is sound" A says nothing. Here A's silence is equivalent to speech and amounts to fraud.

(d) A and B, being traders, enter upon a contract. A has private information of a change in prices which would affect B's willingness to proceed with the contract. A is not bound to inform B.

2.15.1 Essentials

The following essential ingredients must be present in an act to become fraud.

1. There must be an intention to deceive.
2. The act must be done by a party to a contractor, with his connivance or by his agent.
3. There must be a false representation of fact i.e. suggestion falsi.
4. There must be an active concealment of a fact of which he has the knowledge and duty to disclose i.e. suppressio veri.
5. There must be a false promise i.e. a promise made without any intention to perform it.
6. Any other act or omission, which the law considers it to be fraudulent or fitted to deceive which is done with the obvious intention to commit fraud.
7. The party so induced must have acted upon it and suffered loss.

2.15.2 Exceptions

When consent to an agreement is caused by fraud, the agreement is a contract voidable at the option of the party whose consent was so caused. But in the following cases the contract is not voidable.

1. Deceit which does not deceive

A party, who at the time of agreement, knows through diligence that the other is making a false representation and yet enters into the agreement can have no grievance. An attempt to deceive which does not deceive the party has no effect because there is no damage.

2. Negligence

If an element of negligence or carelessness creeps in, it is not fraud.

3. Ignorance

Where a party enters into a contract in ignorance of fraud, the contract is not voidable.

4. Waiver

Where a party deceived takes benefit of the contract or waives the fraud and gives his consent to it, the contract becomes valid.

2.15.3 Mere silence is not Fraud

Mere silence of a party as to certain facts does not generally amount to fraud. A party to the contract is under no obligation to disclose the whole truth to the other party. Similarly there is no duty to disclose facts, which are within the knowledge of both the parties. Silence in such a case will not amount to fraud.

Sri Krishna Vs Kurukshetra University (1976)

A student does not disclose details about attendance shortage in his application though he knew it. He cannot be stopes from appearing examination. The student committed no fraud by not disclosing the attendance shortage. It was the duty of the university to scrutinise forms and call for explanation in case of doubts.

However, silence cannot go too far. It amounts to fraud in certain cases. They are as follows

1. When the party keeping silence under duty to speak. Duty to speak arises when one party responses and the other accepts confidence. For example a father selling a horse to his son, has the duty to tell his son whother the horse was of unsound mind, because the son responses confidence in his father.

2. Silence amounts to fraud when there is a change of circumstances. Sometimes a representation is true when made but may become false when acted upon by the party. This may happen because of changed circumstances. In such cases it is the duty of the person who made the representation to communicate the change of circumstances. For example, a company's prospectus represented that certain persons would be directors of the company but before the allotment took place, there were changes, in the board some directors having retired. The allotee was allowed to avoid the allotment as the change was not communicated to him in time.

3. Finally silence amounts to fraud when a person voluntarily makes a settlement but stops half a way through. Having committed himself to disclose he has duty to speak out remaining truth. Failure to do so amounts to fraud.

2.15.4 Effects

The following remedies are available to the party who has been induced to enter into a contract by fraud.

1. The contract is voidable at the option of the party whose consent was so caused.
2. He may insist that the contract shall be performed and that he shall be put in the position in which he would have been, if the representation made had been true.
3. He may rescind the contract within a reasonable time under the Specific Relief Act, 1963.
4. He has a right to sue for damages.

2.16 MISREPRESENTATION

The word representation means a statement of fact which one party makes in the course of negotiations with a view to inducing the other party to enter into a contract. When the statement is untrue but the person making it believes it to be true, it is known as misrepresentation. In other words, misrepresentation means a statement made which in fact is not true under the belief that it is true. In short, it refers to misstatement of a material fact to a contract. So, it is a false statement, which the person making it honestly believes it to be true, or which he does not know to be false. It also includes non-disclosure of a material fact or facts without any intent to deceive the other party.

According to section 18, misrepresentation means and includes.

1. When a person positively asserts that a fact is true but his information does not warrant it to be so though he believes it to be true.
2. When there is any breach of duty by a person, which brings an advantage to the person committing it by misleading another to his prejudice.
3. When a party causes, however, innocently the other party to the agreement to make a mistake as to substances of the thing, which is the subject of the agreement.

Example

1. A says to B that C's horse is very good and runs 20 miles at a stretch. A believes the statement to be true. B purchases the horse from C on A's information. It turns out that the horse is able to run 2 miles. It is a misrepresentation.
2. A having no time to read the contents of a deed, signed it as he was given the impression by 'B' that it contained nothing but formal matters already settled between them. However, the deed contained a release in favour of B. It is a misrepresentation as it is the duty of B to state fully without concealment all that was essential to knowledge of the contents of a document because A placed confidence in him.

3. A told B that one C would be the director of a company. A obtained this information not from C directly but from another person D. B acting on A's information subscribed for shares in the company. C did not become the director. This was misrepresentation.

2.16.1 Essentials

A misrepresentation is relevant if it satisfies the following requirements:

1. It must be a representation of a material fact. Mere expression of opinion does not amount to misrepresentation even if it turns out to be wrong.
2. It must be made before the conclusion of the contract with a view to inducing the other party to enter into the contract.
3. It must be made with the intention that it should be acted upon by the person to whom it is addressed.
4. It must actually have been acted upon and must have induced the contract.
5. It must be wrong but the person who made it honestly believed it to be true.
6. It must be made without any intention to deceive the other party.
7. It need not be made directly to the plaintiff. A wrong statement of facts made to a third person with the intention of communicating it to the plaintiff also amounts to misrepresentation.

Babul Vs R.A. Singh (1968)

A told his wife within the hearing of their daughter that the bridegroom proposed for her was a young man. The bridegroom however, was over sixty years. The daughter gave her consent to marry him believing the statement by her father. Held the consent was vitiated by misrepresentation and fraud.

2.16.2 Effects

The party, whose consent is caused by misrepresentation shall have the following remedies.

1. He can avoid the contract.
2. He may rescind the contract within a reasonable time under the Specific Relief Act 1963.
3. He may accept the contract but insists that he shall be placed in the position in which he would have been if the representation made had been true.

Comparison between Misrepresentation and Fraud

Misrepresentation	Fraud
1. The person making the statement believes it to be true.	1. The person making the. statement does not believe it to be true.
2. There is no intention to deceive.	2. There is intention to deceive.
3. It makes contract voidable at the option of the party injured.	3. Besides making the contract voidable at the option of the party injured, it gives right to an independent action in tort.
4. The contract cannot be avoided if the party, whose consent was so caused, had the means of discovering the truth with ordinary diligence.	4. The contract is voidable even though the aggreived party had the means of discovering the truth with ordinary diligence.

2.17 MISTAKE

One of the essential elements for the formation of a valid contract is that the offer and acceptance must correspond exactly. If they do not correspond, there is no true consensus ad-idem and either one or both the parties are said to be under mistake.

Mistake is a misconception or error. It means that parties intending to do one thing have by unintentional error done something else. Mistake may be defined as an erroneous belief about something. It refers to either one or both the parties to the contract are not properly understood matters relating to the contract and have done something wrong against their intention.

Mistake is of two types

1. Mistake of law
2. Mistake of fact

2.17.1 Mistake of Law

When the parties are not aware of the law and done something, which ought not to be done, it is said to be mistake of law. It is of two types.

1. Mistake of law of own country

Ignorantia juris non-excu at, i.e. "ignorance of law is no excuse" is a well-settled rule of law. Every citizen is supposed to know the rule of law of his own country. A party cannot be allowed to get any relief on the ground that it had done a particular act in ignorance of law. A mistake of law of own country is, therefore, no excuse, and the contract cannot be voided.

Example: A owed B ₹10,000. B was under the impression that the debt was time barred. However, B pressed A to pay the amount of the debt. A was aware that the debt was not barred by the law of limitation. A offered to pay ₹3,000 in full settlement of B's claim. B accepted the offer thereafter. B found out that the debt was not barred by the law of limitation B desired to avoid the contract. This is a mistake as to the law in force in India and B cannot avoid the contract.

2. Mistake of law of foreign country

Mistake of law of a foreign country vitiates the contract. The contract becomes void. Mistake of law in force in India is treated as a mistake of fact.

2.17.2 Mistake of fact

When one or both the parties to an agreement are under a mistake as to a matter of fact essential to the agreement it is said to be mistake of fact. It is of two types.

1. Bilateral mistake
2. Unilateral mistake

Bilateral Mistake

Where both the parties to an agreement are under a mistake as to a matter of fact essential to the agreement, there is a bilateral mistake or mutual mistake. In such a case, the agreement is void.

Example: A agreed to purchase B's car, which was lying in B's garage. Unknown to either party, the car or garage were completely destroyed by fire a day earlier. The agreement is void.

Bilateral mistake is of two types.

1. Mistake as to the subject matter: Where both the parties to an agreement are working under a mistake relating to the subject matter, the agreement is void. Mistake as to subject matter covers existence, identity, title, price, quantity and quality of the subject matter.

Example: A inspected fifty rifles in B's shop. Later, he wired B "send three rifles" By mistake of the telegraph clerk the message transmitted to B was "Send the rifles" B sent fifty rifles. A, however, accepted three rifles and sent back the rest. B had to accept the rifles returned.

2. Mistake as to possibility of performing the contract

Where both the parties believe that an agreement is capable of being performed when in fact it is not possible to be performed, the agreement is void on the ground of impossibility. It may be physical impossibility or legal impossibility.

Example

(a) A promise to share with B 50% of the treasure provided the treasure is created by magic. It is physically impossible in nature and the agreement is void.

(b) A agrees with B to sell his site which he already made an agreement to sell to C. Now the agreement between A and B is legally impossible and is void.

Unilateral Mistake

Where one of the parties is mistaken about the value or quality of the subject matter or in expressing or understanding the terms or the legal effect of the agreement, the mistake is a unilateral mistake. Section 22 provides that if one party alone is under a mistake of fact, the contract is not rendered voidable. But if the consent is given by a party under an error or mistake which is so fundamental as goes to the root of the agreement, it is void. Thus, in the following cases, even though there is unilateral mistake, the agreement is void.

1. Mistake as to the identity of the person contracted with: It is a fundamental rule of law that if one of the parties represents himself to be some person other than he really is there is a mistake as to the identity of the person contracted with it. A mistake as to the identity of a person contracted with when such identity is essential to the contract would invalidate the contract.

Example

(a) A intends a contract with B but finds that he has contracted with C, there is no contract if the identity of B was a material element of the contract and C knows it.

(b) In May 1938, a lady by name of Ann Robinson was convicted of permitting disorderly conduct in her cafe. In July of the same year she assumed another name, Ann potter and took a lease of Sowler's premises. Held, the lease was void ab initioab because of Sowler's mistaken belief that Ann potter was not Ann Robinson [Sowler Vs Potter (1940)].

Cundy Vs Lindsay (1878)

Blenkaran ordered, by letter, goods from Lindsay and signed it in such a way that Lindsay believed it came from the well-known firm of Blenkiran & Co. Held, there was no contract between Lindsay and as Lindsay never intended to deal with Blenkiran, having never heard of him.

2. Mistake as to the nature of contract

If a person enters into a contract in the mistaken belief that he is signing a document of a different class and character altogether there is a mistake as to the nature of contract and the contract is void. He can successfully plead that it is not his document. Thus, while in signing a document the mind of the singer does not go with the signature, there is a mistake, which would vitiate the contract.

Example: A, an old man of poor sight, signed his cheque thinking that it was a guarantee letter. There was no contract on the ground that the mind of the signer did not accompany the signature.

2.18 LEGALITY OF OBJECT

Legality of object is yet another requirement of a valid agreement. A contract must not only be based upon mutual assent of competent parties but must also have a lawful object. The word 'object' means purpose or design of the contract. It implies the manifestation of intention. The word 'lawful' means permitted by law. So, lawful object means law of the land must permit the purpose of the parties to the contract. If the object of an agreement is the performance of an unlawful act the agreement is not enforceable. Section 23 declares that the object or the consideration of an agreement is not lawful in certain cases. The words 'object' and 'consideration' are not used synonymously. In some cases, consideration for an agreement may be lawful but the purpose for which the agreement is entered into may be unlawful. In such cases the agreement is void. As such both the object and the consideration of an agreement must be lawful otherwise the agreement is void.

2.18.1 When consideration or object is unlawful?

Section 23 declares that the 'consideration' or 'object' of an agreement is not lawful in the following cases.

1. Forbidden by law: If the object or the consideration of an agreement is the doing of an act forbidden by law, the agreement is void. An act is forbidden by law when it is punishable under the Indian Penal Code or by any special legislation. Where the act is forbidden by law, the agreement will be void and the parties cannot recover anything under such an agreement.

Examples

(a) A promises B to drop a prosecution which he has instituted against B for recovery and B promises to restore the value of the thing taken. The agreement is void as its object is unlawful.

(b) A promises to obtain for B an employment in the public services and B promises to pay ₹1,000 to A. The agreement is void as the consideration for it is unlawful.

2. Defeat any law

Sometimes the consideration for an agreement may not be directly forbidden by law but if permitted it might defeat the provisions of any law. Such agreement is also void. So, when an agreement is entered into to defeat the intention of the legislature such an agreement would defeat the provisions of any law and will therefore be unlawful.

Examples

(a) A is employed with B for a salary of ₹5,000 and travelling allowance and daily allowance of ₹8,000. Both the parties knew that more TA and DA given was a device to evade tax. The agreement was unlawful.

(b) A was licensed under an Excise Act to run a liquor shop. The Act forbids the sale, transfer or sub-lease of the licence or the creation of a partnership to run the shop. A took B into partnership. Held, the agreement was void.

(c) A, a Muslim, contracts to marry B. A already has four wives. His marriage with B would be void, as the same would contravene provisions of the Mohammedan law as a Muslim is authorised to only four marriages.

(d) A contracts to give his adopted son B in consideration of an annual allowance to the natural parents. No suit will be allowed to recover any allowance on such a contract as such an agreement defeats the provisions of Hindu law.

3. Fraudulent

An agreement made for fraudulent purpose is void. Where the parties agree to impose a fraud on a third person, their agreement is unlawful. Agreement to defraud creditors or to give fraudulent preferences to a creditor to defraud revenue authorities or investors in a company is illegal.

Examples

(a) A and B agree to distribute themselves gains acquired or to be acquired by them by fraud, the agreement is void.

(b) A being an agent for a landed proprietor, agrees for money, without the knowledge of his principal, to obtain for B a lease of land belonging to his principal. The agreement between A and B is void as it implies a fraud by concealment by A on his principal.

4. Injurious to person or property

An agreement between two persons to injure the person or property of another is unlawful and therefore void. In the same way, if the object of an agreement is such that it involves or implies injury to the person or property of another, the agreement is void.

Examples

(a) A promises to pay B ₹1000 if he published an article defamatory in character against C, so that it would lower his reputation. B publishes the same. A refuses to pay the amount. B cannot recover the amount as the agreement between A and B involved injury to C.

(b) A agrees to pay B ₹1000 if B destroyed the standing crop of C. As agreed B destroyed it. He cannot recover the amount from A because the agreement between them is to injure property of C.

5. Immoral

Every agreement, the object or consideration of which, is immoral. The word immoral means inconsistent with what is right. It takes every aspect of a personal life deviating from the standard norms of life. Anything contrary to good morals, for example, sexual immorality, illicit cohabitation, prostitution etc., would be regarded as immoral.

(a) A agrees to let her daughter to B for concubinage (state of living together as husband and wife without being married) it is immoral.

(b) A married woman was given money to enable her to obtain divorce from her husband and then to marry the lender. Held, the agreement was immoral and the lender could not recover the amount [Bai-Vijli Vs Nansa Nagar 1885 Bom.152].

(c) A tempo traveller was let on hire to a prostitute knowing that it would be used for immoral purpose to attract men, the agreement was held to be illegal and the hire could not be recovered [Pearce Vs Brooks 1886-LRI Ex 213]

6. Public policy

An agreement is unlawful if the court regards it as opposed to public policy. A contract, which is opposed, to public policy, cannot be enforced by either of the parties to it. An agreement, which tends to promote corruption or injustice or is against the interests of the public, is considered to be opposed to public policy.

2.18.2 What is public policy?

An agreement is said to be opposed to public policy when it is harmful to the public welfare. In other words, an agreement which is injurious to the public or is against the interest of the society, is said to be opposed to public policy. Public policy is that principle of law which holds that no subject cart lawfully do that which has a mischievous tendency to be injurious to the interests of the public or which is against the public good or public welfare. However, it is not possible to give a precise or exact definition of the term 'public policy.'

It is a vague and elastic term. The flexibility of the doctrine of public policy is potentially dangerous. It could provide a judge with an excuse for invalidating any contract, which he violently disliked. With this danger in mind, judges have often criticised the doctrine of public policy. In the words of Burrough J in Richardson V sMallish case "public policy was a very unruly horse and when once you get astride it you never know where it will carry you." In another case Janson V s Driefontein Consolidated Mines Ltd, Lord Davey observed that "public policy is always an unsafe and treacherous ground for legal decisions... and that categories of public policy are closed and that no court can invent a new head as narrow views, courts cannot create new head of public policy." According to these views known as narrow views, courts cannot create new head of public policy. A new head of public policy can be coined only when the harm to the public policy is substantially incontestable.

But, according to the current school of thought, known as the broad view school, the principles governing public policy must be and are capable of proper occasion of expansion or modification. One need not shy away from unruly horse. With a good man in the saddle the unruly horse can be kept in control. It can jump over obstacles. Danckwerts J observed in Nagle Vs Fielden case "the law relating to public policy cannot remain immutable, it must change with the passage of time. The wind of change blows upon it."

Rejecting the argument that new heads of public policy should not be evolved for the risk of unruliness and uncertainty involved in such an attempt, it has been held in 'Ratanchand Hirachand Vs Asker Nawaz Jung' case that in a modern progressive society with fast changing social values and concepts, new heads of public policy need to be evolved whenever necessary. Law cannot afford to remain static. It has, of necessity, to keep pace with the progress of society and judges are under an obligation to evolve new techniques to meet the new conditions and concepts.

2.18.3 Agreements opposed to public policy

The following agreements have been held to be opposed to public policy and are unlawful.

1. Trading with an enemy

All agreements made between the citizen of alien countries when two countries are at war with each other, are considered void, illegal and inoperative. It applies to all contracts, which involve intercourse with the enemy or tend to assist the enemy. Only when the Government permits such agreements, they are considered valid. These agreements are held to be against public policy in natural interest as their existence may benefit the country. Besides, it is against national honour in times of national emergency. But contracts which are entered into at the time of peace and subsequently war breaks out between the two countries the obligation of performance of the contract is suspended till the end of hostilities.

2. Agreement to commit a crime

Where the consideration in an agreement is to commit a crime the agreement is opposed to public policy. Such an agreement is not enforceable by court. Likewise an agreement to indemnify a person against consequences of his criminal act is opposed to public policy and hence unenforceable.

Example: A promises to indemnify B in consideration of his beating to C. It is opposed to public policy.

3. Agreements which interfere with administration of justice

An agreement, the object that is to interfere with administration of justice is unlawful, being opposed to public policy. It may take any of the following forms.

(a) Interference with the course of justice

An agreement which obstructs the ordinary process of justice is unlawful. So, an agreement for using improper influence of any kind with the judges or officers of justice is unlawful. But an agreement to refer present or future disputes to arbitration is valid.

(b) Stiffling prosecution

It is in public interest that if a person has committed a crime; he must be prosecuted and punished. Hence, an agreement not to prosecute an offender is an agreement for stiffling prosecution and is unlawful. But a compromise in case of compoundable (offence not a serious one or involves only private rights) is valid.

Example: A promises to drop prosecution which he has instituted against B for robbery and B promises to restore the stolen property. It is an unlawful agreement.

(c) Maintenance and champerty

Maintenance is an agreement to give financial or other assistance to another to enable him to bring or defend legal proceedings, when the person giving assistance has got no legal interest of his own in the subject-matter. In other words, when a person agrees to maintain a suit, which he has, no legal interest for its prosecution or defence, the proceeding is known as maintenance.

Example: A offers to pay B ₹5000 if B will sue C. A's motive is to annoy C.

Champerty is an agreement whereby one party is to assist another to bring an action for recovering money or property and is to share in the proceeds of the action. In other words, when a person bargains for a share in the proceeds to be decreed in a suit in return for assisting another to bring an action is known as champerty.

Example: A files a suit against B to recover ₹10,000. C promises A the cost of litigation and in turn demands 50% of the amount if A succeeds in the suit.

4. Agreements in restrain of legal proceedings

An agreement, which prohibits a person from taking judicial proceedings, in respect of any right arising from a contract, is void. Further, agreements which curtail the period of limitation prescribed by the law of limitations, are also void because their object is to defeat the provisions of law.

5. Trafficking in public offices and titles

Agreements for the sale or transfer of public offices and titles or for the procurement of a public recognition like Padma Sree or Bharatha Ratna for monetary consideration are unlawful being, opposed to public policy. Such agreement, if enforced, would lead to inefficiency and corruption in public life. Similarly, an agreement to pay money to a public servant to induce him to act corruptly or to retire and thus make way for the appointment of the promisor or an agreement with voters to procure votes for money consideration also void.

Examples

(a) A promised to obtain an employment to B in a public office and B promised to pay ₹1000.

(b) R paid a sum of ₹15,000 to A who agreed to obtain a seat for R's son in a Medical College. On A's failure to get the seat, R filed a suit for the refund of amount. Held, the agreement was against public policy [N.V.P. Pandian Vs M.M. Roy AIR (1979) Mad.42].

6. Agreements tending to create interest against duty

If a person enters into an agreement whereby he is bound to do something which is against his public or professional duty, the agreement is void on the ground of public policy.

Example: An agreement by a news reporter not to comment on the conduct of a particular person is unlawful being opposed to public policy.

7. Agreement in restraint of Parental rights

A father and in his absence the mother, is the legal guardian of his/her minor child. A father is entitled by law to the custody of his legitimate child. He cannot enter into an agreement which is consistent with his duties arising out of such custody. If he enters into any such agreements, it shall be void on the ground of public policy.

8. Agreements in restraint of marriage

Every agreement in restraint of the marriage of any person other than a minor is void. Parties of age are capable of giving a free and intelligent consent. So, any agreement interfering with or restraining their choice of marriage is void.

Example: P promised to marry L only and none else and to pay L sum of ₹2,000 if he

(P) married someone else. P married X. Held, L could not recover the sum agreed as the agreement was in restraint of marriage [Lowe V s Peers (1768) Burr 255].

9. Agreements restricting personal liberty

Agreements which unduly restrict the personal freedom of the parties to it, are void as being against public policy.

Example: A debtor agreed with his moneylender that he would not, without the lender's written consent, leave his job, or borrow money, or dispose of his property, or change his residence. Held, the agreement was void.

10. Agreements in restraint of trade

An agreement which interferes with the liberty of a person to engage him in any lawful trade, profession or vocation, is called an agreement in restraint of trade. In other words, an agreement in restraint of trade is one which restricts the right of a person to carry on his trade or profession. Public policy requires that every person should be at liberty to work for himself and should not be at liberty to deprive himself of the fruit of his labour, skill or talent by any contract that he enters into. It is also in the interest of the community that every person should be at liberty to engage him in any trade, profession or business and use his skill to the best of his capacity consistent with the good of the community. Hence, every agreement, by which anyone is restrained from exercising a lawful profession, trade or business of any kind, is to that extent void [Sec.27].

Mahudev Vs Rajcoomar (1874)

A, who was carrying on some business, promised another person B, carrying on a similar trade in the same locality to stop his business in consideration of B giving him a certain amount. Subsequent to A's closing the business, refused to pay. A filed a suit for the recovery of tho amount Held, the agreement was void.

2.18.4 Exceptions

An agreement in restraint of trade can, however, is justified if it is reasonable in the interests of the contracting parties and the public. It is valid if it falls within any of the following exceptions.

1. Sale of Goodwill

A seller of goodwill of a business may be restricted from carrying on a similar business within the specified local limits so long as the buyer or any person deriving title to the goodwill from his carries on a like business provided that such limits appear to the court reasonable regard being had to the nature of the business.

2. Partners agreements

The Partnership Act, 1932 provides certain exceptions with regard to the principle of restraint of trade They are:

(a) a partner shall not carry on a business similar to that of the firm while he is a partner.

(b) a retiring partner may agree with other partners not to carry on a business similar to that of the firm within a specified period or within specified local limits.

(c) partners may, upon or in anticipation of the dissolution of the firm, make an agreement that some or all of them will not carry on a business similar to that of the firm within a specified period or within specified local limits.

3. Trade combinations

Traders and manufacturers in the same line of business normally form association in order to regulate licencing of traders, price fixation, working hours, supply of materials, power supply etc. These restrictions are valid even though they are in restraint of trade because trade combinations are formed to carry on business in an organised way in order to promote the interest of trade and general public. But a combination which tends to create monopoly and which is against the public interest is void.

Example: An agreement between certain ice manufacturing companies not to sell ice below a stated price and to divide the profits in a certain proportion is not void. Such agreements are neither in restraint of trade nor opposed to public policy [S.B. Fraser and Co Vs Bombay lee Mfg Co. (1904) 29 Bom. LR 107].

4. Service contracts

An agreement of service by which a person binds himself during the tenure of the agreement not to take service with anyone else, or directly or indirectly take part in any business in competition with the present employer is valid. The doctors, for example, are usually debarred from private practice during the term of their employment.

Niranjan Shankar JI: Century Spinning and Mfg Co. Ltd (1967)

A contract of employment for five years provided that the employee should not serve anywhere else during the five years even if he left the employment. This condition was imposed because the employee had access to technical information. The employee left the organisation before the expiry of the period and joined another company for better remuneration. The former employer sought injunction and the court granted it. But an agreement to restrain an employee from competing with his employer after the termination of employment is void.

Brahmaputra Tea Company Vs Scartb (1885)

It was held that an agreement restraining an employee from taking service or engaging in any similar business for a period of 5 years after termination of his services was void.

2.19 PERFORMANCE OF CONTRACT

Performance of contract is an essential obligation on the part of both the parties to the contract. Performance of a contract takes place when the parties to the contract fulfil their obligations arising under the contract within the time and in the manner prescribed. Section 37 lays down that the parties to a contract must either perform their respective promises, unless such performance is dispensed with or excused under the provision of this Act or of any other law.

2.19.1 Rules Relating to Performance

Rules relating to performance of promises are summarised as follows.

1. Tender of performance

Sometimes it so happens that the promissor offers to perform his obligation under the contract at the proper time and place but the promisee does not accept the performance. This is known as "attempted performance or tender or offer to perform. Section 38 says that where a promissor has made an offer of performance to the promisee and the offer has not been accepted, the promissor is not responsible for non-performance nor does he thereby lose his rights under the contract. Thus, a tender of performance is equivalent to actual performance. It executes the promissor from further performance and entitles him to sue the promisee for the breach of contract.

Requisites of valid tender

(i) It must be unconditional. It becomes conditional when it is not in accordance with the terms of the contract.

Example: A, a debtor, offers to pay to B, his creditor the amount due to him on the condition that B sells to him certain shares at cost.

(ii) It must be of the whole quantity contracted for or of the whole obligation. A tender of an instalment, when the contract stipulates payment in full, is not a valid offer.

Example: A, a debtor, offers to pay C, his creditor the amount due in instalments and tenders the first instalment.

(iii) It must be by a person who is in a position and is willing to perform the promise.

(iv) It must be made at the proper time and place. A tender of goods after the business hours of goods or money before the date due is not a valid tender.

(v) It must be made to the proper person, i.e. the promisee or his duly authorised agent. It must also be in proper form.

(vi) In case of tender of goods it must give a reasonable opportunity to the promisee for the inspection of the goods.

(vii) It may be made to one of the several joint promisees. In such case it has the same effect as a tender to all of them.

But, according to section 39, when a party to a contract refuses to perform or disables himself from performing, his promise wholly the promisee may put an end to the contract. However, when the promisee has signified, by words or conduct, his assent in the continuance of the contract, he cannot repudiate it.

Example: A, a singer enters into a contract with B, the manager of a theatre, to sing at his theatre two nights in every week for two months and B agrees to pay her ₹100 for each night's performance. On the sixth night A wilfully absents herself from the theatre. He is at liberty to put an end to the contract. But if A sings on the seventh night with the consent of B and B signified his assent in the continuation of the contract, he cannot now put an end to it, but is entitled to claim damages from A.

2. Party to perform contract

According to section 40, the following persons may perform the contract

(a) A Promissor himself

If there is something in the contract to show that it was the intention of the parties that the promissor himself should perform the promise, such promise must be performed by the promissor. Further, in case of contract, which involves the exercise of personal skill, volition or diligence of the promissor or the promissor himself must perform which are found on personal confidence between the parties.

Example:

(i) A promise to paint a picture for B by a certain day at a certain price. A dies before that day. The contract cannot be enforced either by A's representatives or by B.

(ii) A contract to marry B. C cannot marry on behalf of A.

(b) Agent:

Where personal consideration is not the foundation of a contract, the promissor may employ a competent person to perform it. Example: A promises to pay B a sum of money. The amount may be paid to B either by A personally or his agent.

(c) Legal Representatives:

A contract, which involves the use of personal skill or is founded on personal considerations comes to an end on the death of the promissor. As regards any other contract, the legal representatives of the deceased promissor are bound to perform it unless a contrary intention appears from the contract. But their liability under contract is limited to the value of the property they inherit from the deceased.

Example: A promises to deliver goods to B on a payment of ₹1000. A dies before that day. As representatives are bound to deliver the goods to B and B is bound to pay amount to A's representatives.

(d) Third persons

When a promisee accepts performance of the promise from a third person, he cannot afterwards enforce it against the promissor (Section. 41).

(e) Joint promissors

When two or more persons have made a joint promise they are known as joint promissors unless a contrary intention appears from the contract all joint promissors must jointly fulfil the promise. If any of them dies, his legal representatives must jointly with the surviving promissors fulfil the promise. If all of them die, the legal representatives of all of them must fulfil the promise jointly (Section 42).

But, if the parties do not discharge their obligations of their own, unless otherwise stated, the following rules are laid down (Sec. 43).

(i) The promisee may compel anyone or more of the joint promissors to perform the whole of the promise. This means the liability of joint promissors is joint and several.

Example: A, B and C jointly promise to pay D ₹3000. D may compel all or either A or B or C to pay him ₹3000.

(ii) When the joint promissor has been compelled to perform the whole of the promise, he may compel the other joint promissors to contribute equally with himself to the performance of the promise.

Example: A, B and C are under a joint promise to pay D ₹300 A is compelled to pay the whole amount to D. He may recover ₹100 each from B and C.

(iii) When anyone of the joint promissors makes default in the contribution, the remaining joint promissors must bear the loss arising from such default in equal shares.

Example: A B and C are under a joint promise to pay D ₹3000 C is unable to pay anything and A is compelled to pay the whole sum. A is entitled to receive ₹15,000 from B.

Release of a joint promissor (Section 44)

The promisee may release anyone of the joint promissors from the performance of the contract. But it discharges the other promissors from liability and released joint promissor also continues to be liable to the joint promissors.

Example: Deptor-1, Deptor-2 and Deptor-3 jointly owe a debt to C. C releases D1 from his liability and files a suit against D2 and D3 for payment of the debt. D2 and D3 are not released from their liability nor is D1 discharged from his liability to D2 and D3 for consideration.

Devolution of joint rights (Sec. 45)

When a person has made a promise to several persons, these persons are known as joint promissors. Unless a contrary intention appears from the contract the right to claim performance rests with all of the joint promissors. If the joint promissors die, it rests with legal representatives.

2.19.2 Who can demand performance?

It is only the promisee who can demand performance of the promise under contract. It makes no difference whether the promise is for the benefit of the promisee or for the benefit of any other person.

Example: A promises B to pay C a sum of ₹500. A does not pay the amount to C. C cannot take any action against A. It is only B who can enforce the contract.

In the case of death of the promisee his legal representatives can demand performance.

In certain cases a third party can also enforce a promise under a contract even though he is not a party to the contract. For example, trust, marriage settlement, agent etc.

3. Time and place of performance

Time and place of performance of a contract are matters to be determined by an agreement between the parties themselves. Sections, 46 to 50 lay down the following rules in this regard.

(a) Where no application is to be made by the promisee and no time is specified the promise must be performed by the promissor within a reasonable time (Sec 46).

(b) Where time is specified and no application is to be made, by the promisee, the promissor may perform the promise at any time during the usual hours of business on such day and at the place at which the promise ought to be performed.

(c) When a promise is to be performed on a certain day at a certain place the promissor may undertake to perform it after the application is made by the promisee to that effect (Sec. 48).

(d) When a promise is to be performed without application by the promisee and no place is fixed for the performance of it, the promissor has to apply to the promisee to appoint a reasonable place for the performance of the promise and to perform it at such place (Sec 49).

(e) When a promise is to be performed in the manner and time prescribed by the promisee, the promissor has to perform it in the same manner within the time specified (Sec 50).

2.19.3 Reciprocal promises

When a contract consists of an exchange of promises, they are called reciprocal promises. Section 2(f) defines as "promises, which form the consideration or part of the consideration for each other are called reciprocal promises."

Example: A promises to do or not to do something in consideration of B's promise to do or not to do something, the promises are reciprocal.

Rules regarding performance of reciprocal promises

(1) When a contract consists of reciprocal promises to be simultaneously performed the promissor need not perform his promise unless the promisee is ready and willing to perform his reciprocal promise (Sec. 51) Example: A and B contract that A shall deliver certain goods to B to be paid for by B on delivery. A need not deliver the goods unless b is ready and willing to pay for the goods on delivery. B need not pay for the goods unless A is ready and willing to deliver them on payment.

(2) When the order in which reciprocal promises are to be performed is expressly fixed by the contract, they must be performed in that order (Sec. 52).

Example: A and B contract that A shall build a house for B at a fixed price. A's promise to build the house must be performed before B's promise to pay for it.

But when the order is not expressly fixed by the contract they must be performed in that orders which the nature of the transaction requires.

Example: A and B contract that A shall make over his stock-in-trade to B at a fixed price and B promises to give security for the payment of money. A's promise need not be performed until security is given for the nature of the transaction requires that A shall have security before he delivers up his stock.

(3) When a contract contains reciprocal promises, it may happen that one party to the contract prevents the other from performing his promise. In such a case, the contract becomes voidable at the option of the party so prevented. He is entitled to compensation from the other party for any loss which he may sustain in consequence of the non-performance of the contract (Sec. 53).

Example: A and B contract that B shall execute certain work for A ₹1,000. B is ready and willing to execute the work accordingly but A prevents him from doing so. The contract is voidable at the option of B and if he elects to rescind it he is entitled to recover from A compensation for any loss which he has incurred by its non-performance.

(4) Where the nature of the reciprocal promises is such that one cannot be performed or its performance cannot be claimed unless the other party performs his promise in the first place, then if the later fails to perform, he cannot claim performance from the other, but must make compensation to him for his loss (Sec. 54).

Example: A promises B to sell him 100 bales of merchandise to be delivered next day and B promises A to pay for them within in a month. A does not deliver according to his promise. B's promise to pay the amount need not be performed and A must make compensation.

(5) Where persons reciprocally promise, firstly to do certain other things, which are legal and secondly, under specified circumstances to do certain things, which are illegal, the first set of promise is a contract, but the second is a void agreement (Sec. 57).

Example: A and B agree that A shall sell B a house that belongs to A for RS. 10,000 but that if B uses it as a gambling house, B shall pay A ₹50,000 for it. The first, namely sale of house for ₹10,000 is a contract but the second part, namely using it for gambling, being unlawful object, is void agreement.

Time is the essence of the contract (Sec. 55)

Time is the essence of the contract means the time fixed by the parties for the performance of contract is regarded by them as the most important condition of the contract for the breach of which they are entitled to avoid the contract.

Section 55 provides in this regard:

(a) When time is of the essence

If the time is of the essence of the contract and there is a failure on the part of the promissor to perform his obligation within the fixed time, the contract becomes voidable at the option of the promisee and entitled for compensation.

(b) When time is not of the essence

If the time is not of the essence, a failure on the part of the promissor to perform his obligation within the fixed time does not make the contract voidable, but the promisee is entitled to compensation for any loss caused to him by such failure.

4. Appropriation of payments

Appropriation means application of payments. When a debtor owes several distinct debts to a creditor and makes a payment insufficient to discharge all the debts, the question of appropriation of payment will arise. It means to which debt the payment should be adjusted. Sections 59 to 61 lay down the following rules in this regard.

(a) Where the debtor intimates (Sec. 59)

Where the debtor intimates to which particular debt his payment must be applied, the payment should be applied accordingly

(b) Where the debtor does not intimate

Where the debtor does not intimate and there are no other circumstances indicating to which debt the payment is to be applied, the creditor may apply the payment to any debt due from the debtor.

(c) Where the debtor does not intimate and the creditor fails to apply (Sec 61)

In a situation where the debtor fails to intimate and the creditor does not use his discretion to apply to a particular debt, the law gets the right to appropriate the payment. In such case, the law prefers to clear the debts in the order of time in which they were incurred.

5. Assignment of contracts

To 'assign' means to 'transfer.' Assignment of a contract means transfer of contractual rights and liabilities under the contract to a third party with or without the concurrence of the other party to the contract. In other words, it means transfer of contractual right or liability by a party to the contract to some other person who is not a party to it. It may take place (a) by an act of the parties or (b) by operation law.

(a) Assignment by act of parties

Assignment is said to take place by an act of the parties when they themselves make the assignment. So, parties can drop out from the performance of promise and bring in other parties to perform their parts of promise by mutual agreement or on their own accord. However, contracts of personal skill and ability cannot be assigned. For example, a contractual obligation by an opera signer to sing or by a film actor to act in a film or a contract to marry or paint a picture cannot be assigned.

However, benefits or rights can be assigned but not the liability of the contract except with the consent of the parties. A debtor, for instance, cannot relieve himself of his liability except by consent of the creditor and new party to whom the burden is being assigned.

Example: A owes B ₹5,000. A cannot transfer his liability to a third person. But if B agrees to accept C, as his debtor in place of A the liability can then be transferred from A to C.

(b) Assignment by the operation of law

Assignment by the operation of law takes place by intervention of law. This takes place in case of death or insolvency of promissor. In such cases, rights and liabilities are transferred to legal representatives of the deceased promissor or to the Official Assignee or Receiver on becoming promisor a insolvent. However, contracts requiring personal skill or services cannot be transferred.

Contracts which need not to be performed

The following are the circumstances under which contract need not to be performed:

1. When its performance becomes impossible. [Sec. 56]
2. When the parties to it agree to substitute a new contract for it or to rescind or alter it. [Sec 62]
3. When the parties to a contract agree to dispense with or remit performance of promise either wholly or in part the original contracts stands discharged. [Sec. 63]
4. When the person at whose option a contract is voidable rescinds it. [Sec. 64]
5. When the promisee neglects or refuses to afford the promissor reasonable facilities for the performance of his promise. [Sec. 67]
6. When it is illegal.

2.20 DISCHARGE OF CONTRACT

Discharge of contract means termination of the contractual relationship between the parties. A contract is said to be discharged when the parties thereto are freed from the task of performing their respective obligations as arising from the contract. It puts an end to the contract.

Modes of Discharge: It can be shown in the following chart.

Let us explain in detail the various modes of discharge of contract as shown in the below chart to cease the operation of the contract i.e. the rights and liabilities created by it come to an end.

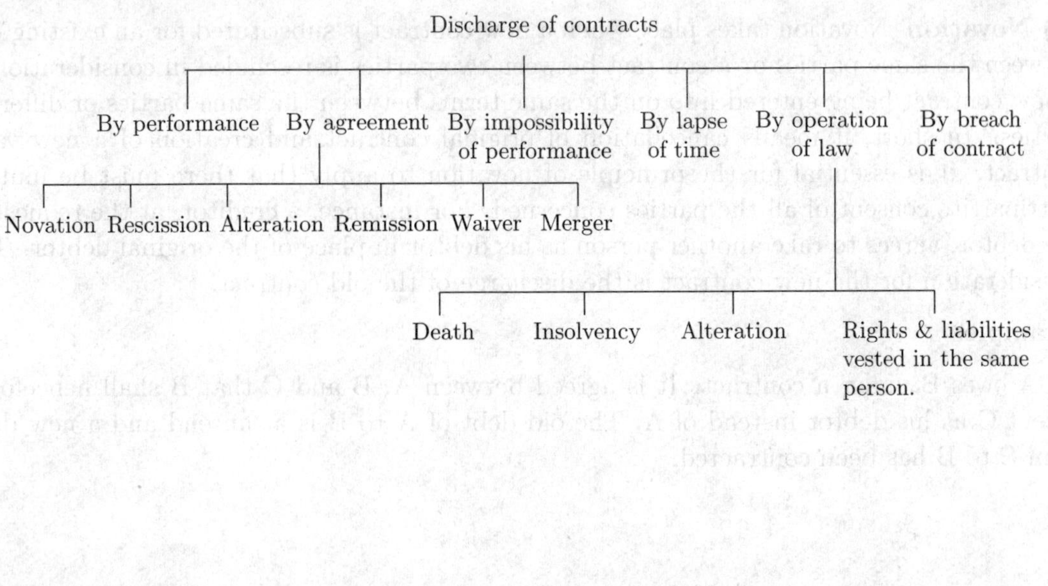

1) Discharge by Performance

Performance means doing of a thing which is required to be done in the contract. Discharge by performance takes place when the parties to the contract fulfil their obligations arising under the contract within the time and in the manner prescribed. In short, a contract is discharged when both the promissor and the promisee perform their respective obligations. In such a case, the parties are discharged and the contract comes to an end. But if only one party performs the promise, he alone is discharged. Such a party gets a right of action against the other party who is guilty of breach.

Example: A agrees to sell his car to B for ₹1,00,000. As agreed A delivered the car and B paid the price. Both the parties performed their mutual obligations and contract is said to be discharged.

2) Discharge by agreement

As a contract is created by means of an agreement, it may be discharged by another agreement between the same parties nullifying the previous contract. It is based on the maxim 'Eodem modo quo quid constituitor, eodem modo destruitur.' It means a thing may be destroyed in the same manner in which it is constituted. It may be discharged either by express or implied agreement.

Example: A agrees to sell his site to B for ₹2,00,000 and received ₹50,000 as advance. A extended time beyond the date of registration by taking an extra amount of ₹10,000 forming a new agreement. The old agreement is discharged by forming a new agreement.

2.20.1 Types of Discharge

Sections 62 and 63 deal with the various types of discharge of a contract by agreement or consent.

(a) Novation Novation takes place when a new contract is substituted for an existing one between the same parties or a contract between two parties is rescinded in consideration of a new contract being entered into on the same terms between the same parties or different parties. In short, it means cancellation of original contract and creation of a new valid contract. It is essential for the principle of novation to apply that there must be mutual or tripartite consent of all the parties concerned. For instance, a creditor, at the request of the debtor, agrees to take another person as his debtor in place of the original debtor. The consideration for the new contract is the discharge of the old contract.

Examples

(a) A owes B under a contract. It is agreed between A, B and C that B shall henceforth accept C as his debtor instead of A. The old debt of A to B is at an end and a new debt from C to B has been contracted.

(b) A owes B ₹10,000. A enters into an agreement with B, and gives B a mortgage of his (A's) estate for ₹5000 in place of the debt of ₹10,000. This is a new contract and discharges the old.

(b) Rescission

Rescission takes place when all or some of the terms of the contract are cancelled. It may occur (i) by mutual consent of the parties, or (ii) where one party fails in performing his obligation, the other party may rescind the contract without prejudice to his right to claim compensation for breach of contract.

Examples

(a) A promises to supply certain goods to B six months after a date. By that time, the goods go out of fashion. A and B may rescind the contract by mutual agreement.

(b) A and B enter into a contract that A shall deliver certain goods to B by the 15th of this month and that 13 shall pay the price on the 1st of the next month. A does not supply the goods. B may rescind the contract and need not pay the price.

(c) Alteration

Alteration takes place when one or more of the terms of the contract is/are altered by the mutual consent of the parties to the contract. In short, alteration means change in one or more of the terms of a contract.

Example: A enters into a contract with B for the supply of 100 bales of cotton at his godown No 1 by the first day of the next month. A and B may alter the term of the contract regarding the period of performance by postponing one week through mutual consent.

(d) Remission

The party to whom an obligation is owed may agree with the other party to accept something different in place of the former obligation. This is known as remission. It means acceptance of a lesser fulfilment of the promise made. For instance, acceptance of a lesser sum than what was contracted for, in discharge of the whole of the debt. It is not necessary that there must be some consideration for the remission of the part of the debt. So the promisee can dispense with or remit the performance of the promise by the promissor or extend the time for performance or accept any other satisfaction instead of performance.

Example: A owes B ₹5,000. A pays to B and B accepts, in satisfaction of the whole debt, ₹2,000 paid at the time and place at which ₹5,000 were payable. The whole debt is discharged.

(e) Waiver

Waiver means the deliberate abandonment of the right by the parties to a contract. It takes place when the parties to a contract agree that they shall no longer be bound by the terms of the contract. It releases the parties from their contractual obligations. Consideration is not necessary for waiver.

Example: A agrees to give B one watch extra along with the delivery of T.V. for some amount. A does not give it and B need to pay the extra amount.

(f) Merger

Merger takes place when an inferior right accruing to a party under a contract merges into a superior right accruing to the same party under the same or some other contract.

Example: A holds a property under a lease. He later buys the property. His rights as a lease merge into his rights as an owner.

3) Discharge by impossibility of performance

Impossibility of performance results in the discharge of the contract. Impossibility may appear on the face of the contract, or may exist, unknown to the parties, at the time of making the contract or may arise after the contract is made. In the first case the contract is void ab initio and creates no rights and obligations between the parties. In the second case also the contract is void on the ground of mutual mistake. In the last case, the contract is not void when the agreement was entered into but becomes void due to impossibility of performance. This is known as the doctrine of subsequent or supervening impossibility. It is based on the maxim Lex non-cogit ad impossibilla i.e. the law does not compel the impossible.

A contract is discharged by supervening impossibility in the following cases:

1. When the subject matter of a contract, subsequent to its formation, is destroyed without any fault of the parties to the contract the contract is discharged.
   A contracted to sell a specific quantity of potatoes to be grown on his farms. The crop largely failed. Held, the contract was discharged [Howell Vs Coupland (1876) Q.B.D. 258].
2. When a contract is entered into between two parties on the basis of a continued existence or occurrence of a particular state of things but there is change in the state of things or state of things, which ought to have occurred does not occur, the contract is discharged.
   Examples
   (a) A and B contract to marry each other. Before the time fixed for marriage A goes mad. The contract becomes void.

(b) H hired a flat from K for witnessing a coronation procession of King Edward VII. The coronation procession was cancelled due to the illness of the king. Held, H was excused from paying the rent for the flat on the ground that existence of the procession was the basis of the contract. Its cancellation discharged the contract [Krell Vs Henry (1903)].

This kind of failure of the object of a contract is called 'frustration of the contract.'

3. Contracts, which are lawful when made but become unlawful later by reason of change in law, become impossible of performance.

   Example: A enters into a contract with B on 1st March for the supply of China silk to be imported in the month of September of the same year. In June by an Act of parliament the import of such silk is banned. The contract is discharged.

4. A contract entered into before the commencement of war remains suspended during the war.

   Example: A contracts to take in cargo for B at a foreign port. A's government afterwards declares war against the country in which the port is situated. The contract becomes void when war is declared.

5. A contract may become impossible of performance or incapable of performance by reason of the death or incapacity or some person whose continued life and health is necessary for the performance of the contract.

Example: An artist undertook to perform at a concert for a certain price. Before she could do so she was taken seriously ill. Held, she was discharged due to illness [Robinson V s Davison (1871) L.R. 6 Ex 269].

4) Discharge by Lapse of time

A contract is also discharged by lapse of time. The Indian Limitation Act 1963 lays down that a contract should be performed within a specified period, called period of limitation. If it is not performed and if no action is taken by the promisee in a law court within the period of limitation, he is deprived of his remedy at law. In other words, we may say that the contract is terminated. For instance, the price of goods sold without any stipulation as to credit should be paid within three year of the delivery of the goods. Where goods are sold on credit to be paid for after the expiry of a fixed period of credit the price should be paid within 3 years of the expiry of period of credit. If the price is not paid and the creditor does not file a suit against the buyer for the recovery of price within 3 years, the debt becomes time barred and hence irrecoverable.

Example: A lends B ₹10, 000 on 1-1-1998. A should recover this amount within 31-12-2000 i.e. 3 years. If B does not repay within this period and A does not take any steps to recover it, he loses the amount.

However, it is upto the parties to rejuvenate a contract by acknowledgements. If the promissor gives a written acknowledgement of debt before the expiry of limitation, a new period of limitation will come into force. These acknowledgements may be an endorsement on the original document or by means of a separate communication.

5) Discharge by operation of Law

A contract is discharged by the operation of other laws. It is discharged in the following cases.

(a) Death

In contracts involving personal skill or ability, the contract is terminated on the death of the promissor. In other contracts, the rights and liabilities of the deceased pass on to the legal representatives of the deceased.

(b) Insolvency

When a person is adjudged insolvent he is discharged from all liabilities incurred prior to his adjudication.

(c) Unauthorised alteration of the terms of the agreement

Where a party to a contract makes any material alteration in the contract without the consent of the other party, the other party can avoid the contract A material alteration is one which changes the legal identity or character of the contract or the rights and liabilities of the parties to the contract.

(d) Rights and liabilities vested in the same person

Where the right and liabilities under a contract vest in the hands of same person, the other parties are discharged. For example, when a bill gets into the hands of the acceptor, the other party is discharged.

6) Discharge by Breach of contract

Parties to a contract are expected to perform their respective obligations. If any party fails to perform his obligation, there takes place a breach of contract. Breach of the contract operates as a discharge of the contract.

Breach of contract may be 'actual' or 'anticipatory.'

(a) Actual breach of contract

The actual breach occurs when, during the performance of the contract or at the time when the performance of the contract is due, one party either fails or refuses to perform his obligation under the contract.

Examples

(a) A agrees to deliver B 10 bags on 1st January. He fails to deliver the rice on 1st January. There is a breach of contract by A.

(b) A agrees to deliver B 10 bags on 1st January. On 1st January, he tenders the rice to B. But B refuses to accept delivery without valid reasons. There is a breach of contract by B.

(b) Anticipatory branch of contract

When a party to a contract refuses to perform his part of the contract before the actual time of the performance of the contact is due, it is called an anticipatory breach of contract. Anticipatory breach of contract may be:

(a) by repudiation of the contract (express renunciation) or

(b) by impossibility of performance (implied renunciation)

When a party communicates his ability to perform his part of the contract before the time fixed for the actual performance is due, he is said to have expressly repudiated the contract.

Example: A undertakes to supply certain goods to B on 1st January 2002. Before this date he informs B that he is not going to supply the goods. This is anticipatory breach of contract by express repudiation.

When the breach takes place by either party to the contract by his own voluntary act, which makes performance of the contract impossible, anticipatory breach of contract is committed by impossibility of performance. Here impossibility is created by one party to the contract before the performance is due. It is a case of implied renunciation of a contract.

Example: A promises to sell his car to B on or before 1st March 2002; but before this date, A sells his car to C. Here A had performed such a voluntary act that the performance of his obligation towards B is impossible therefore anticipatory breach is committed.

2.21 REMEDIES FOR BREACH OF CONTRACT

Generally a contract is entered into between the parties with an intention to perform it. When all the provisions of a contract have been complied with, the contract is said to have been discharged by performance. In effect, the contract is no longer exists. But sometimes, the contract may never reach this stage because one party simply refuses to perform or may handle the agreement in an unsatisfactory manner. This makes the performance of the contract impossible. So, parties to a lawful contract are bound to perform its respective obligations. But when one of the parties fails to perform their respective obligation, he is said have committed a breach of contract.

2.21.1 Remedies

A contract gives rise to correlative rights and obligations. A right accruing to a party under a contract would be no value if there were no remedy to enforce that right in a law court in the event of its infringement or breach of contract. A remedy is the means given by law for the enforcement of right.

When there is a breach of contract by one party, the other party called injured party or aggrieved party shall have certain remedies against him. They are remedies for the breach of contract. The different types of remedies are shown in the following chart.

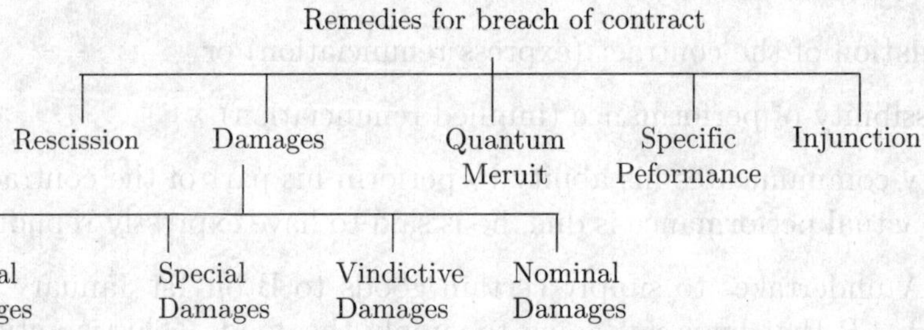

Let us explain the various types of remedies available to an injured person in case of breach of contract by another person.

2.22 RESCISSION

Where one of the parties to a contract commits breach, the other party may sue to treat the contract as rescinded and refuse further performance. In such a case, he is freed from all the obligations under a contract. Under section 64, the party rescinding a voidable contract shall, if he has received any benefit thereunder from another party to such contract, restore such benefit to the person from whom it was received. Further under section 75 a person who rightfully rescinds a contract is entitled to compensation for any damage, which he has sustained through the non-fulfilment of the contract.

Example: A promises B to supply 10 bags of sugar on a certain day. B agrees to pay the price after the receipt of the goods. A does not supply the goods. B is discharged from liability to pay the price.

Under the following circumstances the court may grant recession:

(1) When the contract is voidable by the plaintiff

Example: A sells a field to B. There is a right of passage over the field to which A has direct personal knowledge but which he conceals from B. B is entitled to have the contract rescinded.

(2) Where the contract is unlawful for causes not apparent on its face and the defendant is more to blame than the plaintiff. For example, A, an attorney, induces his client B, a Hindu widow to transfer property to him for the purpose of defrauding B's creditors. Here the parties are not equally in fault and B is entitled to have instruments to transfer rescinded.

However, the court may refuse to rescind the contract under the following circumstances.

1. Where the plaintiff has expressly or impliedly ratified the contract.
2. Where, owing to the change of circumstances since the making of the contract, the parties cannot be restored to their original positions.
3. Where the third parties have, during the subsistence of the contract, acquired right in good faith and for the value.
4. Where only a part of the contract is sought to be rescinded and such part is not severable from the rest of the contract.

2.23 SUIT FOR DAMAGES

Under section 73, where a contract has been broken, the party who suffers by such breach is entitled to receive compensation for any loss or damage caused to him from the party who has broken the contract. Damages are a monetary compensation allowed to the injured party by the court for the loss or injury suffered by him. The object of awarding damages for the breach of a contract is to put the injured party in the same financial position as if the contract had been performed. This is called the doctrine of restitution. The fundamental basis of awarding damages is that law of contract does not seek to punish the guilty but the court will compel the party in breach to make good the loss by paying damages to the other party.

The foundation of modern law of damages is to be found in the judgement of the following case.

Hardley Vs Baxendale

X's mill was stopped by the breakdown of a shaft. He delivered the shaft to Y, a common carrier, to be taken to a manufacturer to copy it and make a new one. X did not make known to Y that delay would result in loss of profit. By some neglect on the part of Y the delivery of the shaft was delayed in transit beyond a reasonable time. Held, Y was not liable for loss of profits during the period of delay, as the circumstances communicated to Y did not show that a delay in the delivery of the shaft would entail loss of profit to the mill. Further, Alderson B observed that "Where two parties have made a contract which one of them has broken, the damages which the other party ought to receive in respect of such breach of contract should be such as may fairly and reasonably be considered either arising naturally i.e. according to the usual course of thing from such breach of contract itself, or such as may reasonably be supposed to have been in the contemplation of both the parties as the time they made the contract as the probable result of the breach of it."

2.23.1 Rules

The rules relating to damages are as follows.

1. General or ordinary damages

General damages are those, which arise, naturally in the usual course of things for the breach of contract. They are awarded with a view to compensate the injured party and not with a view to punish the party at fault. General damages are usually assessed on the basis of actual loss suffered.

Example: A contracts to sell and deliver 100 quintals of rice to B at ₹875 per quintal, the price is to be paid at the time of delivery. The price of rice rises to ₹900 per quintal and A refuses to sell the rice. B can claim damages at the rate of ₹25 per quintal.

In a contract for the sale of goods, the measure of damages on the breach of a contract is the difference between the contract price and the market price of such goods on the date of the breach. If, however, the thing contracted for is not available in the market, the price of the nearest and best available substitute may be taken into account in calculating damages. Where the subject matter of a contract is goods specially made to order and which are not marketable, the price of the goods is the measure of damages.

2. Special Damages

Special damages are those which arise on account of the unusual circumstances affecting the plaintiff. Such damages cannot be claimed as a matter of gift. These can be claimed only if the special circumstances, which would result in a special loss in case of breach of a contract, are brought to the notice of the other party.

If the plaintiff fails to bring to the knowledge of the defendant about the unusual circumstances, he cannot recover the special damages.

Examples

(a) S sent some specimens of his goods for exhibition at an agricultural show. After the show he entrusted some of his samples to an agent of a railway company for carriage to another show ground at New Castle. On the consignment note he wrote "Must be at New Castle Monday certain." Owing to default on the part of the railway company, the samples arrived late for the show. Held, S could claim damages for the loss of profit at the show [Simpson Vs London & N.W. Rail Co. (1876) 1Q.B.D.274].

(b) G delivered a sewing machine and some cloth to a railway company to be delivered at a place where a festival was to be held. He expected to earn some special profit at the festival but he did not bring this fact to the notice of the railway authorities. The goods were delivered after the conclusion of the festival. Held, he could not recover the loss of profit [Madras Rail V s Govinda Rao (1898) 21 Mad, 173].

3. Vindictive or Exemplary damages

Vindictive or exemplary damages are those damages which are awarded with a view to punish the wrongdoer and not primarily with the idea of awarding compensation to the injured party. Hence vindictive damages have no place in the law of contract because they are punitive by nature. But in the case of breach of a promise to marry, dishonour of a cheque by a banker wrongfully, and the issue of a cheque by a customer when he does not possess sufficient funds to his credit, the court may award exemplary damages.

Example: The banker had agreed to give loan to W for a trip to California by crediting his account. But The banker failed to credit the account after W reached California. Held, W was allowed damages for humiliation and mental suffering.

4. Nominal Damages

Nominal damages are those damages which are awarded where the injured party has sustained damages of a short but not of a substantial nature to be reckoned with. Sometimes the plaintiff suffers no loss the court may still award him nominal damages in recognition of his right. The nominal damages are very small. For example, a rupee. These damages merely acknowledge that the plaintiff has proved his case and won.

Example: A firm consisting of four partners employed B for a period of 2 years. After 6 months two partners retired, the business being carried on by the other two. B declined to be employed under the continuing partners. Held, he was only entitled to nominal damages, as he had suffered no loss [Brace Vs Calder (1895) 2 Q.B.253].

2.23.2 Damages and Penalty

Sometimes parties to a contract stipulate at the time of its formation that on the breach of the contract by either of them, a certain specified sum will be payable as damages. Such a sum may amount to either liquidated damages or a penalty. Liquidated damages represent a sum fixed or ascertained by the parties in the contract, which is a fair and genuine pre-estimated of the probable loss that might ensure as a result of the breach. A penalty is a sum named in the contract at the time of its formation, which is disproportionate to the damages likely to accrue as a result of the breach.

2.24 QUANTUM MERUIT

Quantum meruit is another remedy available for a party to a contract on its breach by another. Sometimes, it so happens that one party to the contract has performed part of the promise and fails to perform the remaining part because the other party has committed a breach. The first party must, therefore, be compensated for the part he has performed. This is called the doctrine of quantum meruit. It means as much as meruited or earned or deserved.

The claim for quantum meruit arises only when the original contract is discharged. If the original contract exists, the party not in default cannot have quantum meruit remedy. In such a case, he has to take remedy in damages. Further, only the party who is not at default can bring the claim for quantum meruit.

The claim for quantum meruit arises in the following cases:

(1) When an agreement is discovered to be void (Sec. 65)

When an agreement is discovered to be void, or when a contract becomes void, any person who has received any advantage under such agreement or contract is bound to restore it or to make compensation for it, to the person from whom he received it.

Example: CE was employed as a managing director in a company. After he rendered service for three months, it was found that the directors were not qualified to appoint him. Held, CE could recover remuneration for the services rendered by him on quantum meruit [Craven-Ellis Vs Canon Ltd., (1936) 2 KB. 403].

(2) When something is done non-gratuitously

When a thing is lawfully done or a person without any intention to do so gratuitously to another person goods are supplied by and such other person enjoys the benefit thereof, he is bound to make compensation to the former in respect of, or to restore, the thing so done or delivered.

Example: A, a trader, leaves goods at B's house by mistake. B treats the goods as his own. He is bound to pay A for them.

(3) Where there is an express or implied contract to render services but there is no agreement as to remuneration

In such case a reasonable remuneration is payable. What is reasonable remuneration is determined by the court and this remuneration is quantum meruit.

Example: There was an implied agreement between P and a fire brigade for the services of the brigade. Held, renumeration was payable by P for the services received by him [Upton Rural District Council V s Powell (1942) 1 AII.ER 220].

(4) When the completion of the contract has been prevented by the act of the other party to the contract

Example: C engaged P to write a book on ancient armoury to be published by instalments in a periodical called "The Juvenile Library" for the fee of ₹100. After a few issues of the periodical had appeared, it was abandoned. Held, P could recover on quantum meruit for the work he had done under the contract [Panache Vs Colburn, (1831) 8 Bing, 14].

(5) When a contract is divisible

When a contract is divisible and the party not in default has enjoyed the benefit of the part performance, the party in default may sue on quantum meruit. But if the contract is not divisible i.e. where it requires complete performance as a condition of payment, the party in default cannot claim remuneration on the ground of quantum meruit.

Example: P agreed to pay C, appointed as second mate, 30 guineas on the completion of a voyage from Jamaica to Liverpool. C died before the completion of the voyage. Held, C's widow was not entitled to claim proportionate payment for the part of the voyage completed as the contract imposed one indivisible obligation which had not been performed [Cutter V s Powell (1975) 6T.L.R. 320].

(6) When an indivisible contract is completely performed, but badly

When an indivisible contract for a lump sum is completely performed, but badly the person who has performed the contract can claim the lump sum. But the other party can make a deduction for bad work.

Example: P agreed to decorate D's flat for a lump sum of ₹750, certain requirements having been laid down. P did the work but D complained of faulty workmanship. It cost D ₹204 to remedy that defect. Held P could recover D ₹750 less ₹204 [Hoening Vs Issacs, (1952) All E.R. 176].

2.25 SPECIFIC PERFORMANCE OF CONTRACT

Sometimes damages are not an adequate remedy for breach of contract. The injured party may ask the court to compel the defaulting party to actually carry out promises what should have been agreed as per the terms of contract. In such cases, the court may direct the party in breach to carry out his promise according to the terms of the contract. This is a direction by the court for specific performance of the contract at the suit of the injured party.

However, an injured party cannot claim specific performance as an absolute right. It is the discretion of the court to grant such a remedy. Generally, the court will order for specific performance of the contract in the following cases.

1. When the act agreed to be done is such that compensation in money for its non-performance is not an adequate relief.
2. When there exists no standard for ascertaining the actual damages caused by the non-performance of the act agreed to be done.
3. When it is probable that the compensation in money cannot be got for the non-performance of the act agreed to be done.

But, under the following circumstances, the court will not grant specific performance:

1. When damages are an adequate remedy
2. When the court is not certain or is inequitable to either party.
3. When the contract is in its nature revocable.
4. When the trustees in breach of their trust make the contract.
5. When the contract is of a personal nature e.g. a contract to marry.
6. When the contract is made by a company in excess of its powers as laid down in its Memorandum of Association.
7. When the court supervises its carrying out e.g. a building contract.

2.26 INJUNCTION

When a party is in breach of a negative term of a contract (i.e. where he is doing something which he promised not to do), the court may, by issuing an order, restrain him from doing what he promised not to do. Such an order of the court is known as injunction. In short, an injunction is an order of the court restraining a party from doing a wrongful act. On breach of contract, the court can restrain a party, by an order of injunction, from committing the breach. However, the power of the court to grant injunction is discretionary and may be granted for a temporary or an indefinite period. It is granted when (1) damages would be an inadequate remedy and (2) the specific performance of the contract would involve a general superintendence with the court could not undertake.

Example: N, a film actress, agreed to act exclusively for W for a year and for no one else. During the year she contracted to act for Z. Held, she could be restrained by injunction from doing so. [Warner Bros Vs Nelson (1937) IKB 209]

2.27 CONTINGENT CONTRACTS

A contract may be unconditional or absolute on the one hand and conditional or contingent on the other. The absolute or unconditional contract is one without any reservations or conditions and is to be performed under any event. On the other hand, conditional or contingent contract is one in which a promise is conditional and the contract shall be performed only on the happening or not happening of some future uncertain event. The condition may be precedent or subsequent. This chapter deals with condition precedent.

'Contingent' means that which is dependent on something else. It is uncertain i.e. which may or may not.

Section 31 of the Indian Contract Act, 1872 defines, as "A contingent contract is a contract to do or not to do something if some event, collateral to such contact does or does not happen."

In the words of Pollock and Mulla "collateral event is one which is neither a performance directly promised as part of the contract, nor the whole of the consideration for a promise."

Thus, a contract is said to be contingent when its performance is made to depend upon the happening or not happening of a future event, which is collateral to the contract.

Example

(a) A contract to pay ₹10,000 if B's house is burnt.
(b) A agrees to sell a certain piece of land to B, in case he succeeds in his litigation concerning that land.
(c) A sent some goods to B on approval basis. The contract of sale depends upon the act of B i.e. to accept or reject the goods.

2.27.1 Essential characteristics

There are three essential characteristics of a contingent contract:

1. Its performance depends upon the happening or non-happening in future of some event.
2. The event must be uncertain. If the event is bound to happen and the contract has got to be performed in any case, it is not a contingent contract.
3. The event must be collateral i.e. incidental to the contract. It does not form an essential part of the contract.

2.27.2 Rules

The following rules relate to contingent contract

(1) Happening of a Future Event (Sec. 32)

A contingent contract, dependent on the happening of an uncertain future event, cannot be enforced until the event has happened. In other words, the future uncertain event must happen if the contingent contracts were to be enforced. If the events become impossible, the contingent contracts become void.

Examples

(a) A makes a contract with B to sell a house to B at a specified price if C to whom the horse has been offered, refuses to buy it. The contract cannot be enforced by law unless and until C refuses to buy the house.

(b) A makes a contract with B to buy B's house if A survives C. This contract cannot by enforced by law unless and until C dies in A's lifetime.

(c) A contracts to pay B a sum of money when B marries C. C dies without being married to B. The contract becomes void.

(2) Not happening of a Future Event (Sec. 33)

A contingent contract to do or not to do anything if an uncertain future event does not happen can be enforced when the happening of that event becomes impossible, and not before. In other words, the performance of such contract can be forced only when the happening of event becomes impossible.

Examples

(a) A agrees to pay B a sum of money if a certain ship does not return. The ship is sunk. The contract can be enforced when the ship sinks.

(b) A agrees to sell his car to B if C dies. The contract cannot be enforced so long as C is alive.

(3) Conduct of person at an unspecified time (Sec. 34)

If a contract is contingent upon how a person will act at an unspecified time, the event shall be considered to become impossible when such person does anything within any definite time, or otherwise than under further contingencies.

Examples

(a) A agrees to pay B a sum of money if B marries C. C marries D. The marriage of B to C must now be considered impossible, although it is possible that D may die and that C may afterwards marry B.

(b) A agreed to take shares if the company would appoint him as its sale agent at a certain place. The company went into liquidation before appointing him agent and A was entered on the list of contributors. Held, A was not liable as the contract to take shares was contingent on his appointment as agent which event never took place [Jaunpur Sugar Factory, Re (192) All 658].

(4) Specified uncertain event happening or not happening within a fixed time (Sec. 35)

Contingent contracts to do or not to do anything if a specified uncertain event happens within a fixed time, become impossible before the expiry of that time. On the other hand, contingent contract to do or not to do anything, if a specified uncertain event does not happen within a fixed time, may be enforced if the event does not happen or its happening is impossible before the expiry of that time.

Examples

(a) A promises to pay B a sum of money if a certain ship returns within a year. The contract may be enforced if the ship returns within a year and becomes void if the ship is burnt within the year.

(b) A promises to pay B a sum of money if a certain ship does not return within a year. The contract may be enforced if the ship does not return within the year, or is burnt within the year.

(5) Agreements contingent on impossible event are void (Sec. 36)

Contingent contracts to do or not to do anything if an impossible event happens, are void, whether the impossibility of the event is known or not the parties to the agreement at the time when it is made.

Examples

(a) A agrees to pay B ₹10,000 if two straight lines should enclose a space.

(b) A agrees to pay B ₹10,000 if 13 will marry A's daughter, C. C was dead at the time of the agreement

2.28 WAGERING AGREEMENTS

Wager means a bet. A wager may be defined as an agreement to pay money or money's worth on the happening of a specified uncertain event. It is a game of chance in which the chance of either winning or losing is wholly dependent on an uncertain event. Section 30 of the Act defines wager as "an agreement between two parties by which one promises to pay money or money's worth on the happening of some uncertain event in consideration of the other party's promise to pay if the event does not happen."

The essence of wager is that one party is to win and the other loses upon a future event, which at the time of contract is of uncertain nature. If either of the parties may win, but cannot lose, or may lose but cannot win, it is not a wagering contract.

Examples

(a) A and B enter into an agreement that A shall pay to B ₹I0 if it rains on Monday and that B shall pay to A the same amount if it does not rain, it is a wagering agreement.

(b) A and B each deposited ₹200 with a stakeholder to abide by the issue of a walking match. It was agreed that the loser shall forfeit ₹200. This is a wagering agreement [Diggle Vs Higge - 1877-2 Ex. D 4

2.28.1 Essentials

An agreement becomes a wager if it has the following essential elements in it.

(1) Uncertain Event

An agreement becomes a wager when it is based on the happening or not happening of an uncertain event. Event may be past, present or future but the parties must not be aware of its result or the time of its result or the time of its happening.

(2) Payment of Consideration

The consideration must move from one person to another upon the results of the wagering agreement. So, it must contain a promise to pay money or moneys worth.

(3) Mutual chances of Gain or loss

There must be mutual chance of gain or loss on the determination of an uncertain event. Each side should stand to win or lose according to the result of the uncertain event. The stakes must come out of the pockets of the parties.

(4) No control over the Event

Neither party should have control over the happening of the event one-way or the other. If one of the parties has the event in his own hands, the transaction lacks an essential ingredient of a wager.

(5) No other interest in the event

Finally, neither party should have interest in the happening or non-happening of the event other than the sum or stake he will win or lose. If anyone of them has any proprietary interest in the subject matter of the agreement, the same ceases to be a wagering agreement, but becomes enforceable as a contract. It is on this basis that a wagering agreement is distinguished from a contract of insurance.

Comparison between Insurance contracts and Wagering agreements

Insurance contracts are seem to be synonymous with wagering agreements. But, they have certain superficial resemblance to wagering agreements and really transactions of a different character. The principle differences between these two are as follows.

Insurance contracts	Wagering agreements
1. There is insurable interest.	1. There is no insurable interest.
2. Both parties are interested in the subject-matter,	2. Neither party has any interest in the happening or non-happening of an event.
3. These are contracts of indemnity except life insurance contracts, which are contingent contracts.	3. These are conditional contracts and hence the amount is fixed.
4. It is based on scientific and actuarial calculation.	4. A wagering agreement is just a gambling.
5. These are valid contracts because they are beneficial to the public.	5. These are void agreements because these are opposed to public policy.

Comparison between contingent contracts and wagering agreements

Contingent contract	Wagering agreements
1. It is not necessary that there should be mutual promises. All contingent contracts are not wagers.	1. It is an agreement by mutual promises each of them conditional on all happening or non-happening of an event. All wagers are contingent but all contingent are not wagers.
2. Determination of an uncertain event is not the sole condition of the contingent contract.	2. There must be determination of an uncertain event as the sole condition of the contract.
3. The parties are interested in the occurrence or non-occurrence of event.	3. The parties are not interested in the occurrences or non-occurrences of the event.
4. The future event is merely collateral or incidental to the contract.	4. The future event is the sole determination factor of the contract.
5. It is a valid contract.	5. It is void contract.

Effects of a wagering agreement

Agreements by way of wager are void. Section 30, as stated earlier, states that no suit shall be brought for recovering anything alleged to win on any wager. Such an agreement will not be enforced by any court of law. So also the winner cannot recover money deposited with a person to enable him to pay to the party winning upon a wager. However, before it is paid to the winner the depositor can recover from the person holding such money i.e. the stakeholder.

Examples

(a) A challenges with B that India is going to win a cricket match against Pakistan to be held in Bangalore on Monday. If India loses match B cannot be recover the stake money from A.

(b) Two persons entered into wagering transactions in shares and one becomes indebted to another. A promissory note was executed for the payment of the debt. It was geld that the promissory note was not enforceable by the court [Badrids V s Meghraj AIR (1967) CA 25].

Collateral Transactions

Though wagering agreements are void, agreements collateral, incidental or subsidiary to them are valid. It has been laid down by the Supreme Court that the wager is not forbidden by the law notwithstanding the fact it is void and unenforceable [Gherular Parekh Vs Mahader Das (1959)]. Hence, a wagering agreement is not unlawful under section 23 of the Indian Contract Act and the transactions collateral to the main transaction are enforceable. Accordingly, an agent who pays and loses on wagering transactions can recover the amount from his principal. Similarly, a partner who has paid the loss on wagering transaction may recover proportionate indemnity from his copartners.

2.28.2 Exceptions

The following agreements are not held to be wagering agreements

1. Horse Race

An agreement to contribute or subscribe towards any plate, prize or sum of money ₹500 or more to be awarded to the winners of any horse race is a valid agreement and not a wager.

2. Crossword Competitions

Competitions which involve the application of skill and in which an effort is made to select the best and most skilful competitor are not wagers.

3. Share Market Transactions

Transaction, where there is a clear intention of give and take, and delivery of shares and bonds, are wagers. If there is no such clear intention give and take and parties are intend to gamble only on the rise or fall of share prices, the transaction become wagers.

4. Chit funds

Transactions of chit funds are not wagers. No doubt, some members get some gain in advance but none of the members loses the money. Their periodical contribution is refunded at the end of the chit.

2.29 QUASI CONTRACTS

Sometimes, contracts are created not by the parties but by the law itself. They are not derived from the consent of the parties but are imposed by law regardless of their consent or dissent. These are certain obligations which are not in truth contractual in the sense of resting on agreements, but which the law treats as if they were. Such obligations are called quasi contracts. They are also called constructive contracts implied contracts or certain relations resembling those created by contract.

Strictly speaking, a quasi contract is the principal that the law as well as justice should try to prevent 'unjust enrichment' i.e, enrichment of one person at the cost of another. The law will not allow a person to become rich out of the effort of another. A person who has received benefit from another must pay it. Otherwise, it would be unjust for him to retain such benefit.

In an American case Miller Vs Schloss, 918 NY 400. NE 337, it was observed that:

In truth it (quasi-contract) is not a contract at all. It is an obligation which the law creates in the absence of any agreement, when the acts of the parties or others have placed in the possession of one person, money or its equivalent, under such circumstances that in equity and good conscience he ought not retain it, and which ex aeque et bono (injustice and fairness) belong to another.

Section 73 of the Act lays down that "when an obligation resembling those created by contract has been incurred and has not been discharged, an injured person is entitled to receive the same compensation from the party in default, as if such person had contracted to discharge it and had broken his contract."

Thus, law in such cases, places the parties in the same position, as they would have been if there were contracts between them.

2.29.1 Types of Quasi Contracts

Sections 68 to 72 deal with five kinds of quasi contracts.

1. Supply of Necessaries (Sec.68)

When necessaries are supplied to a person who is incompetent to contract or to some one whom he is legally bound to support, the supplier is entitled to recover the amount from the property of the receiver of such benefit.

Section 68 says that if a person, incapable of entering into a contract or anyone whom he is legally to support is supplied by another person with necessaries suited to his condition in life, the person who has furnished such supplies is entitled to be reimbursed from the property of such incapable person.

Examples

(a) A supplies B, a lunatic, with necessaries suitable to his conditions in life. A is entitled to be reimbursed from B's property.

(b) A supplies the wife and children of B, a minor with necessaries suitable to their condition in life. A is entitled to be reimbursed from the property of B.

What are necessaries?

Necessaries mean things suited to the conditions of incompetent parties. It includes articles required to maintain a particular person in the state and degree in the life in which he is. Things necessary are those without which an individual cannot reasonably exist. For example minor's education expenditure, debt incurred for performing funeral obligations etc.

2. Payment by an interested person (Sec. 69)

When a person who is not bound to pay, makes a payment in which he is interested, is entitled to be reimbursed by such person for and on whose behalf he made the payment.

Section 69 quotes that A person who is interested in the payment of money in which another is bound by law to pay, and who therefore pays it, is entitled to be reimbursed by other.

Example: B holds land in Bengal, on a lease granted by A, the Zamindar. The revenue payable by A to the Government in arrear, his land is advertised for sale by the Government under the revenue law the consequences of such sale will be the annulment of B's lease. B to prevent the sale and consequent annulment of his own lease, pays to the government the sum due from A. A is bound to make good to B the annulment so paid.

Essentials

The following conditions must be satisfied for a suit under this section:

(a) The plaintiff must be interested in making the payment. The interest, which the plaintiff seeks to protect, must be bonafide.

(b) It is necessary that the plaintiff should not be bound to pay. He should only be interested in making the payment in order to protect his own interest.

(c) The defendant should have been bound by law to pay the money.

3. Obligations to pay non-gratuitous acts [Sec 701]

When a person does anything for the benefit of another without intended to do gratuitously, the latter is bound to compensate the former in respect of such benefit.

Section 70 says "When a person lawfully does anything for another person or delivers anything to him not intending to do so gratuitously and such other person enjoys the benefit thereof, the latter is bound to make compensation to the former in respect of, or to restore, the thing so done or delivered."

Examples

(a) A, a trader, leaves goods at B's house by mistake. B treats the goods as his own. He is bound to pay for them.

(b) A saves B's property from fire. A is not entitled to compensation from B, if the circumstances show that he intended to act gratuitously.

Essentials

The following conditions must be fulfilled for any right action according to this section.

(a) The person should lawfully do something for another person or deliver something to him.
(b) The person doing the act should not have intended to do it gratuitously.
(c) The person for whom the act is done must have enjoyed the benefit of the act.

Damodar Mudaliar Vs Secretary of state of India (1894)

A village was irrigated by a tank. The government affected certain repairs to the tank for its preservation and had no intention to do so gratuitously for the Zamindars. They enjoyed the benefit thereof. Held, they were liable to contribute.

4. Responsibility of finder of goods (Sec.71)

When a person finds goods belonging to another and takes them into his custody, he is bound to take care of the goods and must take all necessary measures to trace its owner. If the true owner is found, the finder must hand over goods to him. In case, the true owner cannot be found after reasonable search or he refuses to pay the compensation, the finder may use goods as his own or may sell them.

Section 71 reads "A person who finds goods belonging to another and takes them into his custody is subject to the same, responsibility as a bailee."

Example: F picks up a diamond on the floor of S's shop. He hands it over to S to keep it till the true owner is found. No one appears to claim it for quite some weeks in spite of the wide advertisements in newspaper. F claims the diamond from S who refuses to return.

S is bound to return the diamond to F who is entitled to retain the diamond against the whole world except the true owner.

5. Mistakes or Coercion (Sec. 72)

When a person receives money or anything from another person by mistake or under coercion, the latter must return money or such thing so received to the former.

Section 72 declares, "A person to whom money has been paid, or anything delivered by mistake or under coercion, must repay or return it."

Examples

(a) A and B jointly owe ₹100 to C. A alone pays the amount to C, and B not knowing this fact, pays ₹100 over again to C. C is bound to repay the amount to B.

(b) A pays some money to B by mistake. It is really due to C. B must refund the money to A. C, however, cannot recover the amount from B as there is no privities of contract between B and C.

(c) A railway company refuses to deliver up certain goods to the consignee, except upon the payment of an illegal charge for carriage. The consignee pays the sum charged in order to obtain the goods. He is entitled to recover so much of the charge as is illegally excessive.

Section 72 used coercion in its general sense and not as defined in section 15. Further, it does not draw any distinction between a mistake of fact and a mistake of law.

Examples

(a) K paid sales tax on his forward transactions of bullion. Subsequently this tax was declared ultra wires. Held, K could recover the amount of sales tax and that section 72 is wide enough to cover not only mistake of fact but also a mistake of law [Sales tax officer Banaras Vs Kanhailya lal Mukund Lal Saraf(1959)].

(b) An insurance company paid the amount on a policy under the mistake that goods had been destroyed by a peril insured against. The goods in fact had been sold. Held, the money could be recovered by the insurance company [Norwich etc., Society Ltd. Vs Price (W.H) Ltd (1934) A.C. 455].

QUESTIONS FOR PRACTICE

Section - A (Two Marks Questions)

1. Define a contract.
2. What is a unilateral contract?

3. What is a voidable contract?
4. What is a bilateral contract?
5. What is meant by implied contract?
6. What is unenforceable contract?
7. What is meant by an offer?
8. What are cross offers?
9. What is meant by counter offer?
10. State the differences between an executed contract and an executory contract.
11. What is consensus ad idem?
12. What is meant by revocation of communication?
13. What is an acceptance?
14. State the two kinds of offer.
15. Why is consideration essential for a contract?
16. Who is regarded as a minor?
17. When does silence amount to fraud?
18. What is undue influence?
19. What is the difference between a stranger to a contract and a stranger to consideration?
20. What is specific performance?
21. What is rescission?
22. What is remission?
23. How does consent differ from free consent?
24. Give the meaning of novation.
25. What is novation?
26. What is meant by the term 'public policy'?

27. What is meant by tender?
28. State any three essentials of a valid acceptance.
29. Mention four exceptions to agreements in restraint of trade.
30. What is meant by supervising impossibility?
31. What is meant by novation of a contract?
32. What is meant by doctrine of supervening impossibility?
33. Explain the terms 'offer' and 'acceptance'.
34. State any three essentials of a valid offer.
35. What is meant by bilateral mistake?
36. What is injunction?
37. What is free consent?
38. Give the meaning of capacity to contract.
39. Differentiate between a general offer and a special offer.
40. What is fraud?
41. What is duress?
42. What is doctrine of restitution?
43. What is doctrine of frustration?
44. What is coercion?
45. What is anticipatory breach of contract?
46. What is alteration?
47. What do you mean by vindictive damages?
48. What are the elements opposed to public policy?
49. What are special damages?
50. What are exemplary damages?
51. State the meaning of remission.

52. Give the meaning of misrepresentation.

53. Define the term consent.

Section - B (Five Marks Questions)

1. "A contract without consideration is void". Discuss.
2. "A contract without consideration is void". Discuss.
3. "A stranger to consideration can sue, but a stranger to a contract cannot". Explain.
4. "Agreements in restraint of trade are void". State the exceptions.
5. "The law of contract is not the whole law of agreements, nor is it the whole law of obligations". Discuss.
6. 'All contracts are agreements but all agreements are not contracts'. Explain.
7. Define consideration. State the essentials of a valid consideration.
8. Distinguish between coercion and undue influence.
9. Distinguish between misrepresentation and fraud.
10. Distinguish between novation and alteration.
11. Explain any four modes of discharge of a contract by agreement.
12. Explain breach of contract at a mode of discharge of contract.
13. Explain how a contract is discharged by agreement or consent.
14. Explain the elements of fraud.
15. Explain the essential elements of a valid contract.
16. Explain the exceptions to "an agreement with a minor is void".
17. Explain the various instances in which doctrine of supervening impossibility applies.
18. Mention any four agreements opposed to public policy.
19. State the exception to the rule "an agreement without consideration is void".
20. State the facts and rulings of Mohiribibi Vs. Dharmodas Ghose.

21. State when an offer can be revoked.
22. Under what circumstances can a claim in quantum meruit arises?
23. What are the different modes of rescission?
24. What are the different types of offer?
25. What are the essentials of tender?
26. What are the facts of the case Lalman Shukla Vs. Gauri Dutt?
27. What are the mistakes regarding the subject-matter of a contract?
28. What are the various kinds of contracts?
29. What is a contract? What are the essentials of a valid contract?
30. What is mistake of law and mistake of fact? State the differences between unilateral and bilateral mistake of fact.
31. When does a consent fail to become free consent?
32. When is consideration not necessary in a contract?
33. Who is public policy? Explain any three agreements opposed to public policy.
34. Write the essentials of an offer under the Contract Act.
35. Write the exceptions to the rule "no consideration no contract".
36. Write the exceptions to the rule "stranger to consideration cannot enforce a contract".

Section - C (Fifteen Marks Questions)

1. Define an offer. Explain the essentials of a valid offer.
2. Define consideration. Explain the characteristic feature's of consideration.
3. Define consideration. Explain the essentials of a valid consideration.
4. Define the term acceptance. Explain the essentials of a valid acceptance.
5. Define the term acceptance. What are the essential provisions of a valid acceptance? When can an acceptance be revoked?

6. Describe the legal rules for consideration along with examples.
7. Discuss the various remedies for breach of contract.
8. Discuss the various ways in which a contract may be discharged.
9. Explain the exceptions to the rule "a contract without consideration is void".
10. Explain the instances in which the rule of quantum meruit is applied.
11. Explain the legal rules for acceptance along with examples.
12. Explain the legal rules for consideration.
13. Explain the position of a minor regarding contracts.
14. Explain the various elements of fraud.
15. Explain the various modes by which a contract may be discharged.
16. Explain when an offer can be revoked.
17. What are the agreements opposed to public policy?
18. What are the essentials of a valid contract? Discuss.
19. What are the various kinds of damages paid as a remedy for breach of contract?
20. What is free consent? When is consent not free? Explain with examples.
21. What is meant by breach of contract? Briefly explain the remedies available to an aggrieved party on the breach of contract.
22. What is mistake? Explain the different kinds of mistakes of fact.
23. When and how is a contract discharged?

Chapter 3

Intellectual Property Legislations

3.1 INTELLECTUAL PROPERTY LEGISLATIONS

3.1.1 Background

Modern business world is full of competition. Every businessman wants to grab the maximum share in the market. There are various innovational and research activities carried on to bring in new products but there do exist fake and look-alike products in the market. To avoid any such duplication or to stop unhealthy competition it is always desirable to get legal protection for the products, process or design whatsoever. This legal protection can be obtained by registering the innovation or inventions under Patents Act. Thus, Patent Act gives legal protection to the genuine manufacturers and their products. It also encourages the intelligent class of the society such that the activities related to Research and Development can be carried on without any interference from any unauthorised person. A patent, generally speaking, is a grant from the Government which confers on the grantee, for a limited period of time, the exclusive privilege of making, selling and using the invention for which a patent has been granted and also authorising others to do so. The grant of patents for inventions in India is governed by the Patents Act, 1970 and the Patents Rules 1972. A patent granted under the Act confers upon the patentee where the patent is for an article or substance like an exclusive right itself to the inventor to use it for the benefit of society and for himself. The patents granted under Patent Act, 1970 are operative in the entire country.

3.1.2 Meaning

Patent refers to a right granted under the Patents Act. This Act consists or nearly 163 sections and it applies to whole of India. According to Sec 2(m) of the Indian Patents and Designs Act, 1911 'patents means a patent granted under this Act.'

In fact the word patent is derived from a Latin word 'patere' which means 'to open.' Patent is granted to protect the interest of an inventor such that his invention is recognised and no one should make or gain benefits unauthorisedly. When the patent is granted either to an article or a product such article or product is called 'patented article' or 'patented product.' The person in whose favour a patent is granted is called 'patentee.'

3.1.3 Objectives

The following are the important objectives of obtaining a patent.

1. Patentee obtains an absolute right over his inventions.
2. Patentee gets a right to sue any person who uses his product, design or the inventions without a prior permission of patentee.
3. Patentee gets a right to sell, licence, transfer his invention favouring other party for a due consideration.
4. Patentee, as an absolute owner of his invention, has a right to improve, add on to his finding, modify the product or process any time at his will.
5. The grant of patent declares the patentee as the first owner for his invention officially.

3.1.4 Salient features

The salient features of patent are as under.

1. Patent must be in respect of inventions and discovery.
2. Each invention must be supported by separate patent.
3. Patents must be obtained only in respect of new product process, method, articles, designs but not for marketing these.
4. Patents for process and substance must go together as they cannot be separated.
5. All the details like design, process and methods of new invention must be duly declared while obtaining patent.
6. A patent must be new and useful method especially for the society at large.

3.1.5 Definitions

Invention

According to Sec 2(1)(j) invention means any new and useful art, process, method or manner or manufacture, machine, apparatus or article, substance produced by manufacture. However according to Sec. 4 of the Act any invention relating to atomic energy are not patentable. Inventions also adds to human knowledge, but it necessarily involves some suggestions or an act to be done which results in new product.

Manufacture

Manufacture refers to making of an article or product or a thing which has utility. It also includes the process of converting a raw material into finished product.

Patent [**Sec.2(1)(m)**]

Patent means a right granted under the Patents Act, 1970 or Indian Patents and Designs Act, 1911.

True and First Inventor [Sec. 4(1)(y)]

A patentee is a true and first inventor. A true and first inventor means a person who for the first time makes or declares about his invention through the patent to the rest of the world. The true owner will be decided on the basis of the date on which such patent is obtained.

3.1.6 Specifications

It refers to the details of the design or formula or chemical combination used for the first time to obtain the patent.

Person interested [Sec. 2(1)(t)]

This includes a person who is engaged in or who promotes the research activities for the first time and even helps in modifications of the specification under the patent.

Patentee [Sec. 2(1) (p)]

A patentee means the persons for the time being entered on the register as the grantee or proprietor of the patent.

Government undertaking [Sec. 2(1)(h)]

It means any industrial undertaking carried on by govt. dept. or govt. company or corporation established by the govt.

Patented article or Patented process [Sec. 2(1) (o)]

They mean respectively an article or process in respect of which a patent is in process.

Controller [Sec. 2(1)(b)]

Controller means the Controller General of Patent, Designs and Trade Marks.

Exclusive Licence [Sec. 2(1) (f)]

Exclusive licence means a licence from a patentee which confers on the licencee and a persons authorised by him, any right in respect of the patented invention.

3.1.7 Application and Procedure to obtain patents

Any person who claims himself as the true and first inventor of an invention purely on the basis of invention and not on any idea which is imported unless such person is originally assigned as a true owner by the inventor can apply for a patent. Here one should note that patent can be applied by a legal representative of a deceased person who immediately before his death was entitled to make such an application.

An application may be made by any of the above persons either alone or jointly with any other person at appropriate office of the patent within the territorial limits. Application for each invention shall be made in the form prescribed in schedule II of the Patents rules 1972. Filled in applications are to be filed in the patent office or specific area where the inventor resides. Every application shall contain the information regarding the invention. It shall disclose in detail the process, methods and procedure of using, manufacturing the article, product and state the scope of invention for which the patent is made. Whenever an application is made for some modification, improvements or so information regarding the same shall be furnished properly.

Every complete specification shall fully and particularly describe the invention and its operations or use and the method by which it is to be performed based on which the true inventor can claim the protection in case the patent is infringed by any person. However, before granting a patent the controller shall make sure that the application contains complete specifications. On the acceptance of complete specifications the controller shall give notice thereof to the applicant and shall advertise in official gazette the fact that the specification has been accepted. Once the specifications are accepted and the same has been advertised in the official gazette, the Joint Controller has no power to decide that the complete specifications accepted relate to more than one invention and cannot amend anything thereupon. Thus, a patent granted to a person based on complete specifications confers upon him a bundle of several exclusive rights to use the patent for a specific period or till such period as the grant is confirmed. However the grant of patent is subject to the following conditions:

(a) Any machine, apparatus or other article made by using a process in respect of which a patent is granted, may be imported or made by the government for its own use.
(b) Any process in respect of which the patent is granted may be used by any person for experiment or research including the imparting of instructions to the students who indulge in such research activity.
(c) In case of patent relating to medicine or drug may be imported by the government for its own use having regard to the public service by notifying in the official gazette.

It is not in the interest of general public and society to grant a patent right in respect of certain inventions which are either not in good taste of the society or which directly harms the very interest of public or the process of such a manufacture is injurious to both human beings and other living beings.

3.2 TERM OF PATENTS (SECTION 53)

Every patent granted in respect of any invention, process or manufacturing method shall exist for a period of 5 years from the date of sealing the patent or 7 years from the date of the patent whichever is less and in respect of any other invention the term shall be 14 years from the date of grant of the patent right.

3.3 OPPOSITION TO GRANT OF PATENT

Grant of patents can be opposed by any person within a period of four months from the date of advertisement of the acceptance of complete specifications by giving a notice to the controller of opposition to the grant of patents on the following grounds.

1. Priority dates of claims

The opponent, by issue of notice to the controller, claims that the said invention is that of a later period and the original invention belongs to him based on the prior date of invention, that the claimed invention is claimed in a claim of complete specification in which priority date is earlier than that of applicant's claim.

2. Invention not obtained lawfully

Obtaining refers to finding out about the invention. The applicant for the patent must obtain the patent lawfully i.e. legally claiming the invention that to be of his own. On the other hand any invention obtained unlawfully or wrongfully definitely gives right to the opponent to claim it rightfully. The controller after knowing the fact and prima-facie of the original patentee (proposed) shall take suitable action such that the real patent right shall be given to a person who has the earlier claims, based on the date of invention.

3. Based on publication and public knowledge

The original patentee can be identified by the controller based; H1 the priority of date related to the specific invention. The controller shall also, through the advertisement, make it clear about the original inventor. Sufficient publicity regarding this to create public awareness must be given. The opponent must make it clear that his invention does not have any claims from anyone other than he himself only.

4. Objections to inventions as not inventions only, which cannot be patented

Complete specifications are misleading which itself is the ground that the said invention is obtained illegally from the opponent for which justice is sought from controller of patent rights.

Thus, wherever such notices are given by any person or opponent, it is the duty of the controller to notify the applicant as well as the opponent and inform them that equal opportunity will be given to both to claim their genuine right. Rules 35 and 36 state clearly the process and duties of controller in case an objection is filed with him for the genuine claim of the patent. Further on the completion of the presentation of details and evidences as to the claim of priority by the opponent the controller shall appoint a time for hearing for the opposition by giving not less than 10 days notice. The controller shall then decide the opposition and notify the decision to the parties with reasons.

3.4 LAPSE OF PATENT AND ITS RENEWAL

A patent gets ceased the moment its licence expires. However, in ordinary language a patent has its life intact till its fees are paid and renewed regularly without fail. Whenever the patent ceased to exist it is called as 'Lapse of Patent.'

The patents are to be renewed regularly by paying the fees to the controller of patents. The lapsed patent can be restored by way of an application from the patentee explaining the reasons of such non-payment of renewal fees. The controller after hearing from the inventor, if satisfied, can again restore the lapsed patent with immediate effect. Where a patent is restored, the rights of the patentee shall be subject to the provisions as the controller thinks fit to impose for the protection or compensation of persons who may have began to avail themselves of, or have taken definite steps by contract to avail of the patented invention between the date when the patent ceased to have effect and the date of advertisement of the application for restoration of the patent, controller shall restore the patent and any patent of addition specified in the application which has ceased to have effect.

3.5 SURRENDER OF PATENT

A patent can be surrender at anytime if the patentee so desires by giving notice of surrender to the controller in a specified form as per section 63 of the Act. The controller after receiving the surrender application shall notify the same through an advertisements to seek any opposition to the same. Any person interested in the said patent which is surrendered can, within three months from the date of such advertisement, give notice of opposition to the surrender to the controller as per law. The notice of opposition shall be informed to the patentee and an official hearing from both the parties should be conducted by the controller. After such hearing from both the parties, he may direct the patentee to return the 'patent' and as soon as the controller receives the patent from the patentee he shall revoke the same and notify such revocation of patent in the official gazette.

3.6 REVOCATION OF PATENTS

Subject to the provisions of Patent Act any person interested may claim the patent as his own or on a counter-claim in a suit for infringement of the patent, the central government shall implement the order of revocation of patent passed by the High Court on any of the following grounds:

(i) on a claim of priority of dates of invention and opposing that same should be cancelled in the interest of original patentee.

(ii) that the application for the patent made is not in accordance with the rules of this Act.

(iii) that the said patent was obtained wrongly in contravention of the right of the petitioner or any person under or through whom he claims.

(iv) that the invention in the complete specification is not invention only, which is not useful to the public at large and the specification which definitely mislead the persons of ordinary produce while using the patent.

(vi) that the subject of any claim of the complete specification is not patentable under this Act.

(vii) that the information furnished by the inventor is not of material fact and controller of patent is of the opinion that the same specifications do exist earlier.

(viii) that the applicant has not maintained the secrecy in regard to specifications as per this Act.

(ix) that the revocation of the patent is completely in the interest of public and the society at large.

(x) that the patent has already expired hence is revoked.

Thus, revocation of a patent is final and not appealable. Application of revocation must be made by the person interested in the process to seek its revocation otherwise the application of revocation can be dismissed by the controller stating that there are no specific and valid reasons of revocation of patent.

3.7 INFRINGEMENT AND REMEDIES

'Patent right' is an exclusive right conferred on the original and true inventor. The very purpose of obtaining patent under this Act is to get legal protection against anyone or everyone who is found to use the said patented design or sell the patented product and gains unauthorisedly and freely in the market. If the invention is used by any other person claiming it to be of his, which in reality is not so, amounts to infringement of the patent. In other words, when the invention is used by any other person without a licence from the patentee, it constitutes infringement of patent. Thus, infringement means interference with or the violation or misuse of the exclusive right of the patentee. It directly amounts to the misuse of already conferred rights of the genuine owner of a patent. In a suit for infringement of patent, the plaintiff must prove that during the period of his absolute ownership and right of enjoyment of those lawful rights the defendants have made, sold or used the invention without his licence or the said patent is imitated for gains and profits. In the process of suit it is the responsibility of defendant to prove and furnish all such particulars of the breaches constituting the alleged infringement of the patent as claimed by the plaintiff is totally false and he shall be declared as true owner and possess the genuine patent.

Thus, the onus is on the defendants to prove all objections to the validity of the patent. However, persons liable would be those who actually manufacture the infringing article or use the patented process and others who are indirectly connected with the manufacture or sale of the articles.

As stated earlier an action for infringement may be instituted by way of a legal suit in District Court or in the High Court. The relief which the court may grant in any suit for infringement of a patent include:

(a) an injunction
(b) damages
(c) an account of profit.

In a claim of profits, it is material to ascertain how much of the invention was actually apportioned to determine what portion of the new profit realised by the infringer was attributable to its use. While, in case of assessing the damage, it is normally seen as to what is the nature of loss whether monetary, moral or any other aspect which led to the suit. The loss must be natural and direct consequence of the defendants acts.

3.8 INTELLECTUAL PROPERTY RIGHTS

Patents are aptly described as intellectual property. These are the result of purely intellectual effort. A person expends time, skill and effort to produce something new. It has long been recognised that the inventor of something new will have the exclusive right to use the subject-matter of invention for a certain period. He may also grant a licence to someone to use the subject-matter of invention. If other people were free to use the subject-matter of invention they would be making a profit out of the skill, labour and intellectual effort of the inventor. The law does not permit this. It is to protect the interest of the inventors that the law gives them for a specified period certain exclusive rights in relation to the subject-matter of invention.

3.9 CONCLUSION

Patent Act surely protects the rights of true and original owner of any invention. No doubt the patentee's confidence is morally boosted to work towards the direction of better use of his invention. Not only the patentee but the said Act also controls and puts a legal stamp in the invention for his commercial use. Thus, Patent Act assures the smooth functioning of sales activities in the interest of the inventor as well as the society at large.

QUESTIONS FOR PRACTICE

Section - A (Two Marks Questions)

1. Give two examples of intellectual properties.
2. State the meaning of patent right.
3. State two advantages of obtaining a patent.
4. What are intellectual property rights?
5. What is intellectual property?
6. What is infringement of a patent right?
7. What is invention according to the Patents Act, 1970?
8. Who can apply for the registration of a patent?

Section - B (Five Marks Questions)

1. Explain infringement of patent rights.
2. Give four grounds for opposition to the grant of a patent right.
3. State the advantages of obtaining patents.
4. State the purposes of a patent.
5. State the remedies available to a patentee in case of infringement of his patent right.
6. What are inventions? What are not regarded as inventions by the Patents Act?
7. What are not patentable inventions?
8. What are patent rights? What are the grounds for the opposition of the grant of a patent right?
9. What is patent right? What does it lapse?
10. When does a patent lapse? How can it be restored?
11. Write about revocation of patents.

Section - C (Fifteen Marks Questions)

1. When do the patents lapse and how are they restored?

2. What is revocation of a patent right? What are the circumstances when a patent can be revoked in public interest and by the High Court?

3. What are the rights of the patentee? What are the limitations on the rights of the patentee?

4. Explain the procedure for the registration of a patent.

Chapter 4

Environment Protection Act, 1986

4.1 INTRODUCTION AND BACKGROUND

The mother earth is nature's beautiful gift to mankind. We get everything from the womb of mother earth but it is felt that due to excessive extraction from the earth and due to huge industrialisation man has burdened the mother earth which has resulted in unmanageable problems. It is time that the ecological balance of earth is disturbed and the entire environment is polluted. Even in our own country we have seen tragedies like Bhopal Gas leak tragedy which resulted in many deaths and several people became handicap. It was after the Bhopal Tragedy, the Central Government enacted the Environment (protection) Act 1986 under Article 253 of the constitution. The Act was mainly brought in line with the advice from United Nations Conference on Human Environment of 1972, as the outcome of the conference was very much related with protection and improvement of Human environment and the prevention of hazards to human beings, other living creatures, plants and property. The Environment Act came into effect from November 9, 1986. The Act applies to entire India.

4.2 DEFINITIONS

4.2.1 Environment

According to Chambers Twentieth Century Dictionary the word 'environment' means a surrounding or conditions influencing development or growth. It is evident that environment directly relates to the growth of our neighbourhood, our city or our place and its surrounding.

According to section 2(a) of this Act "Environment includes water, air and land, the inter relationship which exists among and between water, air and land, human beings, other living creatures, plants, micro organism and property".

4.2.2 Environment Pollutant [See 2(b)]

It refers to any solid, liquid or gaseous substance present in such concentration as may be tend to be injurious to environment.

4.2.3 Environment Pollution [See 2(e)]

It refers to the presence in the environment of any environmental pollutant something that befoul physically to contaminate.

4.2.4 Handling [See 2 (d)]

It relates to any substance used in manufacturing processing, treatment of material like storage, distribution, collection, sale, transfer etc, done carefully without harming the environment.

4.2.5 Hazardous substance [See 2(e)]

It means all such substance by which or by its chemical process or handling of such substance causes harm to either human being or other living creatures, property or the environment.

4.2.6 Occupier (See 2(f)]

The modified meaning of the term occupies under the Environment protection Act is related to a place of work like a factory, premise, or a person in whose possession the substance are, which results in polluting the environment.

4.3 OBJECTIVES

The Environment Act is enacted with three main objectives

(a) Protection of Environment
(b) Improvement of Environment and
(c) Prevention of hazardous to:
   (i) Human beings
   (ii) Other living creatures
   (iii) Plants and property.

4.4 POWERS OF CENTRAL GOVERNMENT

The Central Government is empowered to take all such necessary actions under this Act which protects and improve the quality of the environment and also prevent and control the environment pollution.

The Central Government may include certain measures with respect to all or anyone of the following matters

(a) Coordination of actions by the State Governments in respect of protecting the environment and controlling and preventing the Environment pollutant rules and regulations under any other Law which is relatable to the objects of this Act.

(b) Planning and Controlling through the execution of such programmes and policies which help in prevention, controlling of environment pollution.

(c) Fixing the standard for maintaining quality of environment in its various aspects.

(d) Fixing standards for emission or discharge of environmental pollutants from various sources.

(e) Restricting certain industries regarding their production processes not to venture into production of such article, product and the process of manufacture which adds to environmental pollution.

(f) Laying down safe methods of production and maintenance of machinery for the prevention of accidents which may cause environment pollution.

(g) Laying dawn procedures and safeguards for handling, of hazardous substances.

(h) Examination and inspection, of such machineries, plant, equipments and manufacturing processes and directing the owners of such units not to use such machinery, methods or processes which causes environmental pollution.

(i) Establishment or recognition of environmental laboratories and institutions to carry out the functions entrusted ta such environmental laboratories under this Act.

(j) Collection and dissemination of information in respect of matters relating to environmental pollution.

(k) Preparation of manuals, codes or guides relating to the prevention, control and abatement of environmental pollution.

(l) Such other matters as the Central Government deems necessary or expedient for the purpose of securing the effective implementation of the provisions of this Act.

Besides all these, as per Sec 3(3), of this Act, the Central Government is also empowered ta constitute any authority for exercising and performing such powers and functions of the Central Government as may be specified in its order.

4.5 PROTECTION AND PREVENTION OF ENVIRONMENT POLLUTION

Sections 7 ta 14 of Environment Protection Act deal with all such information which was an industrial unit not to indulge in an activity which ultimately causes environmental pollution. Section 7 deals with information on emission pollution in excess of standard accordingly. No person carrying on any industry, operation, or process shall discharge or emitted or permit to be discharged or emitted any environmental pollution in excess of the standards prescribed.

Section 8 of the Act prescribes and informs about procedural safe-guards in case of handling of hazardous substances Section 9 of the Act provides a detailed information authorities and agencies operative in controlling the environmental pollution, it provides as follows:

(a) Where the discharge of any environmental pollutant in excess of the prescribed standards occurs the person responsible for such discharge and the person in charge of such place at which such discharge occurs shall be bound to prevent the environmental pollution caused as a result, of such discharge. Further it is the duty of such person to co-operate in furnishing such information which caused such discharge ta the authorities.

(b) On receiving the information about the discharge of any environmental pollution, the authorities or the agencies appointed to check such occurrences shall immediately take all such measures to mitigate the environmental pollution and further damage.

(c) The authorities or the agencies are empowered to collect all such expenses which have been incurred in taking all the remedial actions, measures to mitigate environmental pollution from the person concerned as per law.

4.6 POWERS OF ENTRY AND INSPECTION [SECTION 10]

As per Section 10 of Environment Protection Act, the Central Government can authorise on its behalf any person and entrust all the nights to him to enter all such places at all reasonable time for:

(a) Performing any of the functions which are directed by the Central Government to him.

(b) Determine whether and if so in what manner any such functions are to be performed or whether any provision of this Act or rules made thereunder or any notice order, or direction given or granted as per this Act being an has been complied with.

(c) The purpose of testing any equipment, plant, any record or document or any other material object in which he has reason to believe that an offence under this Act has been committed and thereupon seize such equipment, plant or record whatsoever for legal enquiries.

Further section 11 of this Act empowers the Central Government to grant such powers to take samples and check the process and procedure to be followed in process, or plant functioning etc. The sample so taken that of water, soil, air or any other substance from an factory, premises or site shall be sent to the laboratory which is established or recognised u/s 12 for conducting the tests of such material or object obtained from any place or site whatsoever claimed to be harmful to the environment in general.

4.7 HAZARDOUS SUBSTANCE

Hazardous substance means any substance or preparation which by reason of its chemical or physiochemical properties or handling is liable to cause harm to human beings, other living creature's plant, micro-organism, property or the environment.

The law states that no person shall handle or cause to be handled any such hazardous substance except in accordance with sue procedure and after complying with such safeguards as may be prescribed. The Central Government may take into account the following factors while prohibiting the handling of hazardous substance in different areas:

(a) The very nature of the substance both qualitative and quantitative and its potentiality to cause the damage to the environment, human beings, other living creatures, plant and property.

(b) The very substance, material available or its substitute which is proposed to be a prohibited or restricted.

(c) The time or period required by the authorities to obtain its technology which will help in either produces the substance of its substitute.

(d) Any other factor as may be considered by the Central Government to be relevant to the protection of environment.

4.8 PREVENTION OF ENVIRONMENT POLLUTION

The Central Board or a State Board for prevention and control water pollution constituted u/s 3 and 4 respectively of water prevention and control of Water Pollution Act, 1974 or the State Board for prevention and control of Air Pollution constituted under section of the Act 1981 may specify more stringent standards from those provided in schedules I, III and IV in respect of any specific industry operation, procedure, process upon quality of the recipient system and after recording therefore in writing. The recipient system means the part of the environment such as soil, water, air or other which receives the pollutants.

The standards of emission or discharge of environment pollutant so specified shall be complied with by an industry or process within, a period of 12 months of being so specified. The industries shall abide by the standards fixed under this Act to control the emission, the parameters are to be strictly followed failing which the Board may specify more stringent standards and even levy punishment in the form of parality.

The Board or the Central Government may directly appoint, person to supervise the procedure of process, manufacturing and monitoring the parameters to protect the environment.

Prohibition and Restriction on the location of industries and carrying on processes and operation in different areas.

The Central Government may take into consideration the following factors while prohibiting or restricting the location of industries and carrying on of the processes and operations:

(a) Standards of quality of environment in its various aspects laid down for an area.

(b) The maximum allowable limits of concentration of various environment pollutants for the area including noise etc.

(c) The emission discharge ot the environmental pollutants from an1 industry, process or operation proposed to be prohibited or restricted.

(d) The topographic and climatic feature of the area.

(e) The Biological diversity of the area which in the opinion of the Central Government needs to be preserved.

(f) Environmentally compatible land use.

(g) Net adverse environmental impact likely to be caused by industry, process or operation proposed to be prohibited or restricted.

(h) Proximity to the prohibited area according to ancient moment and archaeological sites and remains Act 1958 or a sanctuary, park games village area reserved for development of games, closed area or notified area such as wildlife areas etc.

(i) Proximity to Human settlement.

(j) Any other factor as may be considered by the Central Government to be relevant to the protection of environment in an area.

While prohibiting a particular area or location or any operation process of an industry the Central Government shall follow the procedure laid down here under:

1. Whenever it appears to the Central Government that it is expedient to impose prohibition or restriction on carrying on of process and any operations in an area, it may, by notification in the Official Gazette and in such other manner as the Central Government may deem necessary from time to time.

2. Every notification shall briefly describe the location, area, industry or process which such notification pertains and also specify the reasons for imposition of prohibition or restriction or the location, area, industry or process as the case may be.

3. Any person interested in filing the objection may do so in writing to the Central Government within 60 days from the date of publication of such notification in the official Gazette.

4. The Central Government shall within a period of 120 days from the date of publication of the notification in the Official Gazette consider all the objection received against such notification and may impose prohibition or restrictions on location of such industries and the carrying on of any process or operation in an area.

4.9 CONCLUSION

The Environment Protection Act 1986 is enacted to exercise Control and guide those industries, manufacturing units to revise their manufacturing processes in a manner to adhere to the conditions of Board so specified to control or minimise the environment pollutant. The biggest lesson one can learn is from Bhopal Gas Tragedy due to which still there are thousands who are unable to lead a happy life. The Noise pollution, Air and Water are slowly becoming rare products. The Government which is empowered to take action against erring industrialists, the environment awareness movement which has given impends to Eco- friendly products and the very Act itself has made many industrialists to think and adopt such measures which are no harmful to the mankind and other beings in nature. It is the bounded duty of every one of us to protect the virginity of nature and pass it on to next generation in a same way as we all wanted it for the good of every one of us.

QUESTIONS FOR PRACTICE

Section - A (Two Marks Questions)

1. What is a hazardous substance?
2. What is environment?
3. What is environmental pollution?

Section - B (Five Marks Questions)

1. Write about the need for Environment (Protection) Act.
2. Mention the objectives of the Environment (Protection) Act.
3. Explain the power of the government in regulating environmental pollution.

Section - C (Fifteen Marks Questions)

1. Define environment, environmental pollution and occupier as per the Environment (Protection) Act.
2. Discuss the provisions for prevention, control and abatement of environmental pollution.
3. Explain the powers of the government to regulate environmental pollution.
4. Explain the role of the Central Government to prevent and control environmental pollution.
5. What are the powers of the Central Government to protect and improve environment?
6. What are the powers of the Central Government to protect and improve environment?
7. What is environmental pollution? Explain the Central Government's power in protecting the environment.

CHAPTER 5

CONSUMER PROTECTION ACT (COPRA), 1986

5.1 INTRODUCTION AND BACKGROUND

In India consumers spread over the entire length and breadth of the country are unorganised. Many of them are also illiterate, poor and backward. As against this, the producers are relatively much more organised. They have huge resources at their disposal and can deceive and exploit consumers in a number of ways. In a bid to beat competition, increase their market share and maximise their profits, they, at all times, adopt dubious means to push up the sales of their products.

The following are the most popular ways and means will be adopted by the producers and traders to deceive consumers:

1. Prices may be fixed at levels much higher than those dictated by the costs of production.
2. The sellers may first hike prices and then offer discounts to attract consumers.
3. The consumers may not be given the correct weight or quantity of goods.
4. Advertisement might make false claims about the quality of the goods.
5. Advertisement may provide incomplete information not disclosing the risks associated with the use of the products.
6. The goods supplied to the consumers maybe highly adulterated.

On account of the above factors, it needs consumer protection.

5.2 EMERGENCY OF THE CONSUMER RIGHTS

Every year the 15th of March is observed as the "World Consumer Rights Day". The significance of this day is that on this day in 1962, John Fitzerald Kennedy, the then President of U.S.A., declared four consumer rights in his special message to the American Congress. Later on the International Organization of Consumers Union (IOCU) added three more rights to the list. The Government of India also included these rights in its Bill of Consumer Rights, i.e., Consumer Protection Act, 1986. These have also been incorporated in the United Nations Charter of Human Rights. The seven consumer rights are:

Mentioned by the President Kennedy:

1. Right to Safety
2. Right to be Informed
3. Right to Choose
4. Right to be Heard

Added by International Organization of Consumers Union - (IOCU):

5. Right to Redress
6. Right to a Healthy Environment
7. Right to Consumer Education.

According to Human Development Report, 1998 of United Nations Development Program, the rights must be defended through:

(i) Strict standards for consumers health and safety;
(ii) Product labelling about the content and proper use of products and their environmental and social impact;
(iii) Information and awareness campaigns about potential health hazards, such as smoking and the improper use of feeding formula for infants.

The Government of India passed a number of Acts to protect the rights of consumers. These include: The Agricultural Produce (Grading and Marking) Act, 1937, the Essential Commodities Act, 1955, the Weights and Measures Act, 1958, the Prevention and Food Adulteration Act, 1954, the Drugs and Cosmetics Act, 1940, the Fruits Products Order, 1955, the Drugs and Magic Remedies (Objectionable Advertisement) Act, 1940, the Dangerous Drugs Act, 1940, the Indian Standards Institution (Certification Mark) Act, the Indian Sale of Goods Act, 1930, the Indian Contract Act, 1872, the Emblems and Names (Preventing of Improper Use) Act, the Packaged Commodities (Regulation) Order, 1975, the Trade and Merchandise Mark Act, the Monopolies and Restrictive Trade Practices Act, 1969, the Bureau of Indian Standards (BIS) etc.

The most important legislation in the field of consumer protection is the Consumer Protection Act, 1986 (Act 68 of 1986), which is now regarded as the ***magna carta*** of the rights of consumers. It was formulated after studying intensively the consumer protection

Acts of a number of countries and after thorough consultations with the representatives of consumers, traders and industrialists. The enactment of the detailed Consumer Protection Act was also necessitated by the fact that India too have signed the Consumer Protection Resolution No.39/248, dated: 09-04-1985 adopted by the General Assembly of UNO at international level. It has been held that the framework and objectives of the Consumer Act were provided by the aforesaid resolution.

The Act extends to the whole of India except the State of Jammu and Kashmir. This Act has came into force in the whole of India on 15-04-1987 (only Chapter I, II & IV). Chapter III of the Act came into force in the whole of India on 1-07-1987. It has been laid down by clause 4 of Section 1 that save as otherwise expressly provided by the Central Government by Notification that this Act shall apply to all goods and services.

The Act thoroughly Amended in 1991, 1993 and 2002 to make it more purposeful and to increase the powers of Consumer Disputes Redressal Agencies.

5.3 OBJECTIVES OF THE ACT

The objective of legislature envisaged under the Consumer Protection Act is for redressal of grievance of consumers. They wanted to protect the interest of consumers against the exploitation by traders or manufacturers. Therefore, legislation was introduced and enacted with enthusiasm as a benevolent legislation objected to protect consumer from unfair trade practices, exploitation by unscrupulously traders or manufacturers of goods.

The Act provides three-tier form of redressal of consumer grievances: Firstly, the District Forum at district level. Secondly, the State Forum at state level it is called the State Commission and the National Commission at the national level.

The main object behind the Constitution of Forums at three levels, namely, to ensure speedy redressal of consumer disputes where complaint was not required to undergo long-drawn litigation reflecting so much financial burden on him. Under the Act, provision for the establishment of Consumer Councils and other authorities for the settlement of consumer's disputes and for matters connected therewith, hence, to provide protection and ensure welfare of consumers at large.

The basic objectives behind the Act, where laid down very lucidly under the Statement of Object and Reasons of the Act, 1986 which are as under:

1. The Consumer Protection Bill, 1986 seeks to provide for better protection of the interests of consumers and for that purpose, to make provision for the establishment of Consumer Protection Councils and other authorities for the settlement of consumer disputes and for matters connected therewith.

2. It seeks ***inter alia***, to provide and protect the rights of consumer such as:
   (a) the right to be protected against marketing of goods, which are hazardous to life and property;
   (b) the right to be informed about the quality, quantity, potency, purity, standard and price of goods to protect the consumer against unfair trade practices;
   (c) the right to be assured, whenever possible access to variety of goods at competitive prices;
   (d) the right to be heard and to be assured that consumer's interest will receive due consideration at appropriate forums;
   (e) the right to seek redressal against unfair trade practices or unscrupulous exploitation of consumers; and
   (f) the right to consumer education.
3. These objects are sought to be promoted and protected by the Consumer Protection Councils to be established at the Central and State levels.
4. To provide speedy and simple redressal to consumer disputes, a quasi-judicial machinery is sought to be set up at the District, State and Central levels. These quasi-judicial bodies will observe the principle of natural justice and have been empowered to give reliefs of a specific nature and to reward, wherever appropriate, compensation to consumers. Penalties for noncompliance of the orders given by the quasi-judicial bodies have also been provided.
5. The Bill seeks to achieve the above objects.

5.4 DEFINITIONS

(Section-2 of Chapter-I, deals with the Definitions):

In the Consumer Protection Act, 1986 various terms have been defined so as to avoid any ambiguity in the inter-presentation of the provisions of the Act. The definitions of these terms also help in ascertaining the scope and ambit of consumer disputes covered under the Act. Hence, definition of some of the terms like 'consumer', 'consumer dispute', 'complaint', 'complainant', 'defect', 'deficiency', 'goods', 'services' is necessary.

Consumer-[Section 2(1)(D)]

Consumer means any of the following persons:

(i) A person who buys any goods for a consideration, which has been paid or promised or partly paid and partly promised, or under any system of deferred payment and includes any user of such goods other than the person who buys such goods for consideration paid or promised or partly paid or partly promised, or under any system of deferred payment when such use is made with the approval of such person, but does not include a person who obtains such goods for resale or for any commercial purpose; or

(ii) A person who hires or avails of any services for a consideration which has been paid or promised or partly paid and partly promised, or under any system of deferred payment and includes any beneficiary of such services other than the person who hires or avails of the services for consideration paid or promised, or partly paid and partly promised, or under any system or deferred payment, when such services are availed of with the approval of the first mentioned person but does not include a person who avails of such services for any commercial purpose.

Explanation: For the purposes of this clause, "commercial purpose" does not include use by a person of goods bought and used by him and services availed by him exclusively for the purpose of earning his livelihood by means of self-employment.

Consumer Dispute-[Section 2(1)(E)]

"Consumer Dispute" means a dispute where the person against whom a complaint has been made, denies or disputes the allegations contained in the complaint.

Complaint-[Section 2(1)(C)]

"Complaint" means any allegation in writing is made by a complainant that:

(i) an unfair trade practice or a restrictive trade practice has been adopted by any trader or service provider;

(ii) the goods bought by him or agreed to be bought by him suffer from one or more defects;

(iii) the services hired or availed of or agreed to be hired or availed of by him suffer from deficiency in any respect;

(iv) the trader or service provider, as the case may be, has charged for the goods or for the services mentioned in the complaint, a price in excess of the price:

   (a) fixed by or under any law for the time being in force;
   (b) displayed on the goods or any package containing such goods;
   (c) displayed on the price list exhibited by him or under any law for the time being in force; (d) agreed between the parties;

(v) goods which will be hazardous to life and safety when used, are being offered for sale to the public:

(a) in contravention of any standards relating to safety of such goods to be complied with, by or under any law for the time being in force;

(b) if the trader could have known with due diligence that the goods so offered are unsafe to the public;

(vi) service which are hazardous or likely to be hazardous to life and safety of the public when used, or being offered by the service provider which such person could have known with due diligence to be injurious to life and safety; with a view to obtaining any relief provided by or under this Act.

Complainant-[Section 2(1)(B)]

A "Complainant" means any of the following and having made a complaint:

(i) a consumer; or

(ii) any voluntary Consumer Association registered under the Companies Act, 1956 (1 of 1956) or under any other law for the time being in force; or

(iii) the Central Government or any State Government; who or which makes a complaint;

(iv) one or more consumers, where there are numerous consumers having the same interest; or

(v) in case of death of a consumer; his legal heir or representative; who or which makes a complaint;

Defect-[Section 2(1)(F)]

"Defect" means any fault, imperfection or shortcoming in the quality, quantity, potency, purity or standard which is required to be maintained by or under any law for the time being in force or under any contract, express or implied or as is claimed by the trader in any manner whatsoever in relation to any goods.

Deficiency-[Section 2(1)(G)]

"Deficiency" means any fault, imperfection, shortcoming or inadequacy in the quality, nature and manner of performance which is required to be maintained by or under any law for the time being in force or has been undertaken to be performed by a person in pursuance of a contract or otherwise related to any service.

Goods-[Section 2(1)(I)]

"Goods" under this Act shall have the same meaning as assigned to it under the Sale of Goods Act, 1930. Accordingly, "Goods" means every kind of movable property other than actionable claims and money; and includes stock and shares, growing crops, grass and things attached to or forming part of the land, which are agreed to be severed before sale or under the contract of sale. [Section 2(7) of the Sale of Goods Act, 1930).

Service-[Section 2(1)(O)]

"Service" means service of any description which is made available to potential users and includes, but not limited to, the provision of facilities in connection with banking, financing, insurance, transport, processing, supply of electrical or other energy boarding or lodging or both, housing construction, entertainment, amusement or the purveying of news or other information, but dose not include the rendering of any service free of charge or under a contract of personal service.

Spurious Goods and Services-[Section 2(1)(OO)]

A new definition under Section 2(oo) has been added to the Act of spurious goods and services, as under:

"Spurious Goods and Services" means such goods and services which are claimed to be genuine but they are actually not so.

5.5 CONSUMER PROTECTION COUNCIL

The Government had the idea that the interest of consumers in India were not being protected by the manufacturers and traders. In order to give due importance to the interest of consumers Government had created a machinery under the name Consumer Protection Council under the Act which has been entrusted with the functions of promoting and protecting various interests of the consumers. In order to give these interests proper recognition in the Indian legal system, the Act has recognised these interests in the shape of various rights. The Act recognises Central Consumer Protection Council at the Center and State Consumer Protection Councils at the State level and District Consumer Protection Councils at District level, which are to look after the rights of the consumers.

Central Consumer Protection Council-[Section 4 to 6]

Section 4 of the Act, provides that:

1. The Central Government shall, by notification, establish with effect from such date as it may specify in such notification, a council to be known as the Central Consumer Protection Council, hereinafter referred to as the Central Council.

2. The Central Council shall consist of the following members, namely:
   (a) the Minister in charge of the Consumer Affairs in the Central Government, who shall be its Chairman, and
   (b) such number of other official or non-official members representing such interests as may be prescribed.

   According to Rule 3 of the Consumer Protection Rules, 1987, the Central Council shall consist of the following 150 members namely:

   (a) the Minister in charge of Consumer Affairs in the Central Government, who shall be Chairman of the Central Council;
   (b) the Minister of State (where he is not holding independent charge) or Deputy Minister in charge Consumer Affairs in the Central Government who shall be the Vice-Chairman of the Central Council;
   (c) the Minister of Food and Civil Supplies or Minister in charge of Consumer Affairs in States;
   (d) eight Members of Parliament, 5 from the Lok Sabha and 3 from Rajya Sabha;
   (e) the Secretary of the National Commission for the Scheduled Castes and Scheduled Tribes;
   (f) representatives of the Central Government Departments, autonomous organisations concerned with consumer interest, not exceeding 20;
   (g) representatives of the Consumer Organisations for Consumers, not less than 35;
   (h) representative of Women, not less than 10;
   (i) representative of Farmers, Trade and Industries, not exceeding 20;
   (j) persons capable of representing consumer interest not specified above, not exceeding 15;
   (k) the Secretary in charge of Consumer Affairs in the Central Government shall be the Member Secretary of the Central Council.
3. The term of the Council shall be three years.
4. Any member may, by writing under his hand to the Chairman of the Central Council, resign from the Council. The vacancies so caused or otherwise, shall be filled from the same category by the Central Government and such person shall hold office so long as the members whose place he fills would have been entitled to hold office, if the vacancy had not occurred.
5. For the purpose of monitoring the implementation of the recommendations of the Central Council and to suggest the working of the Council, the Central Government may constitute from amongst the members of the Council, a Standing Working Group, under the Chairmanship of the Members Secretary of the Council. The Standing Working Group shall consists of not exceeding 30 members and shall meet as and when considered necessary, the Central Government.

Procedure for Meetings of the Central Council-(Section 5)

1. The Central Council shall meet as and when necessary and at least one meeting of the Council shall be held every year.
2. It shall meet at such time and place as the Chairman may think fit and shall observe such procedure in regard to the transaction of its business as may be prescribed.

Objects of the Central Council-(Section 6)

The objects of the Central Council shall be to promote and protect the rights of the consumers such as:

Rights of Consumers

(a) the right to be protected against the marketing of goods and services, which are hazardous to life and property;
(b) the right to be informed about the quality, quantity, potency, purity, standard and price of goods or services as the case may be, so as to protect the consumer against unfair trade practices;
(c) the right to be assured, wherever possible, access to a variety of goods and services at competitive prices;
(d) the right to be heard and to be assured that consumer's interests will receive due consideration at appropriate forums;
(e) the right to seek redressal against unfair trade practices restrictive trade practices or unscrupulous exploitation of consumers; and
(f) the right to consumer education.

The Central Council shall give wide publicity to the rights of the consumers and the consumer dispute redressal agencies and procedure of filing complaints therein through television, radio, newspapers and magazines to give impetus to consumer movement in the country.

5.6 THE STATE CONSUMER PROTECTION COUNCIL-[SECTIONS 7 & 8]

Section 7 of the Act, provides that:

1. The State Government shall, by notification, establish with effect from such date as it may specify in such notification, a Council to be known as the Consumer Protection Council for: hereinafter referred to as the State Council.
2. The State Council shall consist of the following members, namely:

(a) the Minister in charge of Consumer Affairs in the State Government who shall be its Chairman;

(b) such number of other official or non-official members representing such interests as may be prescribed by the State Government;

(c) such number of other official or non-official members, not exceeding 10, as may be nominated by the Central Government.

3. The State Council shall meet as and when necessary but not less than two meetings shall be held every year.

4. The State Council shall meet at such time and place as the Chairman may think fit and shall observe such procedure in regard to the transaction of its business as may be prescribed by the State Government.

Objects of the State Council-(Section 8)

The objects of every State Council shall be to promote and protect within the State, the rights of consumers laid down in clauses (a) to (f) of Section 6.

5.7 THE DISTRICT CONSUMER PROTECTION COUNCIL-[SECTIONS 8A AND 8B]

Section 8-A as inserted by the Consumer Protection (Amendment) Act, 2002 provides that:

1. The State Government shall establish for every district, by notification, a council to be known as the District Consumer Protection Council with effect from such date as it may specify in such notification.

2. The District Consumer Protection Council hereinafter referred to as the District Council shall consist of the following members, namely:

   (a) the Collector of the District (by whatever name called), who shall be its Chairman; and

   (b) such number of other official and non-official members representing such interests as may be prescribed by the State Government.

3. The District Council shall meet as and when necessary but not less than two meetings shall be held every year.

4. The District Council shall meet at such time and place within the district as the Chairman may think fit and shall observe such procedure in regard to the transaction of its business as may be prescribed by the State Government.

Objects of the District Council-(Section 8B)

Section-8B: Inserted by the Consumer Protection (Amendment) Act, 2003. The objects of every District Council shall be to promote and protect within the district the rights of the consumers laid down in clauses (g) to (f) of Section 6.

5.8 CONSUMER DISPUTES REDRESSAL AGENCIES

Chapter-III deals with the Consumer Disputes Redressal Agencies. Under the Act, Consumer Disputes Redressal Agencies have been established at District State and National level. These are "District Forum" (DF), "State Consumer Disputes Redressal Commission" (SCDRC), and "National Consumer Disputes Redressal Commission" (NCDRC). Above these the Supreme Court of India is the Final Court of appeal.

It has been held that the Consumer Disputes Redressal Agencies are vested with powers of adjudication of all types of consumer disputes. Finality is attached to the orders of the Redressal Agencies and provision has been made for execution and implementation of the orders passed by them treating as orders and decrees of Courts. The scheme ensures speedy and prompt redressal of the complaints. The Supreme Court recognised these agencies as quasi-judicial bodies; hence these agencies should arrive at a conclusion based on reason. Their obligation not only introduces clarity but it also excludes, or at any rate minimise, the chances of arbitrariness and the higher forum can evaluate the correctness of those reasons.

Establishment of Consumer Disputes Redressal Agencies-(Section 9)

These shall be established for the purpose of this Act, the following agencies, namely:

1. a Consumer Disputes Redressal Forum to be known as the "District Forum" established by the State Government in each district of the State by notification; provided that the State Government may, if it deems fit, establish more than one District Forum in a district;
2. a Consumer Disputes Redressal Commission to be known as the "State Commission" established by the State Government in the Sate by notification; and
3. a National Consumer Disputes Redressal Commission established by the Central Government by notification.

5.9 DISTRICT FORUM

Composition of the District Forum-(Section 10)

1. Each District Forum shall consists of:
   - (a) a person who is, or has been or is qualified to be a District Judge, who shall be its President;
   - (b) two other members, one of whom shall be women, who shall have the following qualifications, namely:
     - i. be not less than thirty-five years of age;
     - ii. possess a bachelor's degree from a recognised university; and
     - iii. be persons of ability, integrity and standing, and have adequate knowledge and experience of at least ten years in dealing with problems relating to economics, law, commerce, accountancy, industry, public affairs or administration;

   Provided that a person shall be disqualified for appointment as members if he:
   - (a) has been convicted and sentenced to imprisonment for an offence which, in the opinion of the State Government, involves moral turpitude; or
   - (b) is an un-discharged insolvent; or
   - (c) is of unsound mind and stands so declared by a competent court; or
   - (d) has been removed or dismissed from the service of the Government or a Body Corporate owned or controlled by the Government; or
   - (e) has in the opinion of the State Government, such financial or other interest as is likely to affect pre-judicially the discharge by him of his functions as a member; or
   - (f) has such other disqualifications as may be prescribed by the State Government.

(1-A)Every appointment under sub-section (1) shall be made by the State Government on the recommendation of a Selection Committee consisting of the following, namely:

- (i) the President of the State Commission-Chairman.
- (ii) the Secretary, Law Department of the State-Member.
- (iii) the Secretary, in charge of the Department dealing with Consumer Affairs in the State-Member.

Provided that where the President of the State Commission is, by reason of absence or otherwise, unable to act as Chairman of the Selection Committee; the State Government may refer the matter to the Chief Justice of the High Court for nominating a sitting Judge of that High Court to act as Chairman.

2. Every Member of the District Forum shall hold office for a term of five years or up to a age of 65 years, whichever is earlier.

   Provided that a member shall be eligible for re-appointment for another term of five years, or up to the age of sixty-five years, whichever is earlier, subject to the condition that he fulfils the qualifications and other conditions for appointment mentioned in clause (b) of sub-section (1) and such re-appointment is also made on the basis of the recommendation of the Selection Committee.

   Provided further that a member may resign his office in writing under his hand addressed to the State Government and on such resignation being accepted, his office shall become vacant and may be filled by appointment of a person possessing any of the qualifications mentioned in sub-section (1) in relation to the category of the member who is required to be appointed under the provisions of sub-section (1-A) in place of the person who has resigned;

   Provided also that a person appointed as the President or as a member, before the commencement of the Consumer Protection (Amendment) Act, 2002, shall continue to hold such office as President or Member, as the case may be, till the completion of his term.
3. The salary or honorarium and other allowances payable to and other terms and conditions of service of the members of the District Forum shall be such as may be prescribed by the State Government:

   Provided that the appointment of a Member on whole time basis shall be made by the State Government on the recommendation of the President of the State Commission taking into consideration such factors as may be prescribed including the workload of the District Forum.

Jurisdiction of the District Forum-(Section 11)

1. Subject to the other Provisions of this Act, the District Forum shall have jurisdiction to entertain complainants where the value of the goods or services and the compensation, if any, claimed does not exceed rupees twenty lakh.
2. A complaint shall be instituted in a District Forum within a local limits of whose jurisdiction:
   (a) the opposite party or each of the opposite parties, where there are more than one, at the time of the institution of the complaint, actually and voluntarily resides or carries on business or has a branch office or personally works for gain; or
   (b) any of the opposite parties, where there are more than one, at the time of the institution of the complaint, actually and voluntarily resides, or carries on business or has a branch office, or personally works for gain, provided that in such

case either the permission of the District Forum is given, or the opposite parties who do not reside, or carry on business or have a branch office or personally work for gain, as the case may be acquiesce in such institution; or

(c) the cause of action, wholly or in part, arises.

In order to do justice to the consumers and also to ensure that traders are not harassed, a limitation period has also be prescribed under the Act vide the Amendments made in 1993 by the addition of Section 24-A. Thus a complaint can only be lodged within two years from the date on which the cause of action has arisen.

Limitation Period-(Section 24-A)

1. The District Forums, the State Commission or the National Commission shall not admit a complaint unless it is filed within two years from the date on which the cause of action has arisen.
2. Notwithstanding anything contained in sub-section (1), a complaint may be entertained after the period specified in sub-section (1), if the complainant satisfies the District Forums, the State Commission or the National Commission, as the case may be, that he had sufficient cause for not filing the complaint within such period; Provided that no such complaint shall be entertained unless the National Commission, the State Commission or the District Forum, as the case may be, records its reasons for condoning such delay.

Manner in which Complaint shall be Made-(Section 12)

1. A Complaint in relation to any goods sold or delivered or agreed to be sold or delivered or any service provided or agreed to be provided may be filed with a District Forum by:
   (a) the consumer to whom such goods are sold or delivered or agreed to be sold or delivered or such service provided or agreed to be provided;
   (b) any recognised Consumer Association whether the consumer to whom the goods sold or delivered or agreed to be sold or delivered or service provided or agreed to be provided is a member of such Association or not;
   (c) one or more consumer, where are numerous consumers having the same interest with the permission of the District Forum, on behalf of, or for the benefit of, all consumers so interested; or
   (d) the Central Government or the State Government, as the case may be, either in its individual capacity or as a representative of interests of the consumers in general.

2. Every complaint filed under sub-section (1) shall be accompanied with such amount of fee and payable in such manner as may be prescribed.
3. On receipt of a complaint made under Sub-section (1), the District Forum may, by order, allow the complaint to be proceeded with or rejected;

   Provided that a complaint shall not be rejected under this sub-section unless an opportunity of being heard has been given to the complainant;

   Provided further that the admissibility of the complaint shall ordinarily be decided within twenty-one days from the date on which the complaint was received.
4. Where a complaint is allowed to be proceeded with under sub-section (3), the District Forum may proceed with the complaint in the manner provided under this Act:

   Provided that where a complaint has been admitted by the District Forum, it shall not be transferred to any other Court or Tribunal or any authority set up by or under any other law for the time being in force.

Explanation: For the purpose of this section "Recognised Consumer Association" means any voluntary consumer association registered under the Companies Act, 1956 (1 of 1956) or any other law for the time being in force.

5.9.1 Admission of Complaint

A new feature has been added by the Amendment Act, 2002, regarding the procedure adopted by the Redressal Forums. This new step is the admission of complaint. Thus before a complaint is entertained for detailed inquiry at the preliminary stage the Forum shall be required to decide the admissibility only when a ***prima facie*** case is made out. However, the complaint can only be rejected after an opportunity of hearing has been given to the complainant. Further, to avoid delay a limitation of 21 days has been fixed for deciding the admissibility.

Procedure on Admission of Complaint-(Section 13)

1. District Forum shall, on admission of a complaint, it is relates to any goods:

   Procedure:

   (a) refer a copy of the admitted complaint, within twenty one days from the date of its admission to the opposite party mentioned in the complaint directing him to give version of the case within a period of thirty days or such extended period not exceeding fifteen days as may be granted by the District Forum;

   (b) where the opposite party on receipt of a complaint referred to him under clause (a) denies or disputes the allegations contained in the complaint, or omits or fails to take any action to represent his case within the time given by the District Forum, the District Forum shall proceed to settle the consumer dispute in the manner specified in clauses (c) to (g);

(c) where the complaint alleges a defect in the goods which cannot be determined without proper analysis or test of the goods, the District Forum shall obtain a sample of the goods from the complainant, seal it and authenticate it in the manner prescribed and refer the sample to the appropriate laboratory along with a direction that such laboratory make an analysis or test, whichever may be necessary, with a view of finding out whether such goods suffer from any defect alleged in the complaint or suffer from any other defect and to report its findings thereon to the District Forum within a period of forty-five days of the receipt of the reference or within such extended period as may be granted by the District Forum.

(d) before any sample of the goods is referred to any appropriate laboratory under clause (c), the District Forum may require the complainant to deposit to the credit of the Forum such fees as may be specified, for payment to the appropriate laboratory for carrying out the necessary analysis or test in relation to the goods in question.

(e) the District Forum shall remit the amount deposited to its credit under clause (d) to the appropriate laboratory to enable it to carry out the analysis or test mentioned in clause (c) and on receipt of the report from the appropriate laboratory, the District Forum shall forward a copy of the report along with such remarks as the District Forum may feel appropriate to the opposite party;

(f) if any of the parties disputes the correctness of the finding of the appropriate laboratory, or disputes the correctness of the methods of analysis of test adopted by the appropriate laboratory, the District Forum shall require the opposite party or the complainant to submit in writing his objections in regard to the report made by the appropriate laboratory;

(g) the District Forum shall thereafter give a reasonable opportunity to the complainant as well as the opposite party of being heard as to the correctness or otherwise of the report made by the appropriate laboratory and also as to the objection made in relaticn thereto under clause (f) and issue an appropriate order under Section 14.

2. The District Forum shall, if the complaint admitted by it under Section 12 relates to goods in respect of which the procedure specified in sub-section (1) cannot be followed, or if the complaint relates to any services:

   (a) refer to a copy of such complaint to the opposite party directing him to give his version of the case within a period of thirty days or such extended period not exceeding fifteen days as may be granted by the District Forum.

(b) where the opposite party, on receipt of a copy of the complaint, referred to him under clause (a) denies or disputes the allegations contained in the complaint, or omits or fails to take any action to represent his case within the time given by the District Forum; the District Forum shall proceed to settle the consumer disputes:

i. on the basis of evidence brought to its notice by the complainant and the opposite party, where the opposite party denies or disputes the allegations contained in the complaint, or

ii. ***ex parte*** on the basis of evidence brought to its notice by the complainant where the opposite party omits or fails to take any action to represent his case within the time given by the Forum.

Dismissal of Default

(c) where the complainant fails to appear on the date of hearing before the District Forum the District Forum may either dismiss the complaint for default or decide it on merits.

3. No proceedings complying with the procedure laid down in sub-sections (1) and (2) shall be called in question in any Court on the ground that the principles of natural justice have not been complied with.

Time limit for disposal of complaint

(a) Every complaint shall be heard as expeditiously as possible and endeavour shall be made to decide the complaint within a period of three months from the date of receipt of notice by opposite party where the complaint does not require analysis or testing of commodities and within five months if it requires analysis or testing of commodities;

Provided that no adjournment shall ordinarily be granted by the District Forum unless sufficient cause is shown and the reasons for grant of adjournment have been recorded in writing by the Forum;

Provided further that the District Forum shall make orders as to the costs of occasioned by the adjournment as may be provided in the regulations made under this Act;

Provided also that in the event of a complaint being disposed of after the period so specified the District Forum shall record in writing, the reasons for the same at the time of disposing of the said complaint.

Power to pass interim orders

(b) Where during the pendency of any proceeding before the District Forum, it appears to it necessary, it may pass such interim order as is just and proper in the fact, and circumstances of the case.

4. For the purpose of this section, the District Forum shall have the same powers as are vested in a Civil Court under the code of Civil Procedure, 1908 (5 of 1908) while trying a suit in respect of the following matters, namely:

Powers of District Forum

(a) the summoning and enforcing attendance of any defendant or witness and examining the witness on oath;
(b) the discovery and production of any document or other material object producible as evidence;
(c) the reception of evidence on affidavits;
(d) the requisitioning of the report of the concerned analysis or test from appropriate laboratory or from any other relevant source;
(e) issuing of any commission for the examination of any witness; and
(f) any other matter which may be prescribed.

5. Every proceeding before the district Forum shall be deemed to be a judicial proceeding within the meaning of Sections 193 and 228 of the Indian Penal Code (45 of 1860), and the District Forum shall be deemed to be a Civil Court for the purposes of Section 195, and Chapter XXVI of the Code of Criminal Procedure, 1973 (2 of 1974).
6. Where the complainant is a consumer referred to in sub-clause (iv) of clause (b) of sub-section (1) of Section 2, the provisions of Rules 8 of Order 1 of the First Schedule to the Code of Civil Procedure, 1908 (5 of 1908) shall apply subject to the modification that every reference therein to a suit or decree shall be construed as a reference to a complaint or the order of the District Forum thereon.

Substitution of Petties

7. In the event of death of a complainant who is a consumer or of the opposite party against whom the complaint has been filed, the provisions of Order XII of the First Schedule to the Code of Civil Procedure, 1908 (5 of 1908) shall apply subject to the modification that every reference therein to the plaintiff and the defendant shall be construed as reference to a complainant or the opposite party, as the case may be.

Findings of the District Forum-[Section 14]

1. If, after the proceeding conducted under section 13, the District Forum is satisfied that the goods complained against suffer from any of the defects specified in the complaint or that any of the allegations contained in the complaint about the services are proved,

it shall issue an order to the opposite party directing him to do one or more of the following things, namely:

Relief available:

(a) to remove the defect pointed out by the appropriate laboratory from the goods in question;

(b) to replace the goods with new goods of similar description which shall be free from any defect;

(c) to return to the complainant the price, or as the case may be, the charges paid by the complainant;

(d) to pay such amount as may be awarded by its as compensation to the consumer for any loss or injury suffered by the consumer, due to the negligence of the opposite party;

Provided that the District Forum shall have the power to grant punitive damages in such circumstances as it deems fit;

(e) to remove the defects in goods or deficiencies in the services in question;

(f) to discontinue the unfair trade practices or the restrictive trade practices or not to repeat them;

(g) not to offer the hazardous goods for sale;

(h) to withdraw the hazardous goods from being offered for sale;

i. to cease manufacture or hazardous goods and to desist from offering services which are hazardous in nature;

ii. to pay such sum as may be determined by it, if it is of the opinion that loss or injury has been suffered by a large number of consumers who are not identifiable conveniently.

Provided that the minimum amount of sum so payable shall not less than five percent of the value of such defective goods sold or services provided, as the case may be, to such consumers;

Provided further, that the amount so obtained shall be credited in favour of such person and utilised in such manner as may be prescribed;

iii. to issue corrective advertisement to neutralise the effect of misleading advertisement at the cost of the opposite party responsible for issuing such misleading advertisement;

(i) to provide for adequate costs to parties.

2. Every proceeding referred to in sub-section (1) shall be conducted by the President of District Forum and at least one member thereof sitting together:

Provided that where the member, for any reason, is usable to conduct a proceeding till it is completed, the President and the other member shall continue the proceeding from the stage at which it was last heard by the previous member.

(a) Every order made by the District Forum under sub-section (1) shall be signed by its President and the member or members who conducted the proceeding:

Provided that where the proceeding is conducted by the President and one member and they differ on any point or points, they shall state the point or points on which they differ and refer the same to the other member for hearing on such point or points and the opinion of the majority shall be the order of the District Forum.

3. Subject to the foregoing provisions, the procedure relating to the conduct of the meetings of the District Forum, its settings and other matters shall be such as may be prescribed by the State Government.

Appeal-(Section 15)

Any person aggrieved by an order made by the District Forum may prefer an appeal against such order to the State Commission within a period of thirty days from the date of the order, in such form and manner as may be prescribed;

Provided that the State Commission may entertain an appeal after the expiry of the said period of thirty days if it is satisfied that there was sufficient cause for not filing it within that period;

Provided further, that no appeal by a person who is required to pay any amount in terms of an order of the District Forum, shall be entertained by the State Commission unless the appellant has deposited in the prescribed manner fifty per cent of that amount or twenty-five thousand rupees, whichever is less.

5.10 STATE COMMISSION

Composition of the State Commission-(Section 16)

(1) Each State Commission shall consist of:

Qualification

(a) a person who is or has been a Judge of a High Court, appointed by the State Government, who shall be its President:

Provided that no appointment under this clause shall be made except after consultation with the Chief Justice of the High Court;

(b) not less than two, and not more than such number of members as may be prescribed, and one of whom shall be a woman, who shall have the following qualifications, namely:

i. be not less than thirty-five years of age;
ii. possess a bachelor's degree from a recognised university; and
iii. be persons of ability, integrity and standing, and have adequate knowledge and experience of at least ten years in dealing with problems relating to economics, law, commerce, accountancy, industry, public affairs or administration;

    Provided that no more than fifty per cent of the members shall be from amongst persons having a judicial background;

Explanation: For the purposes of this clause, the expression "persons having judicial background" shall mean persons having knowledge and experience for at least a period of ten years as a Presiding Officer at the district level Court or any Tribunal at equivalent level;

Disqualification:
Provided further that a person shall be disqualified for appointment as a member if he:

(a) has been convicted and sentenced to imprisonment for an offence which, in the opinion of the State Government, involves moral turpitude; or
(b) is an un-discharged insolvent; or
(c) is of unsound mind and stands so declared by a competent court; or
(d) has been removed or dismissed from the service of the Government or a body corporate owned or controlled by the Government; or
(e) has, in the opinion of the State Government, such financial or other interest, as is likely to affect prejudicially the discharge by him of his functions as a member; or
(f) has such other disqualifications as may be prescribed by the State Government.

Process of Appointment

(1A) Every appointment under sub-section (1), shall be made by the State Government on the recommendation of the Selection Committee consisting of the following members, namely:

(i) President of the State Commission - Chairman;
(ii) Secretary of the Law Department of the State - Member;
(iii) Secretary-in-charge of the Department dealing with Consumer Affairs in the State - Member.

Provided that where the President of the State Commission is, by reason of absence or otherwise, unable to act as Chairman of the Selection Committee, the State Government may refer the matter to the Chief Justice of the High Court for nominating a sitting Judge of that High Court to act as Chairman.

Benches

(1B)

(i) The jurisdiction, powers and authority of the State Commission may be exercised by benches thereof:

(ii) A bench may be constituted by the President with one or more members as the President may deem fit.

(iii) If the members of a bench differ in opinion or any point, the points shall be decided according to the opinion of the majority, if there is a majority, but if the members are equally divided, they shall state the point or points on which they differ, and make a reference to the President who shall either hear the point or points himself or refer the case for hearing on such point or points by one or more or the other members and such point or points shall be decided according to the opinion of the majority of the members who have heard the case including those who first heard it.

(2) The salary or honorarium and other allowances payable to, the other terms and conditions of service of, the members of the State Commission shall be such as may be prescribed by the State Government.

Provided that the appointment of a member on whole-time basis shall be made by the State Government on the recommendation of the President of the State Commission taking into consideration such factors as may be prescribed including the workload of the State Commission.

Terms of Office

(3) Every member of the State Commission shall hold office for a term of five years or up to the age of sixty-seven years, whichever is earlier;

Provided that a member shall be eligible for a re-appointment for another term of five years or up to the age of sixty-seven years, whichever is subject to the condition that he fulfils the qualifications and other conditions for appointment mentioned in clause (b) of sub-section (1) and such re-appointment is made on the basis of the recommendations of the Selection Committee;

Provided further that a person appointed as President of the State Commission shall also be eligible for re-appointment in the manner provided in clause (a) of sub-section (1) of this section;

Provided also that a member may resign his office in writing under his hand addressed to the Government and on such resignation his office shall become vacant and may be filled by appointment of a person possessing any of the qualifications mentioned in sub-section (1) in relation to the category of the members who is required to be under the provisions of the sub-section (1A) in place of the person who has resigned.

(4) Notwithstanding anything contained in sub-section (3), a person appointed as the President or as a member, before the commencement of the Consumer Protection (Amendment) Act, 2002, shall continue to hold such office as president of member, as the case may be, till the completion of his term.

This section after amendment gives a detailed procedure for appointment, qualification, disqualification, constitution of selection committee, term of office, etc., of the members of the State Commission, to provide a wholesome arrangement for disposal of consumer cases at state level. It also makes provision for creation of benches for quicker disposal of cases.

Jurisdiction of the State Commission-(Section 17)

1. Subject to the other provisions of this Act, the State Commission shall have jurisdiction:
   (a) to entertain:
      i. complaints where the value of the goods or services and compensation, if any, claimed exceeds rupees twenty lakh but does not exceed rupees one crore, and
      ii. appeals against the orders of any District Forum within the State; and
   (b) to call for the records and pass appropriate orders in any consumer dispute which is pending before or has been decided by any District Forum within the State, where it appears to the State Commission that such District Forum has exercised a jurisdiction not vested in it by law, or has filed to exercise a jurisdiction so vested or has acted in exercise of its jurisdiction illegally or with material irregularity.
2. A complaint shall be instituted in a State Commission within the limits of whose jurisdiction:
   (a) the opposite party or each of the opposite parties, where there are more than one, at the time of the institution of the complaint, actually and voluntarily resides or carries on business or has a branch office or personally works for gain; or
   (b) any of the opposite parties, where there are more than one, at the time of the institution of the complaint, actually and voluntarily resides, or carries on business or has a branch office or personally works for gain, provided that in such case either the permission of the State Commission is given or the opposite parties who do not reside or carry on business or have a branch office or personally work for gain, as the tile case may be, acquiesce in such institution; or
   (c) the cause of action, wholly or in part, arises.

Transfer of Cases and Creation of Circuit Benches

Through Amendment Act of 2002 two new provisions have been added for facilitating the ends of justice. The State Commission has been given the power to transfer cases from one District Forum to another, that too at any stage of proceeding. The transfer of case can be ordered either on the application of the complainant or on its own by the State Commission. However, the defendant cannot move for transfer of cases.

Transfer of Cases-(Section 17A)

On the application of the complainant or of its own motion, the State Commission may, at any stage of the proceeding, transfer any complaint pending before the District Forum to another District Forum within a State if the interest of justice so requires.

To reduce the workload of District Forums provision has also been made for the creation of Circuit Benches of the State Commission. This is to be done by the State Governments with a consultation of the State Commission. The decision may be taken by the State Government from time to time.

Circuit Benches-(Section 17B)

The State Commission shall ordinarily function in the State capital but may perform its functions at such other place as the State Government may, in consultation with the State Commission, notify in the Official Gazette from time to time.

Procedure Applicable to State Commission-(Section 18)

The provisions of Sections 12, 13 and 14 and the rules made thereunder for the disposal of complaints by the District Forum shall, with such modifications as may be necessary, be applicable to the disposal of disputes by the State Commission.

Thus the provision for the procedure to be applicable to the State Commission is the same as is applicable to District Forums, subject to modifications. Notably Section 18A of the Act has been omitted by the Amendment Act, 2002, which deals with the cases of vacancy in the office of the President.

Appeals-(Section 19)

Any person aggrieved by an order made by the State Commission in exercise of its powers conferred by sub-clause (i) of clause (a) of section 17 may prefer an appeal against such order to the National Commission within a period of thirty days from the date of the order in such form and manner as may be prescribed;

Provided that the National Commission may entertain an appeal after the expiry of the said period of thirty days if it is satisfied that there was sufficient cause for not filing it within that period;

Provided further, that no appeal by a person, who is required to pay any amount in terms of an order of the State Commission, shall be entertained by the National Commission unless the appellant has deposited in the prescribed manner fifty per cent of the amount or rupees thirty-five thousand, whichever is less.

Hearing of Appeal-(Section 19A)

An appeal filed before the State Commission or the National Commission shall be heard as expeditiously as possible and an endeavour shall be made to finally dispose of the appeal within a period of ninety days from the date of its admission;

Provided that no adjournment shall be ordinarily granted by the State Commission or the National Commission, as the case may be, unless sufficient cause is shown and the reasons for grant of adjournment have been recorded in writing by such Commission;

Provided further, that the State Commission or the National Commission, as the case may be, shall make such orders as to the costs occasioned by the adjournment as may be provided in the regulations made under this Act.

Provided also that in the event of an appeal being disposed of after the period so specified, the State Commission or the National Commission, as the case may be, shall record in writing the reasons for the same at the time of disposing of the said appeal.

5.11 NATIONAL COMMISSION

Composition of the National Commission-(Section 20)

(1) The National Commission shall consist of:

Qualification:

(a) a person who is or has been a Judge of the Supreme Court, to be appointed by the Central Government, who shall be its President;
Provided that no appointment under this clause shall be made except after consultation with the Chief Justice of India;

(b) not less than four, and not more than such number of members, as may be prescribed, and one of whom shall be a woman, who shall have the following qualifications, namely:

  (i) be not less than thirty-five years of age;

(ii) possess a bachelor's degree from a recognised university; and

(iii) be persons of ability, integrity and standing and have adequate knowledge and experience of at least ten years in dealing with problems relating to economics, law, commerce, accountancy, industry, public affairs or administration;

Provided that not more than fifty per cent of the members shall be from amongst the persons having a judicial background.

Explanation: For the purposes of this clause, the expression "persons having judicial background" shall mean persons having knowledge and experience for at least a period of ten years as a Presiding Officer at the District level Court or any Tribunal of equivalent level:

Disqualification:

Provided further that a person shall be disqualified for appointment if he:

(a) has been convicted and sentenced to imprisonment for an offence which, in the opinion of the Central Government, involves moral turpitude; or

(b) is an un-discharged insolvent; or

(c) is of unsound mind and stands so declared by a competent Court; or

(d) has been removed or dismissed from the service of the Government or a body corporate owned or controlled by the Government; or

(e) has in the opinion of the Central Government such financial or other interest as is likely to affect prejudicially the discharge by him or his functions as member; or

(f) has such other disqualifications as may be prescribed by the Central Government:

Procedure of Selection

Provided also that every appointment under this clause shall be made by the Central Government on the recommendation of a Selection Committee consisting of the following, namely:

(a) a person who is a Judge of the Supreme Court, to be nominated by the Chief Justice of India - Chairman.

(b) the Secretary in the Department of Legal Affairs in the Government of India - Member.

(c) secretary of the Department dealing with Consumer Affairs in the Government of India - Member.

Benches

(1A)

(i) The jurisdiction, powers and authority of the National Commission may be exercised by Benches thereof.

(ii) A Bench may be constituted by the President with one or more members as the President may deem fit.

(iii) If the members of a bench differ in opinion on any point, the points shall be decided according to the opinion of the majority, if there is a majority, but if the members are equally divided, they shall state the point or points on which they differ, and make a reference to the President who shall either hear the point or points himself or refer the case for hearing on such point or points by one or more or the other members and such point or points shall be decided according to the opinion of the majority of the members who have heard the case, including those who first heard it.

(2) The salary or honorarium and other allowances payable to and the other terms and conditions of service of the members of the National Commission shall be such as may be prescribed by the Central Government.

Term

(3) Every member of the National Commission shall hold office for a term of five years or up to the age of seventy years, whichever is earlier;

Provided that a member shall be eligible for re-appointment for another term of five years or up to the age of seventy years, whichever is earlier, subject to the condition that he fulfils the qualifications and other conditions for appointment mentioned in clause (b) of sub-section (1) and such re-appointment is made on the basis of the recommendation of the Selection Committee;

Provided further that a person appointed, as a President of the National Commission shall also be eligible for re-appointment in the manner provided in clause (a) of sub-section (1);

Provided also that a member may resign his office in writing under his hand addressed to the Central Government and on such resignation being accepted, his office shall become vacant and maybe filled by appointment of a person possessing any of the qualifications mentioned in subsection (1) in relation to the category of the member who is required to be appointed under the provisions of sub-section (1A) in place of the person who has resigned.

(4) Notwithstanding anything contained in sub-section (3), a person appointed as a President or as a member before the commencement of the Consumer Protection (Amendment) Act, 2002 shall continue to hold such office as President or member, as the case may be, till the completion of his term.

Jurisdiction of the National Commission-(Section 21)

Subject to the other provisions of this Act, the National Commission shall have jurisdiction:

(a) to entertain:

   (i) complaints where the value of the goods or services and compensation, if any, claimed exceeds rupees one crore; and
   (ii) appeals against the orders of any State Commission; and

(b) to call for the records and pass appropriate orders in any consumer dispute which is pending before or has been decided by any State Commission where it appears to the National Commission that such State Commission has exercised a jurisdiction not vested in it by law, or has failed to exercise a jurisdiction so vested, or has acted in the exercise of its jurisdiction illegally or with material irregularity.

Power and Procedure Applicable to the National Commission-(Section 22)

1. The provisions of Section 12, 13 and 14 and the rules made thereunder for the disposal of complaints by the District Forum shall, with such modifications as may be considered necessary by the Commission, be applicable to the disposal of disputes by the National Commission.
2. Without prejudice to the provisions contained in sub-section (1), the National Commission shall have the power to review any order made by it, when there is an error apparent on the face of record.

5.11.1 Special Powers

Similar to the newly vested powers to the State Commission by the Amending Act, 2002, National Commission too has been given additional powers to deal with the transfer of cases and for creation of Circuit Benches, with a avowed objective of delivery justice at door-step. This will obviously lessen the number of appeals from going to the Supreme Court from the orders of the National Commission.

Power to Set Aside Ex-Parte Orders-(Section 22A)

Where an order is passed by the National Commission ex-parte against the opposite party or a complainant, as the case may be, the aggrieved party may apply to the Commission to set aside the said order in the interest of justice.

Transfer of Cases-(Section 228)

On the application of the complainant or of its own motion, the National Commission may, at any stage of the proceeding, in the interest of justice, transfer any complaint pending before the District Forum of one State to a District Forum of another State or before one State Commission to another State Commission.

Circuit Benches-(Section 22C)

The National Commission shall ordinarily function at a New Delhi and perform its functions at such other place as the Central Government may, in consultation with the National Commission, notify in the Official Gazette, from time to time.

Vacancy in the Office of the President-(Section 220)

When the Office of the President of a District Forum, State Commission, or of the National Commission, as the case may be, is vacant or a person occupying such office is, by reason of absence or otherwise, unable to perform the duties of his office, these shall be performed by the senior-most member of the District Forum, the State Commission or of the National Commission, as the case may be;

Provided that where a retired Judge of a High Court is a Member of the National Commission, such member or where the number of such members is more than one, the senior-most person among such members, shall preside over the National Commission in the absence of the President of that Commission.

Appeal-(Section 23)

Appeal to the Supreme Court

Any person, aggrieved by an order made by the National Commission in exercise of its powers conferred by sub-clause (i) of clause (a) of Section 21, may prefer an appeal against such order to the Supreme Court within a period of thirty days from the date of the order;

Provided that the Supreme Court may entertain an appeal after the expiry of the said period of thirty days if it is satisfied that there was sufficient cause for not filing it within that period;

Provided further that no appeal by a person who is required to pay any amount in terms of the order of the National Commission shall be entertained by the Supreme Court unless that person has deposited in the prescribed manner fifty per cent of that amount or rupees fifty thousand, whichever is less.

Finality of Orders-(Section 24)

Every order of a District Forum, the State Commission or the National Commission shall, if no appeal has been preferred against such order under the provisions of this Act, be final.

Limitation Period-(Section 24A)

1. The District Forum, the State Commission or the National Commission shall not admit a complaint unless it is filed within two years from the date on which the cause of action has arisen.
2. Notwithstanding anything contained in sub-section (1), a complaint may be entered after the period specified in sub-section (1), if the complainant satisfies the District Forum, the State Commission or the National Commission, as the case may be, that he had sufficient cause for not filing the complaint within such period.

Provided that no such complaint shall be entertained unless the National Commission, the State Commission or the District Forum, as the case may be, records its reasons for condoning such delay.

Administrative Control-(Section 24B)

1. The National Commission shall have administrative control over all the State Commissions in the following matters, namely:
   (a) calling for periodical returns regarding the institution, disposal, pendency of cases;
   (b) issuance of instructions regarding adoption of uniform procedure in the hearing of matters, prior service of copies of documents produced by one party to the opposite parties, furnishing of English translation of Judgments written in any language, speedy grant of copies of documents;
   (c) generally overseeing the functioning of the State Commission or the District Forum to ensure that the objects and purposes of the Act are best served without in any way interfering with their quasi-judicial freedom.
2. The State Commission shall have administrative control over the District Forum within its jurisdiction in all matters referred to in sub-section (1).

5.12 ENFORCEMENT OF ORDERS OF THE DISTRICT FORUM, THE STATE COMMISSION OR THE NATIONAL COMMISSION-(SECTION 25)

1. Where an interim order made under this Act, is not complied with, the District Forum or the State Commission or the National Commission, as the case may be, may order the property of the person, not complying with such order to be attached.

2. No attachment made under sub-section (1) shall remain in force for more than three months at the end of which, if the non-compliance continues, the property attached may be sold and out of the proceeds thereof, the District Forum or the State Commission or the National Commission may award such damages as it thinks fit to the complainant and shall pay the balance, if any, to the party entitled thereto.

3. Where any amount is due from any person under an order made by a District Forum, State Commission or the National Commission, as the case may be, the person entitled to the amount may make an application to the District Forum, the State Commission or the National Commission, as the case may be, and such District Forum or the State Commission or National Commission may issue a Certificate for the said amount to the Controller of the District (by whatever name called) and the Collector shall proceed to recover the amount in the same manner as arrears of land revenue.

Dismissal of Frivolous or Vexatious Complaints-(Section 26)

Where a complaint instituted before the District Forum, the State Commission or, as the case may be, the National Commission is found to be frivolous or vexatious, it shall, for reasons to be recorded in writing, dismiss the complaint and make an order that the complainant shall pay to the opposite party such cost, not exceeding ten thousand rupees, as may be specified in the order.

Penalties-(Section 27)

1. Where a trader or a person against whom a complaint is made [or the complainant] fails or omits to comply with any order made by the District Forum, the State Commission or the National Commission, as the case may be, such trader or person [or complainant] shall be punishable with imprisonment for a term which shall not be less than one month but which may extend to three years, or with fine which shall not be less than two thousand rupees but which may extend to ten thousand rupees, or with both;

2. Notwithstanding anything contained in the Code of Criminal Procedure, 1973 (2 of 1974), the District Forum or the State Commission or the National Commission, as the case may be, shall have the power of a Judicial Magistrate of the first class for the trial of offences under this Act, and on such conferment of powers, the District Forum or the State Commission or the National Commission, as the case may be, on whom the powers are so conferred, shall be deemed to be a Judicial Magistrate of the first class for the purpose of the Code of Criminal Procedure, 1973.

3. All offences under this Act may be tried summarily by the District Forum or the State Commission or the National Commission, as the case may be.

Appeal Against Order Passed under Section 27-(Section 27A)

1. Notwithstanding anything contained in the Code of Criminal Procedure, 1973, an appeal under section 27, both on facts and on law, shall lie from:
   (a) the order made by the District Forum to the State Commission;
   (b) the order made by the State Commission to the National Commission; and (c) the order made by the National Commission to the Supreme Court.
2. Except as aforesaid, no appeal shall lie to any court from any order of a District Forum or a State Commission or the National Commission.
3. Every appeal under this section shall be preferred within a period of thirty days from the date of an order of a District Forum or a State Commission or, as the case may be, the National Commission.

Provided that the State Commission or the National Commission or the Supreme Court, as the case may be, may entertain an appeal after the expiry of the said period of thirty days, if, it is satisfied that the appellant had sufficient cause for not preferring the appeal within a period of thirty days.

QUESTIONS FOR PRACTICE

Section - A (Two Marks Questions)

1. Who can be a complainant as per the Consumer Protection Act?
2. What is a consumer dispute?
3. What do you mean by consumer protection?
4. State the two objects of the Consumer Protection Act.
5. State the rights of a consumer under COPRA.
6. State the meaning of consumer as per the Consumer Protection Act.

Section - B (Five Marks Questions)

1. Explain the need for Consumer Protection Act.
2. State the objectives of Consumer Protection Act.

Section - C (Fifteen Marks Questions)

1. Briefly explain the formation and the working of the different consumer redressal agencies.

2. Explain the purpose of Consumer Protection Act and describe the functions, jurisdiction and composition of consumer redressal agencies.

3. What is consumer dispute? Briefly explain the composition and working of the various redressal agencies.

4. What is Consumer Protection Act, 1986? What are its objectives and how does it work?

5. Who is a consumer? Explain the nature of rights protected under the Consumer Protection Act, 1986.

6. Write notes on various consumer redressal agencies.

CHAPTER 6

FOREIGN EXCHANGE MANAGEMENT ACT, 1999

6.1 INTRODUCTION

With effect from 1st June 2000 the Foreign Exchange Management Act, 1999 (FEMA) has been brought into force repealing the Foreign Exchange Regulation Act, 1973 (FERA). The provisions of FERA which were found harsh and draconian both by trade and industries were required to be repealed to usher in the new millennium era.

6.2 BACKGROUND

As foreign exchange resources and reserves were scarce the need to conserve the resources of the State was felt necessary particularly after the second world war. Conservation and exchange control measures were found more so desirable after the independence. Foreign Exchange Regulation Act, 1947 was enacted initially for a period of 10 years. FERA was made permanent in 1957. FERA, 1947 was repealed when Foreign Exchange Regulation Act, 1973 was enacted. FERA 1973, was enacted to consolidate and amend the law relating to certain payments, dealings in foreign exchange and securities transactions indirectly affecting foreign exchange and the import and export of currency for the conservation of foreign exchange resources of the country and the proper utilisation thereof in the interests of the economic development of the country. The provisions of 1973 Act were strengthened and was more stringent in view of the then prevailing economic scenario with global economy opening up and in the light of liberalisation since 1991, the provisions of 1973 Act were relaxed in 1993. However, Indian economy needed to keep pace with global liberalisation. Provisions of FERA, 1973 though relaxed in 1993 were still found repressive and a blockade to the new economic and free exchange policies to which the Government was committed. A new liberalised Foreign Exchange Management Act, 1999 was therefore, enacted.

6.3 OBJECTS AND REASONS FOR ENACTMENT OF FEMA

FEMA was enacted to consolidate and amend the law relating to foreign exchange with the objective of facilitating external trade and payments and for promoting the orderly development and maintenance of foreign exchange market in India (preamble). The statement of objects and reasons set the tone of the enactment of new legislation:

(i) The Foreign Exchange Regulation Act 1973, was reviewed in 1993 and several amendments were enacted as part of the ongoing process of economic liberalisation relating to foreign investments and foreign trade for closer interaction with the world economy. At that stage, the Central Government decided that a further review of the Foreign Exchange Regulation Act, would be undertaken in the light of subsequent developments and experience in relation to foreign trade and investment. It was subsequently felt that a better course would be to repeal the existing Foreign Exchange Regulation Act and enact a new legislation. Reserve Bank of India was accordingly asked to undertake a fresh exercise and suggest a new legislation. A task force constituted for the purpose submitted its report in 1994 recommending substantial changes in the existing Act.

(ii) Significant developments have been taking place since 1993 such, as substantial increase in foreign exchange reserves, growth in foreign trade, rationalisation of tariffs, current accounts convertibility, liberalisation of Indian investments abroad, increased access to external borrowings by Indian corporate and participation of foreign investors in the stock markets.

Accordingly, a bill to repeal and replace Foreign Exchange Regulation Act, 1973 was introduced in Lok Sabha on 4th August 1998. On reference to the standing committee, modification and suggestions were submitted by the standing committee, the Central Government decided to introduce the new law, the Foreign Exchange Management Bill and ropeal the Foreign Exchange Regulation Act, 1973.

6.4 SALIENT FEATURES OF FEMA

FEMA extends to whole of India. It shall apply to all branches, offices and agencies outside India owned or controlled by a person resident in India and also to any contravention thereunder committed outside India by any person to whom the Act applies. It came into force from 1st June 2002. Therefore joint ventures or wholly owned subsidiaries though outside India, but controlled from India are intended to be covered by the Act.

The new Act is meant to be user friendly with the object to facilitate external trade and payments and for promoting the orderly development of foreign exchange of India. By the new Act, the current account convertibility is now complete under the provisions FERA, 1973 had a greater thrust on offences being treated as criminal offences and contravention was visited with prosecution. Onus was on the accused to prove himself innocent. Violations under FEMA have a thrust on penalties and are more dealt with as civil offences which are compoundable. Arrests shall be resorted to only if the defaulter has dishonestly transferred or cancelled any part of property or despite having the means to pay the penalty refuses or neglect to pay the same. Imprisonment under the new law is only in rear cases.

Under the new law the emphasis for determining the residential status is on the actual period of stay in India, whereas under FERA the emphasis was on the intention of the person. Under the new law it is not necessary that the person should be continuously and physically present in India. It will be sufficient if the total stay in India is 182 days or more during the year.

The Central Government may from time to time give general or special directions to the Reserve Bank and the Reserve Bank shall comply with such direction (Sec 41). The Central Government may, by notification, make rules to carry out the provisions of the Act (Sec. 46). The Reserve Bank may, by notification, make regulations to carry out the provisions of the Act and the rules thereunder (Sec. 47). Every rule and regulation made under the Act shall as soon as after it is made, be laid before each house of the Parliament Sec (48).

If any difficulty arises in giving effect to the provisions of the Act, the Central Government may, by order, do anything not inconsistent with the provisions of the Act for the purpose of removing the difficulty. No such order shall be made after the expiry of two years from 1st June 2000 (Sec. 45).

6.4.1 Suspension of Operation of FEMA (Sec. 40)

If the Central Government is satisfied that circumstances have arisen rendering it necessary that any permission granted or restriction imposed by the Act should cease to be granted or imposed, or if it is considered necessary or expedient to do so in public interest, the Central Government may, by notification, suspend or relax to such extent either indefinitely or for such period as may be notified, the operation of all of the provisions of the Act, has been suspended or relaxed. Such suspension or relaxation may be removed at any time by the Central Government by notification.

6.4.2 Bar of Legal Proceedings (Sec 44)

No suit, prosecution or other legal proceedings shall lie against the Central Government or the Reserve Bank or any officer of that Government or of the Reserve Bank or any other person exercising any power or discharging any function performing any duties under the Act for anything done in good faith or intended to be done under the Act or any rule, regulation, notification, direction or order made thereunder.

6.5 REPEAL, SAVINGS AND COGNIZANCE OF OFFENCES (SEC. 49)

With the enactment of FEMA, FERA stands repealed and the Appellate Board constituted under FERA shall stand dissolved. No court and adjudicating officer shall take cognizance or notice of any offence or any contravention under FERA after the expiry period of 2 years from 1st June 2000. However, while FERA was in force all offences committed under FERA shall continue to be governed by FERA as if FERA had not repealed. Anything done or any action taken shall in so for as it is not inconsistent with the provisions of FEMA be deemed to have been done or taken under FEMA. Any appeal referred to the Appellate Board under FERA but not disposed of before the commencement of FEMA, shall stand transferred and shall be disposed of by Appellate Tribural constituted under FEMA.

Note: *Case law referred and cited in the text to this topic is under FERA, but can be made applicable to harmonious provisions under FEMA.*

6.6 REGULATION AND MANAGEMENT OF FOREIGN EXCHANGE

6.6.1 Capital Account Transaction [Sec. 2(e)(ze) 86]

Capital account transaction means a transaction which alters the assets or liabilities including contingent liabilities, outside India of persons resident in India or alters the assets or liabilities in India of persons resident outside India [Sec 2(e)]. Unlike current account transaction which generally arises in the course of business, capital account transaction is not arise in the ordinary course of business. Capital account transactions are those which are restricted or regulated by Reserve Bank of India. All other capital account transactions not controlled by Reserve Bank of India are not covered by the Act.

Subject to the regulations, any person may sell to or draw foreign exchange from an authorised person for a capital account transaction. The Reserve Bank may, in consultation with the Central Government, specify the regulations in case of:

(i) any class or classes of capital account transactions which are permissible.
(ii) the limit upto which foreign exchange shall be admissible for such transactions.

It is obvious that regulations will relate to outflow of foreign exchange. Inflow of foreign exchange is most welcome.

The Reserve Bank shall not however, impose any restrictions

(i) on the drawal of foreign exchange for payments due to account of amortisation of loans, or
(ii) for depreciation of direct investments in the ordinary course of business.

The Reserve Bank may by regulations prohibit restrict or regulate the following transactions.

(a) transfer or issue of any foreign security by a person resident in India. Transfer includes sale, purchase, exchange, mortgage, pledge, gift, loan or any other form of transfer of right, title, possession or lien [Sec. 2 (ze)).

(b) transfer or issue of any security (not being a foreign security) by a person resident outside India.

(c) transfer or issue of any security by any branch office or agency in India of a person resident outside India.

(d) any borrowing or lending in foreign exchange in whatever form or by whatever name called.

(e) any borrowing or lending in rupees in whatever form or by whatever name called between a person resident in India and a person resident outside India.

(f) deposits between persons resident in India and persons resident outside India.

(g) export, import, or holding of currency or currency notes.

The prohibition does not apply to gold coins with foreign markings as the same are not a legal tender (P. V. Varghese v. Collector of Central Excise 1987 (29) ELT 337 TRI). Import means bringing into India any goods or services, export means taking out of India to a place outside India any goods and provision of services from India to any place outside India. To take or send out of India indicates taking to a place or highseas which is beyond the territorial waters of India (Collector of Customs V. Sun Industries 1988 (35) ELT 241 SC).

(h) transfer of immovable property outside India can hold immovable property in India, other than a lease not exceeding five years by a person resident in India.

(i) acquisition or transfer of immovable property in India, other than a lease not exceeding five years, by a person resident outside India.

No non-Indian citizen and a person resident outside India can hold immovable property in India without the prior permission of Reserve Bank of India (Union of India V. Mahender Singh 1956 (10) ECC 301). To hold means to have a legal title and actual possession (K.K. Handique V. Agri 1. T. Board Assam 1996 (60) ITR 216 SC).

(j) giving of a guarantee or surety in respect of any debt, obligation or other liability incurred-

(i) by a person resident in India and owed to a person, resident outside India, or

(ii) by a person resident outside India

Lease of immovable property in India or outside India not exceeding 5 years will not be regulated

A person resident in India, may hold, own, transfer or invest in foreign currency, foreign currency, foreign security or any immovable property situated outside India, if such currency, security or property was acquired held or owned by such person when he was resident outside India or inherited from a person who was resident outside India. A person resident outside India may hold own, transfer or invest in Indian currency, security, or any immovable property situated in India, if such currency, security or property was acquired, held or owned by such person when he was resident in India or inherited from a person who was resident in India.

Without prejudice to the above provisions, the Reserve Bank may by regulation, prohibit, restrict or regulate, establishment in India of a branch office or other place of business by a person resident outside India, for carrying on any activity relating to such branch, office of other place of business.

In Arun Kumar & Co V. Reserve Bank of India [1983 (54) Company Case 176] Delhi High Court while considering the issue as to whether any restrictions on establishment of place of business in India are violative of Article 19(1)(g) of the Constitution of India held that there was need for preserving and augmenting foreign exchange and therefore such provisions have to be liberally construed so as to arm the state with sufficient powers to deal with the matters so vital to the nation's economy.

Current account transaction means a transaction other than a capital account transaction. The current account transaction includes:

(i) payments due in connection with foreign trade, viz., imports and exports, other current business, services and short-term banking and credit facilities in the ordinary course of business whatever is done in ordinary course of business is permissible
(ii) payments due as interests on loans and as net income from investments
(iii) remittances for living expenses of parents, spouse and children residing abroad, and
(iv) expenses in connection with foreign travel, education and medical care of parents, spouse and children [Sec 2 (1)].

Current account transactions, therefore, are those which arise in the course of business and for living expenses like education, medical foreign travel etc.

Any person may sell to or draw foreign exchange from an authorised person if such sale or drawal is a current account transaction. The Central Government may, in public interest and in consultation with Reserve Bank, impose such reasonable restrictions as deemed fit to be imposed by the Reserve Bank. A free flow of foreign exchange currency for goods and services is however, a rule subject to reasonable restriction, in keeping pace with international trade and global and open market economy.

While granting any permission, the Central Government or the Reserve Bank of India should not impose any condition which does not have a rational connection with the object proposed by the statute (Enforcement Directorate vs Bhahka 1978-48 camp, cas, 649 Cal)

6.6.2 Foreign Exchange [Sec 2 (n) 2(m)]

Foreign exchange means foreign currency. Foreign currency means any currency other than Indian currency. Foreign currency includes:

(i) deposits, credits and balances payable in any foreign currency
(ii) drafts, travellers cheques, letters of credit or bills of exchange expressed or drawn in Indian currency but payable in any foreign currency, and
(iii) drafts, travellers' cheques, letters of credit or bills of exchange drawn by banks, institutions or persons outside India, but payable in Indian currency.

Foreign exchange would, thus, include transaction drawn in Indian currency in India but payable in foreign currency or transactions drawn outside India but payable in India currency.

6.6.3 Indian Currency [Sec 2 (g)(h)(i)]

Indian currency means currency notes, postal notes, postal orders, money orders, cheques, drafts travellers' cheques, letters of credit, bills of exchange and promissory notes, credit cards or such other similar instruments, as may be notified by the Reserve Bank.

Currency notes means and includes cash in the form of coins and bank notes.

6.6.4 Security [Sec 2 (za)]

Security means shares, stocks, bonds and debentures, Government Securities as defined in the Public Debt Act 1944, as Savings certificates to which the Government Savings Certificates Act 1959 applies, deposit receipts in respect of deposits in securities and Unit Trust of India established under Sec 3 (1) of the Unit Trust of India Act, 1963 or of any mutual fund and includes certificates of title to securities but does not include bills of exchange or promissory note other than Government promissory note or any other instruments which may be notified by the Reserve Bank as security.

6.6.5 Foreign Security [Sec 2 (0)]

Foreign Security means any security in the form of shares, stocks bonds debentures or any other instrument denominated or expressed in foreign currency and includes securities expressed in foreign currency, but where redemption or any form of return such as interest or dividends is payable in Indian currency.

6.7 RESTRICTIONS OF DEALINGS IN FOREIGN EXCHANGE [SEC 3 AND 4]

No personnel shall:

(i) deal in or transfer any foreign exchange or foreign security to any person not being an authorised person,

(ii) make any payment to or for the credit of any person resident outside India in any manner.

(iii) receive otherwise through an authorised person, any payment or on behalf of any person resident outside India in any manner. Where any person resident in India receives any payment by order or on behalf of any person resident outside India through any other person (including an authorised person) without a corresponding inward remittance from any place outside India, then, such person shall be deemed to have received such payment otherwise than through an authorised person, and

(iv) enter into any financial transaction in India as consideration for or in association with acquisition or creation or transfer of a right to acquire any asset outside India by any person. Financial transaction means making any payment to, or for the credit of any person or receiving any payment for, by order or on behalf of any person, or drawing, issuing or negotiating any bill of exchange or promissory note or transferring any security or acknowledging any debt.

Any payment received through any person or an authorised person from outside India has to be supported by a foreign inward remittance. These restrictions are intended to prevent money laundency or hawala transactions.

All the above dealings in India shall acquire, hold, own, possess or transfer any foreign exchange, foreign security or any immovable property situated outside India. No person resident in India shall acquire, hold, own, possess or transfer any foreign exchange, foreign security or any immovable property situated outside India.

Receipt of out of pocket expenses abroad by an employee of an Indian company from a foreign national without the permission of the Reserve Bank of India is in contravention of the Act (E Merck India Ltd V. Director of Enforcement 1988 (39) Taxman47)

In Ram Ratan Gupta V Director of Enforcement (AIR 1966 SC 495), Supreme Court has observed that though a loan creates a debt there may be a debt created without contracting a loan, for instance, a barter trader. Borrowing and lending must, therefore, be proved by a contract of a loan. There should be a creation of legal lender-borrower relationship.

There is, however, no legal presumption, express or implied, that if a person has acquired any goods of foreign trade, he will be deemed to have illegally acquired the foreign exchange equivalent to the price of such goods (Neo Pharma (P) Ltd., V. Director of Enforcement 1989 (47) Taxman 12). Foreign exchange acquired by an Indian resident by way of gift outside India cannot be spent or utilised by the donee for any purpose as the donee is required to surrender the same (S. Raman V. Director of Enforcement 1993 (66) Taxman 428). The obligation arises only if the whole or part of the foreign exchange received as gift is brought to India (K.T. Pavanny. V. Director of enforcement 1991 (56) Taxman 142).

Supreme Court of India in Shanti Prasad Jain V. Director of Enforcement (AIR 1964 SC 1023) has held that even a person resident in India, who receives foreign exchange as gift during his trip abroad is required to comply with the provisions of the Act. Once a person is found to own and hold the foreign exchange, there arises no question of any mensrea on his part for the purpose of proving contravention (Gayathri Devi. V. Director of Enforcement 1990 (50) Taxman 510).

No payment can be made to the decree holder who is a foreigner without obtaining permission from Reserve Bank of India (A.B. Lobo V. Fatchkhan - AIR 1972 Mad 323). Department has to prove that the amount is received through unauthorised channels and there was no corresponding issue and remittance (E.V. Marabbar V. Deputy Director of Enforcement 1989 (21) ECC 164) Payment thereof received in rupees from a person who has accounted inward remittances in foreign exchange duly received from an authorised dealer or payment received in rupees from resident outside India, provided before making payment the person in India has received foreign exchange and has converted the same into Indian rupees.

Mere acknowledgement of a debt is not a violation unless such acknowledgement results in the creation of a right to receive payment in favour of any person resident outside India. (Asian Electronics Ltd. V. Director of Enforcement 1992 (64) Taxman 13).

There is no prohibition on a person, who earn foreign money while residing abroad from spending money on himself. Similarly, any amount spent on hand and stay abroad out of sale proceeds of his property abroad is not against the above provision (B.M. Ishak Masical v. Spl Director, Enforcement 1983 L.J.1210).

6.7.1 Realisation and Repariation of Foreign Exchange [Sec, 2 (7, 8 and 9)]

Repatriate to India means bringing into India the realised foreign exchange and

(i) the selling of such foreign exchange to an authorised person in India in exchange for rupees, or

(ii) the holding of realised amount in an account with an authorised person in India to the extent notified by the Reserve Bank and includes use of the realised amount for discharge of a debt or liability denominated in foreign exchange.

Where any amount of foreign exchange is due or is occurred to any person resident in India, such person shall take all reasonable steps to realise and repatriate to India such foreign exchange and in such manner as may be specified by the Reserve Bank.

Any person who becomes entitled to receive any foreign exchange must take every possible step to secure its receipt without any delay (G. Ramaiah Kandiar V. Addl Director of Enforcement) 1988 (36) Taxman 54). The provisions are attracted where there is a right to receive foreign exchange, for instance, legally enforceable right. Mere claim of a person to receive foreign exchanges does not attract the provisions of the Act. IR.K. Enterprises V. Director of Enforcement 1991 (57) Taxman (28)].

6.7.2 Exemption from Realisation and Repatriation of Foreign Exchange

In the following cases the above provisions of holdings, realisation and repatriation of foreign exchange shall not apply:

(i) possession of foreign currency or foreign coins by any person upto such limit as the Reserve Bank may specify;

Foreign coins can be held by any person resident in India upto US $ 500. This is an exception for persons collecting foreign coins as a hobby. Foreign currency held upto a value equivalent to US $ 2000 for personal purpose is exempted (Central Government notification No. 10/22/90-NRI- cell dated 17-7-1992);

(ii) foreign currency account held or operated by such person and the limit upto which the Reserve Bank may specify;

(iii) foreign exchange acquired or received before 8-7-1997 or any income arising or accuring thereon which is held outside India by any person in pursuance of a general or special permission granted by the Reserve Bank;

(iv) foreign exchange held by a person resident in India upto such limit as the Reserve Bank may specify, if such foreign exchange was acquired by way of gift or inheritance from a person holding general or special permission, including any income arising therefrom;

(v) foreign exchange acquired from employment, business, trade, vocation, services, honorarium, gifts, inheritance or any other legitimate means up to such limit as the Reserve Bank may specify; and

(vi) such other receipts in foreign exchange as the Reserve Bank may specify.

6.7.3 Person Sec. 2 (4)

Person includes

a) an individual
b) a Hindu undivided family
c) a company
d) a firm
e) an association of persons or a body of individuals, whether incorporated or not
f) every artifical judicial person, not falling within any of the above clauses, and
g) any agency, office or branch owned or controlled by such person.

The term 'person' includes an individual, a company and a body corporate, a firm and other association of individuals [Agrawal Trading Corporation V Asst, Collector of customs 1972 (42) comp, cases 532 SC]

6.7.4 Person Resident in India [Sec. 2 (v)]

A person resident in India means

(i) a person residing in India for more than 182 days during the course of the preceding financial year but does not include:

(A) a person who has gone out of India or who stays outside India, in either case

a) for or on taking up employment outside India,
b) for carrying on a business or vocation outside India, or
c) for any other purpose in such circumstances as would indicate to stay outside India for an uncertain period.

(B) a person who has come to or stays in India, in either case, otherwise than

a) for or on taking up employment in India,
b) for carrying on in India, or
c) for any other purpose, in such circumstances as would indicate his intention to stay in India for an uncertain period.

(ii) any person or body corporate registered or incorporated in India,
(iii) an office, branch or agency in India owned or controlled by a person resident outside India; and
(iv) an office, branch or agency outside India or controlled by a person resident in India.

A foreigner can become a resident in India if he indicates his intention to stay in India for an uncertain period or if he takes up employment in India or carries on a business or vocation in India. An Indian non-resident citizen on his return will become a resident after the expiry of 182 days of his residence in India, if he does not take up employment or is not able to carry on business or vocation in India or if he does not indicate his intention to stay in India for an uncertain period. If such a person wants to acquire a property immediately on return he shall be required to obtain approval of the Reserve Bank.

Intention of a person plays a crucial role in determining the residential status of a person. A person who proceeds abroad without any intention to stay outside India for an indefinite or uncertain period, will be considered a person resident in India during his temporary absence from India. A mere intention to go abroad is immaterial. The same analogy applies to non-Indian citizens who come to India. A temporary stay in India by a non-Indian citizen will categorise him as resident outside India. A non-Indian citizen is generally a resident outside India (L. Ramabrahmam & Sons (P) Ltd, V. FERA Board 1987 (62) Comp, Cos 80). In Babulal Dayaljee Dudhela V. Director of Enforcement (1991 (57) Taxman 89), it has been held that proof of residential status has to be established by deeds and acts. Residence of a person is a question of fact. It must be established by positive proof. The burden to prove that a person is a non-resident lies on the department (Director of Enforcement v. Ankur Exports Pvt. Ltd - 1988 (41) Taxman 11).

6.7.5 Person Resident outside India [Sec. 2 (w)]

Person resident outside India means a person who is not resident in India.

6.7.6 Export of Goods and Services [Sec. 2 (1) (zb) & 7]

Export means

(i) taking out of India to a place outside India any goods.
(ii) provision of services from India to any person outside India.

Taking goods out of India for sale or purchase would be export. Taking goods out of India for personal use during travel or for repairs and return cannot obviously be export. Service means service of any description which is made available to potential users. Service includes the provision of facilities in connection with banking, financing insurance, medical assistance, legal assistance, chit-fund, real estate, transport, processing, supply of electrical or other energy, boarding or lodging or both, entertainment, amusement or the purveying of news or other information. Service does not include, rendering of any service free of charge or under a contract of personal service.

Foreign exchange earned out of exports of goods or rendering of services are regulated by the Act. Every exporter of goods shall:

(i) Furnish to the Reserve Bank or such other authority a declaration in such form and in such manner as may be specified containing true and correct material particulars including the amount representing the full export value. If the export value of the goods is not ascertainable at the time of export, the value which the exporter, having regard to the prevailing market conditions, expects to receive on the sale of the goods in a market outside India.

(ii) Furnish to the Reserve Bank such other information as may be required by the Reserve Bank for the purpose of ensuring the realisation of the export proceeds by such exporter.

The Reserve Bank may, for the purpose of ensuring that the full export value of the goods or such reduced value of the goods as the Reserve Bank determines, having regard to the prevailing market conditions, is received without any delay, direct any exporter to comply with such requirements as it thinks fit.

Every exporter of services shall also furnish to the Reserve Bank or to such other authorities a declaration containing the true and correct material particulars in relation to payment for such services.

The main purpose and object of the enactment is to get a declaration from the exporter that he has then brought or will bring back the full export value of the goods exported (K. Janardhanan Pillai. V. Collector of customs 1988 (38) ELT 647 (TRI). The declaration of the exporter is, therefore, obtained with a stipulation that it must be affirmed as a true declaration, and not a false or untrue in any material particular (Union of India V. Haim Aghajaw Jer Menor - AIR 1968 130M 366, South India Coir mills V. Addl Collector of customs 1977 (47) comp. Cas 681 SC). In the absence of a declaration the exporter cannot be allowed to ship the goods out of India.

In view of Supreme Court judgement in Director, Enforcement Directorate vis K.O. Krishnaswamy (AIR 1979-SC 1969), the words "full amount payable by the foreign buyers in respect of the goods" were substituted by the words "full export value is over invoiced the exporter" can be proceeded against for non-repatriation of the declared value (J.K. A. Rajappa Chettiar V. Director of Enforcement - 1982 cr LJ. (1562) MAD) Exporter cannot realise the reduced value of the goods, if offered by the foreign buyer without the permission of Reserve Bank of India (A.R. Sarangal V. Director of Enforcement 1993 (66) Taxman 51). No mensrea is required for imposition of penalty for non-realisation of the full export value of the goods. Any act or omission is sufficient to constitute an offence (P. Varada Reddy V. Addl, Director 1988 (37) Taxman 35).

Reasonable efforts should be made to realise the full export value of the goods. Any act or omission is sufficient to constitute an offence (P. Varda Reddy V. Addl. Director 1988 (37) Taxman 35). Reasonable efforts should be made to realise the full export value in order to overcome the offence (Allied Industrial Enterprises V. Director of Enforcement 1988 (41)

Taxman 74). There should be no act or omission on the part of the exporter resulting into non-realisation of full export value. What are reasonable efforts made is a question of fact in each case.

Institution of legal proceedings against foreign buyer may constitute reasonable steps taken in a given case. But where legal proceedings may cost more than the recovery the same if not taken may not constitute a failure to take reasonable steps (Escorts Ltd v. FERA Board 1988 cr. L.J. (240) Delhi)

Goods exported without a declaration constitutes an offence under the Customs Act 1962. The realisation of export proceeds is looked after by Enforcement Directorate and/or by the Reserve Bank of India. An attempt to export goods without a declaration or failure to declare the true and full export value of the goods or export the goods contrary to the prohibitions imposed under the Customs Act, render the goods liable to confiscation under Customs Act, 1962.

6.7.7 Foreign Trade Development

For the development and regulation of foreign trade, Foreign Trade (Development and Regulation) Act, 1992 (herein after referred to as "the said Act") with Foreign Trade (Regulation) Rules, 1993 (herein after referred to as "the said Rules") have been enacted to facilitate imports into, and augment exports from India.

For regulating the clearances of the imported goods and for export of goods from customs station/area/customs Act, 1962 enacted, regulates the law relating to customs.

The Central Government also notifies by notification in the Official Gazette, the Export and Import Policy. The policy announced each time is for a period of five years subject to amendments in public interest from time to time. Along with the policy, handbook of procedures and ITC (I-IS) classification of import and import items are also notified by the Central Government.

6.7.8 Objectives

The principal objectives of the policy are:

(i) To accelerate the country's transition to globally oriented vibrant economy with a view to derive maximum benefits from expanding global market opportunities.

(ii) To stimulate sustained economic growth by providing access to essential raw materials, intermediates, components, consumables and capital goods required for augmenting productions.

(iii) To enhance the technological strength and efficiency or Indian agriculture, industry and services, thereby improving their competitive strength while generating new employment opportunities and encourage the attainment of internationally accepted standards of quality.

(iv) To provide consumers with good quality products at reasonable prices.

The objective of the handbook is to implement the provision of the Foreign Trade (Development and Regulation) Act 1992, the rules and orders thereunder made and the Export and Import Policy by laying down simple and transparent procedures which are easy to comply with and administer a more efficient management of the foreign trade.

The above objectives are to be achieved through coordinated effort of all the departments of the government in general and the Ministry of Commerce and the Directorate General of Foreign Trade and its network of regional offices in particular, with a shared vision and commitment and in the best spirit of facilitation in the interest of export promotion.

6.7.9 Procedure in Brief

1. Code No: No person shall make any import or export except under an Importer - Exporter IEC code number granted by the Director General Registration with licensing authorities is sufficient before commencing export or import by obtaining IEC code number obtaining Exporters Code number from the Reserve Bank of India is no longer required since 1st January 1997.

2. Licence: On an application made to the Director General and after an enquiry as deemed fit by the Director General, a licence to import or export such class or classes of goods as prescribed may be granted or may be refused. The licence granted may also be suspended or cancelled by the Director General for good and sufficient reasons as set out in Rules 9 and 10 respectively of the said Rules. The licence issued will be subject to conditions as set out in Rules 6 of the said Rules.

6.8 CONDITIONS OF LICENCE

Conditions of Licence for Export

(a) No person shall transfer or acquire by transfer any licence issued by the licensing authority except in accordance with the provisions of the policy.

(b) The goods for the export of which a licence is granted shall be the property of the licensee at the time of export.

Conditions of Licence for import

The licensing authority may issue a licence for import subject to one or more of the following conditions.

(a) that the goods covered by the licence shall not be disposed of except in accordance with the provisions of the policy or in the manner specified by the licensing authority in the licence.

(b) that the applicant for a licence shall execute a bond for complying with the terms and conditions of the licence; and

6.8.1 Deemed Conditions of Licence for Import

The following shall be deemed conditions of every licence for import.

a) No person shall transfer or acquire by transfer any licence issued by the licensing authority except in accordance with the provisions of the policy; b) the goods for the import of which a licence is granted shall be the property of the licensee at the time of import and after the time of clearance through the customs; c) the goods for the import of which a licence is granted shall be the new goods, unless otherwise stated in the licence and d) that the goods covered by the licence for import shall not be exported without the written permission of the Director General.

Authorised dealers should, upon letters of credit, allow remittances for the import of goods only when the importer submits a licence marked "For Exchange Control Purposes". Compliance of special conditions on the licences should be strictly adhered to.

3. Declarations: On the importation into, or exportation out of any customs ports of any goods whether liable to duty or not, the owner of such goods shall, in the Bill of Entry or the Shipping Bill or any other documents prescribed under the Customs Act, 1962, state the value, quality and description of such goods, to the best of his knowledge and belief. In case of exportation of goods the owner shall certify that the quality and specification of the goods as stated in the documents are in accordance with the terms of the export contract entered into with the buyer or consignee in pursuance of which the goods are being exported. The owner shall subscribe to a declaration of the truth of such statement at the foot of such Bill of Entry or Shipping Bill or any other document.

The exporter shall also file a declaration with the Commissioner of Customs in duplicate for realisation of export value within the prescribed time and in the prescribed manner. One copy therefore is forwarded by the Commissioner of Customs to the Reserve Bank of India.

No person shall make or sign any declaration, statement or document for the purposes of obtaining a licence or importing any goods knowing or having reason to believe such declaration or statement is false in any material particular. No person shall employ any corrupt or fraudulent practice for the purposes of obtaining any licence or importing or exporting any goods.

4. Utilisation of Imported Goods: No person shall dispose of any goods imported by him against a licence except in accordance with the terms and conditions of such licence.

No person shall use any imported goods allotted to him by the State Trading Corporation of India or any other agency recognised by the Central Government in a manner and for the purpose, otherwise than as declared by him in his application for such allotment or in any document submitted by him in support of such application.

6.8.2 Authorised Person (Sees. 2 (e) 10, 11 & 12)

Authorised person means an authorised dealer, money-changer, offshore banking unit or any other person for the time being authorised to deal in foreign exchange or foreign securities.

The Reserve Bank may on an application made to it, authorise any person to be known as authorised person to deal in foreign exchange or in foreign securities as an authorised dealer, money-changer or offshore banking unit or in any other manner as it deem fit. Thus, an authorised person can now deal in foreign securities apart from foreign exchange. An offshore banking unit is also now an authorised person. An authorisation shall be in writing and shall be subject to the conditions laid down thereon. An authorisation may be revoked by the Reserve Bank at any time if the Reserve Bank is satisfied that:

(a) it is in public interest so to do so, or

(b) the authorised person has failed to comply with the conditions subject to which the authorisation was granted or has contravened any of the provisions of the Act or any rule, regulation, notification, direction or order made thereunder. However, no such authorisation shall be revoked unless the authorised person has been given reasonable opportunity of making a representation in the matter.

An authorised person shall, in all his dealings ill foreign exchange or foreign security, comply with such general or special directions or orders as the Reserve Bank may, from time to time, think fit to give. Except with the previous permissions of the Reserve Bank, an authorised person shall not engage in any transaction involving any foreign exchange or foreign security which is not in conformity with the terms of this authorisation.

An authorised person shall, before undertaking any transaction in foreign exchange on behalf of any person, require that person to make such a declaration and to give such information as will reasonably satisfy him that the transaction will not involve and is not designed for the purpose of any contravention or evasion of the provision of the Act or any rule, regulation, notification, direction or order made thereunder. Where the said person refuses to comply with any such requirement or makes only unsatisfactory compliance therewith the authorised person shall refuse in writing to undertake the transaction. If an authorised person has reason to believe that any such contravention or evasion is contemplated by the person, he shall report the matter to the Reserve Bank.

Any person other than an authorised person who has acquired or purchased foreign exchange for any purpose mentioned in the declaration made by him to authorised person, does not use it for such purpose or does not surrender it to authorised person within the specified period or uses the foreign exchange so acquired or purchased for any other purpose for which purchase or acquisition of foreign exchange is not permissible under the provision of the Act, or the rules or regulation or directions or order made thereunder, shall be deemed to have committed contravention of the provisions of the Act.

6.8.3 Reserve Bank Powers to Issue Directions to Authorised Persons

The Reserve Bank may, for the purpose of securing compliance with the provisions of the Act, and of any rules, regulations, notifications or directions made thereunder give to the authorised persons any directions in regard to making a payment or the doing or desist from doing any act relating to foreign exchange or foreign security. The Reserve Bank may also direct any authorised person to furnish such information, in such manner, as it deems.

Where any authorised person contravenes any direction given by the Reserve Bank or fails to file any return as directed, the Reserve Bank may, after giving reasonable opportunity of being heard. impose on the authorised person a penality, which may extend 10 ₹10,000 and in the ease of continuing contravention with an additional penality which may extend to ₹2000 for everyday during which such contravention continues.

6.8.4 Power of the Reserve Bank to Inspect Authorised Person

The Reserve Bank may, at any time, cause an inspection to be made by any officer of the Reserve Bank specially authorised in writing of the business of any authorised person as may appear it to be necessary or expedient for the purpose of:

(a) verifying the corrections of any statement information or particulars furnished to the Reserve Bank;
(b) obtaining any information on particulars which such authorised person has failed to furnish as being called upon to do so; and
(c) securing compliance in the provisions of the Act or of any rules, regulations, directions or orders made thereunder.

It shall be the duty of every authorised person and where such person is a company or a firm, of every director, partner or other officer of such company or firm as the case may be, to produce to any officer making an inspection, such books, accounts and other documents in his custody or power and to furnish any statement or information relating to the affairs of such person, company or firm as the said offer may require within such time and in such manner as the said officer may direct.

QUESTIONS FOR PRACTICE

Section - A (Two Marks Questions)

1. Who is a money-changer?
2. Who is an authorised dealer?

Section - B (Five Marks Questions)

1. What are the objects of FEMA?
2. State the restrictions regarding the use of foreign exchange under FEMA.

Section - C (15 Marks Questions)

1. Explain the provisions relating to an authorised person.
2. Explain the main provisions of FEMA.
3. Explain offences, and penalties for offences.
4. Briefly state the provisions of the Foreign Exchange Management Act, 1999.

Cyber Laws and the Information Technology Act, 2000

Chapter 7

7.1 BACKGROUND AND INTRODUCTION

Traditionally the business activities done face to face and people used to transact everything in physical forms, but as the development of technology spread its wings to every nook and corner of the globe, the very exercise in business transaction changed. People started transacting through the Internet and major part of the business activities are done through electronic media. No longer the buyer and seller met at a place called market, all the 'give' and 'take' were monitored by computers though websites and the entire domain of traditional business emerged into a latest technology friendly device and process. Cyber cafe became very common scene and people involved themselves with the cyber world and different cyber instruments, thus cyber activities were very common so also the cyber crimes and other mis-practices like hacking, cracking etc., due to which authorities and legal experts throughout the world thought of having a separate and special Act related to cyber activities, thus emerged a new law called cyber-law. As the internet activities totally dominated over the routines called traditional business activities, even the mistakes, irregularities and ultimately the frauds and crime were in the forefront of cyber activities.

Meaning and Definition of Cyber Law

Cyber law was framed to regulate and control the unwanted activities over the Internet trade by the authorities. Though till today there is no definite quote available in legal paralance to define what exactly is the cyber law, but in general terms one can state that now there exist a regulatory reference for cyber operators, to control them from going long way to commit cyber crimes.

However, it needs to define the term 'Cyber Crime', i.e. any act which is punishable under the Information Technology Act. Cyber Crime is "any act of untowardness which results in an illegal gain to the generator of such act through an electronic device called computer through its coverages or devices or domain spread in the form of the Internet throughout the world, accessible though websites without any restrictions from authorities. Cyber crimes and its domain are restrictions. Sometimes the damage is so huge that the entire web-domain suffers both financially and technically.

Thus, the authorities very shortly felt that there must be source controlling rules and regulations on the free domain of cyber world, and a latest Act was framed even in India which is called "Cyber Lays and the Information Technology Act, 2000". This act provides the legal structure needed to be followed by the web operators in free domain and any violation of it will attract an act of crime termed cyber crime.

7.2 NEED AND SCOPE OF CYBER LAW

The popularity of computer, application in day-to-day activities not only by business but also at personal levels of people have resulted in huge Internet transaction which in turn has resulted in the tremendous growth of e-business activities. The domain of electronic concurrence has paved the way for cyber laws. Though there is no direct impact of e-business on any specific crime but there are certain instances which require to be monitored under cyber activities. In a country like India accessibility to the Internet is just next door, people may enter into cyber malpractices without their knowledge. The use of plastic cards to settle the claims is the major source of cyber crimes. In the routine business transactions that cyber crimes are increasing, as the normal user of the Internet is not that careful. The persons who are involved in cyber crimes are extraordinary intelligent and they also go scott-free as they normally do not leave any weak-link to trace the crimes. No doubt malpractices do exist in internet business as they exist in routine business. As the volume of business increase, need to be curbed at the right level to stop any significant damage. The technology is like electricity, used properly will result in development or else if used carelessly causes huge loss both to the user and the society at large.

One should not disagree to the fact that in spite of probable chance of cyber crimes, at large it only helps for development. But the developing countries like India may fail to sustain the burn of such huge malpractices that too when it is interacted globally. The sole reason which can be traced for cyber crimes in the free flow of information from one end to another end, it may look like an entertainment in the beginning but as it crops up into a huge activity may result in causing an irreparable damage to the entire world. Cyber crimes grow and flourish in a democratic society as there is no restriction over its receivability, usability by each and everyone. The information uploaded at one end emerges as a raw material for the fraudulent brains at the other end, and most of the occasions it results as a 'game'. As the crimes have increased in numbers so also the people involved in it, especially the internet malpractices have gave birth to all the different types of crime operators. The following are the types of cyber crimes:

(a) Internet Frauds or Crimes

(i) Fraudulent activities on the Internet
(ii) Credit card frauds
(iii) Altering the digital information
(iv) Forgery of signatures through scanning
(v) E-mail on line frauds

(b) Mastermind Web Frauds

(i) Hacking
(ii) Cracking
(iii) Sniffers
(iv) Securities re-locking process
(v) Protocol spoofing
(vi) Password cyber crimes
(vii) Software piracy
(viii) Hardware/software sabotage

(c) Other Frauds

(i) Time theft
(ii) False data entry
(iii) Programme manipulations
(iv) Piggy hacking
(v) Distribution of anti-social information.

A. Internet frauds or crimes

(i) Fraud on the Internet

This is a form of white collar crime. Internet fraud is a common type of crime whose growth has been proportionate to the growth of the Internet itself. The Internet provides companies and individuals with the opportunity of marketing their products on the net. It is easy for people with fraudulent intention to make their messages look real and credible. There are innumerable scams and frauds most of them relating to investment schemes and have been described in detail below as follows:

(a) Online investment newsletters

Many newsletters on the Internet provide the investors with free advice recommending stocks where they should invest. Sometimes these recommendations are totally bogus and cause loss to the investors.

(b) Bulletin boards

This is a forum for sharing investor information and often fraud is perpetrated in this zone causing loss of millions who bank on them.

(c) E-mail seams

Since junk mail (Email which contains useless material) is easy to create, fraudsters often find it easy to spread bogus investment schemes or spread false information about a company.

(ii) Credit card fraud

With the electronic commerce rapidly becoming a major force in national economies it offers rich pickings for criminals prepared to undertake fraudulent activities. In D.S.A. the ten most frequent fraud reports involve undelivered and online services; damaged, defective, misrepresented or undelivered merchandise; auction sales; pyramid schemes and multilevel marketing and of the most predominant among them is credit card fraud. Something like half a billion dollars lost to consumers in card fraud alone.

(a) Making available digital signature for fraudulent purpose

This is an offence punishable under section 74 of the above-mentioned act, with imprisonment for a term that may extend to two years or with fine of two lakh rupees or with both.

(iii) Alteration and destruction of digital information

The corruption and destruction of digital information is the single largest menace facing the world of computers. This is introduced by a human agent with the help of various programs which have been described in detail below as follows:

Virus just as a virus can infect the human immunity system there exist programs, which, can destroy or hamper computer systems. A computer virus is a program designed to replicate and spread, generally with the victim being oblivious to its existence. Computer viruses spread by attaching themselves to programmes like word processor or spreadsheets or they attach themselves to the boot sector of a disk. When an infected file is activated or when the computer is started from an infected disk, the virus itself is also executed.

B. Mastermind Web Frauds

(a) Hacking

It is the most common type of cyber crime being committed across the world. Hacking has been defined in section 66 of The Information Technology Act, 2000 as follows "whoever with the intent to cause or knowing that he is likely to cause wrongful loss or damage to the public or any person destroys or deletes or alters any information residing in a computer resource or diminishes its value or utility or affects it injuriously by any means commits hacking".

Punishment for hacking under the above-mentioned section is imprisonment for three years or fine which may extend up to two lakh rupees or both. A hacker is a person who breaks in or trespasses a computer system. Hackers are of different types ranging from code hackers to crackers to cyber punks to freaks. Some hackers just enjoy cracking systems and gaining access to them as an ordinary pastime; they do not desire to commit any further crime. Whether this itself would constitute a crime is a matter of fact. At most such a crime could be equated with criminal trespass.

(b) Cracking

The term *cracking* means, 'illegal access'. Now, 'access' comprises the entering of the whole or any part of a computer system (hardware, components, stored data of the system installed, directories, traffic and content-related data). However, it does not include the mere sending of an e-mail message or file to that system. 'Access' includes the entering of another computer, system, where it is connected via public telecommunication networks or to a computer system on the same network, such as a LAN (local area network) or the Intranet within an organisation. The method of communication (e.g. from a distance, including via wireless links or at a close range) does not matter. So if a virus is sent through an e-mail, it is not an illegal 'access' and hence cannot be termed 'cracking'.

(c) Security Related Crimes

With the growth of the Internet, network security has become a major concern. Private confidential information has become available to the public. Confidential information can reside in two states on the network. It can reside on the physical stored media, such as hard drive or memory or it can reside in the transit across the physical network wire in the form of packets. These two information states provide opportunities for attacks from users on the internal network, as well as users on the Internet.

(d) Network Packet Snifters

Network computers communicate serially where large information pieces are broken into smaller ones. The information stream would be broken into smaller pieces even if networks communicated in parallel. These smaller pieces are called network packets. Since these network packets are not encrypted they can be processed and understood by any application that can pick them off the network and process them. A network protocol specifies how packets are identified and labeled which enables a computer to determine whether a packet is intended for it. The specifications for network protocols such as TCP/IP are widely published. A third party can easily interpret the network packets and develop a packet snifter. A packet snifter is a software application that uses a network adapter card in a promiscuous mode (a mode in which the network adapter card sends all packets received by the physical network wire to an application for processing) to capture all network packets that are sent across a local network. A packet snifter can provide its users with meaningful and often sensitive information such as user account names and passwords.

(e) Internet Protocol Spoofing

An IP attack occurs when an attacker outside the network pretends to be a trusted computer either by using an JP address that is within its range or by using an external JP address that you trust and to which you wish to provide access to specified resources on your network. Normally an JP spoofing attack is limited to the injection of data or commands into an existing stream of data passed between client and server application or a peer to peer network connection.

(f) Password attacks

Password attacks can be implemented using several different methods like the brute force attacks, Trojan horse programmes. JP spoofing can yield user accounts and passwords. Password attacks usually refer to repeated attempts to identify a user password or account. These repeated attempts are called brute force attacks.

At the core of these security breaches is the distribution of sensitive information to competitors or others who use it to the owners' disadvantage. While an outside intruder can use password and JP spoofing attacks to copy information, an internal user could place sensitive information on an external computer or share a drive on the network with other users. Man-in-the-middle-attacks.

This attack requires that the attacker have access to network packets that come across the networks. The possible use of such attack are theft of information, hijacking an ongoing session to gain access to your internal network resources, traffic analysis to drive information about one's own network and its users, denial of service, corruption of transmitted data, and introduction of new information into network sessions.

Pornography on the Net

The growth of technology has flip side to it causing multiple problems in everyday life. Internet has provided a medium for the facilitation of crimes like pornography. Cyber porn as it is popularly called widespread. Almost 50% of the websites exhibit pornographic material on the Internet today. Pornographic materials can be reproduced more quickly and cheaply on new media like hard disks, floppy discs and CD-ROMs. The new technology is not merely an extension of the existing forms like text, photographs and images. Apart from still pictures and images, full motion video clips and complete movies are also available. Another great disadvantage with a media like this is its easy availability and accessibility to children who can now log on to pornographic websites from their own houses in relative anonymity and the social and legal deterrents associated with physically purchasing an adult magazine from the stand are no longer present. Furthermore, there are more serious offences which have universal disapproval like child pornography and far easier for offenders to hide and propagate through the medium of the Internet.

The Information and Technology Act, 2000 makes the publishing of information which is obscene in electronic form punishable as under:

"Whoever publishes or transmits or causes to be published in the electronic form, any material which is lascivious or appeals to the prurient interest or if its effect is such as to tend to corrupt persons who are likely, having regard to all relevant circumstances, to read, see or hear the matter contained or embodied in it, shall be punished on first conviction with imprisonment of either description for a term which may extend to five years and with fine which may extend to one lakh rupees and in the event of a second or subsequent conviction, with imprisonment of either description for a term which may extend to ten years and also with fine which may extend to two lakh rupees."

Cryptography, privacy and national security concerns

The Internet has provided its users with a new forum to express their views and concerns on a worldwide platform. As a necessary corollary to the freedom to communicate and speak is the fact that this must be allowed with as little state interference as possible; in other words, in the absence of state intrusion. This immediately raises the controversial issue of the right to privacy. It can be considered a logical corollary to the freedom of speech and expression. At the same time it is common knowledge that liberty cannot thrive without certain restrictions put on them so that each individual in society can be best protected. The practice of encryption and its study which is known as cryptography provides individuals with means of communication that no third party can understand unless specifically permitted by the communicators themselves. It would therefore seem that this practice is a legitimate utilisation of the right to freedom of speech and expression and the right to have a private conversation without intrusion.

Breach of Confidentiality and Privacy

According to section 72 of the Information Technology Act, 2000 if a person has secured access to any electronic record, book, register correspondence, information, document or other material without the consent of the person concerned and discloses the same to any other person then he shall be punishable with imprisonment up to two years, or with fine which may extend to one lakh rupees, or with both.

Encryption and Cryptography

Encryption is like sending a postal mail to another party with a lock code on the envelope which is known only to the sender and the recipient. This therefore has the effect of ensuring total privacy even in open networks like the Internet. Encryption involves the use of secret codes and ciphers to communicate information electronically from one person to another in such a way that the only person so communicating, would know to use the codes and ciphers. The field of cryptography on the other hand deals with the study of secret codes and ciphers and the innovations that occur in the field. It is also defined as the art and the science of keeping messages secure. Thus while encryption is the actual process, cryptography involves a study of the same and is of wider connotation.

The Right to Privacy and Encryption

It is usually agreed upon that in most democracies there do exist private and public spheres in every citizen's life and that these two spheres are distinct and have to be treated as such. Although the line of distinction is blurred and continues to be the subject of much debate especially with regard to certain subjects such as pornography or the use of narcotics, it is generally agreed that the liberal democratic state has no power to interfere with the private aspect of its citizen's lives. There is a common misconception that the right to privacy is merely a weapon to ensure confidentiality in human affairs. This however does not present the complete picture. It must be remembered that the right to confidentiality arises only after information regarding human transaction or affairs have reached third parties. It may be said that privacy involves the right to control one's personal information and the ability to determine it and how that information should be used and obtained. This principle has sometimes been referred to as the right to "informational self-determination". This principle becomes all the more relevant with the onset of the Internet and e-commerce. The volume and the varying nature of the transaction carried out on the net are such that the right to privacy must extend at least to a limited extent. At the same time, the very same factors, volume and the nature of transactions also raise the issue of security concerns as to the political, social and economic health of the country. Encryption of the details of our personal transactions would certainly assure us of greater degree of privacy but may also encroach upon the domain of national security concerns and two ends may be said to be in conflict.

Restrictions on Cryptography In India

The use of the cryptography and encryption in India is a relatively new phenomenon. The use of this technology for the purposes of communication has begun only over the last 15-20 years in India. According to a recent report in India there are very few companies involved in the development of cryptography, further, cryptography remains within the domain of the defence sector. It is only as late as 1995 that India introduced a list of items that required licensing before export. The list only included encryption software for telemetry systems in specific and did not relate to encryption software in general.

The Information Technology Act, 2000 seeks to introduce some sort of control over the use of encryption for communication in India.

Preventing of Computer Crime

By Educating Everyone: For example, users and systems operators, people who hold personal data and the people about whom it is held, people who create intellectual property and those who buy it and the criminals. We must educate people to:

Understand how technology can be used to help or hurt others.

Think about what it would be like to be the victim of a computer hacker or computer pirate.

By Practising Safe Computing

Always ask: Who has or may have access to my log-in address?

Remember: People such as computer hackers and pirates who hurt others through computer technology are not "cool." They are breaking the law.

Authentication of Electronic Records Using Digital Signatures (Section 3)

The section provides the conditions subject to which an electronic record may be authenticated by means of affixing digital signature. The digital signature is created in two distinct steps. First the electronic record is converted into a message digest by using a mathematical function known as "hash function" which digitally freezes the electronic record thus ensuring the integrity of the content of the intended communication contained in the electronic record. Any tampering with the contents of the electronic record will immediately invalidate the digital signature. Secondly, the identity of the person affixing the digital signature is authenticated through the use of a private key which attaches itself to the message digest and which can be verified by anybody who has the public key corresponding to such private key. This will enable anybody to verify whether the electronic record is retained intact or has been tampered with since it was so fixed with the digital signature. It will also enable a person who has a public key to identify the originator of the message.

For the purpose of this sub-section, "hash function" means an algorithm mapping or translation of one sequence of bits into another generally smaller, set known as "hash result" such that an electronic record yields the same hash result every time the algorithm is executed with the same electronic record as its input making it computationally infeasible:

1. to derive of reconstruct the original electronic record from the hash result produced by the algorithm; and
2. that two electronic records can be produced the same hash result using the algorithm.

7.3 ELECTRONIC GOVERNANCE (SECTIONS 4-10)

Section 4 - This section provides for *"legal recognition of electronic records"*. It provides that where any law requires that any information or matter should be in the typewritten or printed form then such requirement shall be deemed to be satisfied if it is in an electronic form.

Section 5 - This section provides for *legal recognition of Digital Signature.* Where any law requires that any information or matter shooed be authenticated by affixing the signature of any person, then such requirement shall be satisfied if it is authenticated by means of digital signatures affixed in such manner as may be prescribed by the Central Government.

For the purposes this section, "signed", with its grammatical variations and cognate expressions, shall with reference to a person, mean affixing of his hand written signature or any mark on any document and the expression "signature" shall be construed accordingly.

Section 6 - lays down the foundation of electronic governance. It provides that the filing of any from, application or other documents, creation, retention or preservation of records, issue or grant of any licence or permit or receipt or payment in government offices and its agencies may be done through the means of electronic form. The appropriate government has the power to prescribe the manner and format of the electronic records and the method of payment of fee in that connection.

Section 7 - This section provides that the documents, records or information which has to be retained for any specified period shall be deemed to have been retained if the same is retained in the electronic form provided the following conditions are satisfied:

(i) the information therein remains accessible so as to be usable subsequently.
(ii) the electronic record is retained in its original format or in a format which accurately represents the information contained.
(iii) the details which will facilitate the identification of the origin, destination, dates and time of despatch or receipt of such electronic record are available therein.

This section does not apply to any information which is automatically generated solely for the purpose of enabling an electronic record to be dispatched or received.

Moreover, this section does not apply to any law that expressly provides for the retention of documents, records or information in the form of electronic records.

Section 8 - provides for the publication of rules, regulations and notifications in the Electronic Gazette. It provides that where any law requires the publication of any rule, regulation, order, bye-law, notification or any other matter in the Official Gazette, then such requirement shall be deemed to be satisfied if the same is published in an electronic form. It also provides where the Official Gazette is published both in the printed as well as in electronic form, the date of publication shall be date of publication of the Official Gazette which was first published in any form.

However, **Section 9** of the Act provides that the conditions stipulated in Sections 6, 7 and 8 shall not confer any right to insist that the document should be accepted in an electronic form by any Ministry or department of the Central Government or the State Government.

Power to Central Government to Make Rules (Section 10)

This section provides that the Central Government, in respect of digital signature may prescribe by rules the following:

(a) the type of digital signature;
(b) the manner and format in which the digital signature shall be affixed;
(c) the manner or procedure which facilitates identification of the person affixing the digital signature;
(d) control processes and procedures to ensure adequate integrity, security and confidentiality of electronic records or payments; and
(e) any other matter which is necessary to give legal effect to digital signatures.

7.4 INFORMATION TECHNOLOGY ACT, 2000

It is very common that every business transaction must be duly supported by a documentary evidence. The electronic media though very popular and user friendly but has failed on many fronts as for as document-generation is concerned. The very purpose of inducting a new leaf into the corporate laws in the form of Information Technology Act 2000 is to give a sort of confidence in the minds of those business people who mainly deal through electronic media. To facilitate electronic form of business and to give legal protection to electronic records and digital signatures, electronic records and digital signatures, Government of India has aptly placed a new law titled as 'Information Technology Act 2000'.

Scope of the Act

This Act extends and applies to the entire union of India, and also to an extent to all those offences, which were commissioned with a view to involve any person of certain bilateral restrictions imposed by countries with India.

However, as a special feature of this Act, openly states that, this act shall not apply to negotiable instrument other than a cheque as defined in Section 13 of NI Act, 1881.

Definitions of various terms under the Act

Section 2, 2007 of the Information Technology Act defines various terms used in the Act, they are:

(i) **Access [Section 2(11)(a)]** means as gaining an entry into, instructing or communicating with the logical, arithmetical or memory function resources of a computer, computer system or computer network.

(ii) **Addressee [Section 2(1)(b)]** means a person who is intended by the originator to receive the electronic record, but does not include any intermediary.

(iii) **Computer [Section 2(11)(i)]** means any electronic, magnetic, optical or other high speed data processing device or system which performs logical, arithmetic and memory functions by manipulations of electronic, magnetic or optical impulses and includes all input, output, processing, storage, computer software or communication facilities which are connected or related to the computer in a computer system or computer network.

(iv) **Computer Network [Section 2(1)(j)]** means the interconnection of one or more computers through

(a) the use of satellite, microwave, terrestrial line or other communication media; and

(b) terminals or a complex consisting of two or more interconnected computers whether or not the interconnection is continuously maintained.

(v) **Affixing Digital Signature [Section 2(1)(d)]** means adoption of any methodology or procedure by a person for the purpose of authenticating an electronic record by means and digital signature.

(vi) **Digital Signature [Section 2(1)(p)]** means authentication of any electronic record by a subscriber by means of an electronic method or procedure in accordance with the provisional of section 3 of the Act.

(vii) **Digital Signature Certificate [Section 2(1)(q)]** means a digital signature certificate issued under sub-section (4) of section 35.

(viii) **Data [Section (1)(o)]** means a representation of information, knowledge, facts, concepts or instructions which are being prepared or have been prepared in a formalised manner, and is intended to processed is being process or has been processed in a computer system or computer network, may be in any form (including the print material) in the memory of the computer.

(ix) Appropriate Government, means the Central Government expect in the following two cases; where it means the State Government:

  (a) in matters enumerated in list II of the seventh schedule of the Indian Constitution; and

  (b) relating to any state law enacted under List III of the seventh schedule of the Indian constitution.

(x) **Computer resources [Section 2(1)(k)]** means computer, computer system, computer network, data, computer database or software.

(xi) **Computer System [Section 2(1)(l)]** means a device or collection of devices, including input and output support devices and excluding calculators which are not programmable and capable of being used in conjunction with external files, which contain computer programs, electronic instructions, input data and output data that performs logic, arithmetic, data storage and retrieval, communication control and other function.

(xii) **Asymmetric Cryptosystem [Section 2(1)(f)]** means a system of a secure key pair consisting of a private key for creating a digital signature and a public key to verify the digital signature.

(xiii) **Certifying Authority [Section 2(1)(g)]** means a person who has been granted a licence to issue a digital signature certificate under Section 24 of the Act.

(xiv) **Key Pair [Section 2(1)(x)]** means a private key and its mathematically related public key which are so related that the public key can verify a digital signature created by the private key.

(xv) **Information [Section 2(1)(v)]** means and includes data, text, images, sound, voice, codes, computer programmes, software and databases or micro film or computer generated microfiche.

(xiv) **Subscriber [Section 2(1)(2Q)]** means a person in whose name the digital signature certificate is issued.

Objectives of the Act

The objectives of the Act are:

(a) to grant legal recognition for transactions carried out by means of electronic data interchange and other means of electronic communication commonly referred to as "electronic commerce" in place of paper based methods communication;
(b) to give legal recognition to digital signature for authentication of any information or matter which requires authentication under any law;
(c) to facilitate electronic filing of documents with government departments;
(d) to facilitate electronic storage of data;
(e) to facilitate and give legal sanction to electronic fund transfers between banks and financial institutions; and
(f) to give legal recognition for keeping books of account by bankers in electronic form. Evidence act, 1891 and the reverse bank of India Act, 1934.

7.5 ATTRIBUTION, RECEIPT AND DESPATCH OF ELECTRONIC RECORDS (SECTIONS 11-13)

Section 11 Deals with attribution, receipt and despatch of electronic records 'Attribution' with regard to a certain means 'to consider it to be written or made by someone'. Hence, this section lays down how an electronic record is to be attributed to the person who originated it.

Section 12 provides for the manner in which acknowledgement of receipt of an electronic record by various modes shall be made.

Section 13 provides for the manner in which the time and place of despatch and receipt of electronic record sent by the originator shall be identified. It is provided that in general, an electronic record is deemed to be despatched at the place where the originator has his place of business and received where the addressee has his place of business.

For the purpose of this section:

(a) if the originator or the addressee has more than one place of business, the principal place of business shall be the place of business;

(b) if the originator or the addressee does not have a place of business, his usual place of residence shall be deemed to be the place of business; and

(c) "usual place of residence", in relation to a body corporate, means the place where it is registered.

7.6 SECURE ELECTRONIC RECORDS AND SECURE DIGITAL SIGNATURES (SECTION 14-16)

The I.T. Act sets out the conditions that would apply to qualify electronic records and digital signatures as being secure. It contains sections 14 to 16.

Section 15 provides for the security procedure to be applied to digital signatures for being treated as a secure digital signature.

Section 16 provides for the power of the Central Government to prescribe the security procedure in respect of secure electronic records and secure digital signatures. In doing so, the Central Government shall take into account various factors like nature of the transaction, level of sophistication of the technological capacity of the parties, availability and cost of alternative procedures, volume of similar transactions entered into by other parties etc.

7.7 REGULATION OF CERTIFYING AUTHORITIES (SECTIONS 17-34)

The IT Act contains detailed provisions relating to the appointment and powers of the controller and certifying Authorities. It contains sections 17 to 34.

Section 17 provides for the appointment of controller and other officers to regulate the Certifying Authorities.

Section 18 lays down the functions which the controller may perform in respect of activities of Certifying Authorities.

Section 19 provides for the power of the controller with previous approval of the Central Government to grant recognition to foreign Certifying Authorities subject to such conditions and restrictions as may be imposed regulations.

Section 20 This section provides that the controller shall be acting as repository of all Digital Signature Certificates issued under the Act. He shall also adhere to certain security procedure to ensure secrecy and privacy of the digital signatures and also to satisfy such other standards as may be prescribed by the Central Government. He shall maintain a computerised database of all public keys in such a manner that they are available to the general public.

Section 21 This section provides that a licence to be issued to a certifying authority to issue Digital Signature Certificates by the controller shall be in such from and shall be in such form and shall be accompanied with such fees and other documents as may be prescribed by the Central Government. Further, the controller after considering the application may either grant the licence or reject the application after giving reasonable opportunity of being heard.

Section 22 This section provides that the application for licence shall be accompanied by a certification practice statement and statement including the procedure with respect to identification of the applicant. It shall be further accompanied by a fee not exceeding ₹25,000 and other documents as may be prescribed by the Central Government.

Section 23 provides that the application for renewal of a *licence* shall be in such form and accompanied by such fees not exceeding ₹5,000 which may be prescribed by the Central Government.

Section 24 deals with the procedure for *grant or rejection of licence* by the controller on certain grounds.

However, that no application shall be rejected under this section unless the applicant has been given a reasonable opportunity of presenting his case.

Section 25 provides that the controller may revoke a licence on grounds such as incorrect or false material particulars being mentioned in the application and also on the ground of contravention of any provisions of the Act, rule, regulation or order made thereunder.

However, no licence shall be revoked unless the Certifying Authority has been given a reasonable opportunity of showing cause against the proposed revocation. Also, no licence shall be suspended for a period exceeding ten days unless the Certifying. Authority has been given a reasonable opportunity of showing cause against the proposed suspension. Thereafter, the controller shall publish a notice of suspension or revocation, as the case may be, shall be made available through a website which shall be accessible round the clock. It also provided that the controller may, if he considers necessary, publicise the contents of database in such electronic or other media, as he may consider appropriate.

Controller's power to delegate: Under section 27 the controller may in writing authorise the Deputy Controller, Assistant controller or any officer to exercise any of his powers under the Act.

Other powers: The controller shall have power to investigate contravention of the provisions of the Act or rules or regulations made thereunder either by himself or through any officer authorised in this behalf. The controller or any person authorised by him, shall have access to any computer system, data or any other material connected with such system if he has reasonable cause to suspect that contravention of the provision of Act or the rules or regulation is being committed.

Duties of Certifying Authorities (Section 30)

1. This section provides that every Certifying Authority shall follow certain procedures in respect of Digital Signature as given below:
   (a) make use of hardware, software, and procedures that a secure from intrusion and misuse;
   (b) provide a reasonable level of reliability in its services which are reasonably suited to the performance of intended functions;
   (c) adhere to security procedures to ensure that the secrecy and privacy of the digital signatures are assured; and
   (d) observe such other standards as may be specified by regulations.
2. Every Certifying Authority shall also ensure that every person employed by him complies with provisions of the Act, or rules, regulations or orders made thereunder.
3. A Certifying Authority must display its licence at a conspicuous place of the premises in which it carries on its business and a Certifying Authority whose licence is suspended or revoked shall immediately surrender the licence to the Controller.
4. Section 34 further provides that every Certifying Authority shall disclose its Digital Signature Certificate which contains the public key corresponding to the private key used by that Certifying Authority and other relevant facts.

7.8 DIGITAL SIGNATURE CERTIFICATION (SECTIONS 35-39)

Section 35 lays down the procedure for issuance of a Digital Signature Certificate. It provides that an application for such certificate shall be made in the prescribed form and shall be prescribed by the Central Government, and different fees may be prescribed for different classes of applicants. The section also provides that no Digital Signature Certificate shall be granted unless the Certifying Authority is satisfied that:

(a) the applicant holds the private key corresponding to the public key to be listed in the Digital Signature Certificate;
(b) the applicant holds a private key, which is capable of creating a digital signature; and
(c) the public key to be listed in the certificate can be used to verify a digital signature affixed by the private key held by the applicant.

However, no application shall be rejected unless the applicant has been given a reasonable opportunity of showing cause against the proposed rejection.

While issuing a Digital Signature Certificate the Certifying Authority should certify that it has complied with the provisions of the Act, the rules and regulations made thereunder and also with other conditions mentioned in the Digital Signature Certificate.

Suspension of Digital Signature Certificate

The Certifying Authority may suspend such certificate if it is of the opinion that such a step needs to be taken in public interest. Such certificate shall not be suspended for a period exceeding 15 days unless the subscriber has been given an opportunity of being heard. Section 38 provides for the revocation of Digital Signature Certificates under certain circumstances. Such revocation shall not be done unless the subscriber has been given an opportunity of being heard in the matter. Upon revocation or suspension the certifying Authority shall publish the notice of suspension or revocation of a Digital Signature Certificate.

7.9 DUTIES OF SUBSCRIBERS (SECTIONS 40-42)

1. On acceptance of the Digital Signature Certificate the subscriber shall generate a key pair using a secure system.

   A subscriber shall be deemed to have accepted a Digital Signature Certificate if he publishes or authorises the publication of such a signature to one more persons or otherwise demonstrates his approval of the Digital Signature Certificate. By so accepting the certificate, the subscriber certifies to the public the following.

   (a) that he holds the private key corresponding to the public key listed in the Digital Signature Certificate; and
   (b) that all the information contained in the certificate as well as material relevant to them are true.

2. The subscriber shall exercise all reasonable care to retain control of his private key corresponding to the public key. If such private key has been compromised (i.e, endangered or exposed), the subscriber must immediately communicate the fact to the Certifying Authority.

   Otherwise, the subscriber shall be liable till he has informed the Certifying Authority that the private key has been compromised.

7.10 PENALTIES AND ADJUDICATION (SECTIONS 43-47)

The Act provides for awarding compensation or damages for certain types of computer frauds. It also provides for the appointment of Adjudicating Officer for holding an inquiry in relation to certain computer crimes and for awarding compensation.

Types of Penalties

Penalty for damage to computer, computer system or network: Section 43 deals with penality for damage to computer, computer system, etc. by any of the following methods:

(a) securing access to the computer, computer system or computer network;
(b) down loading or extracting any data, computer database of information from such computer system or those stored in any removable storage medium;
(c) introducing any computer contaminant or computer virus into any computer, computer system or network;
(d) damaging any computer, computer system or network or any computer dat¡!, database or programme;
(e) disrupting any computer, computer system or network;
(f) denying access to any person authorised to access any computer, computer system or network; and
(g) providing assistance to any person to access any computer, computer system or network in contravention of any person by tampering with or manipulating any computer, computer system or network.

Explanation: For the purposes of this section

1. "computer contaminant" means any set of computer instructions that are designed:
   (a) to modify, destroy, record, transmit data or program residing within a computer, computer system or computer network; or
   (b) by any means to usurp the normal operation of the computer, computer system, or computer network;
2. "computer database" means a representation of information, knowledge, facts, concepts or instructions in text, image, audio, video that are being prepared or have been prepared in a formalised manner or have been produced by a computer, computer system or computer network and are intended for use in a computer, computer network;
3. "computer virus" means any computer instruction, information, data or program that destroys, damages, degrades or adversely affects the performance of a computer resource or attaches itself to another computer resource and operates when a programme data or instruction is executed or some other event takes place in that computer resource; and
4. "damage" means to destroy, alter, delete, add, modify or rearrange any computer resource by any means.

Section 46 confers the power of adjudicate contravention under the Act to an officer not below than the rank of a Director to the Government of India or an equivalent officer of a State Government. Such appointment shall be made by the Central Government. In order to be eligible for appointment as an adjudicating officer, a person must possess adequate experience in the field of Information Technology and such legal or judicial experience as may be prescribed by the Central Government. The adjudicating officer so appointed shall be responsible for holding an inquiry in the prescribed manner after giving reasonable opportunity of being heard and thereafter, imposing penalty where required.

Section 47 provides that while deciding upon the quantum of compensation, the adjudicating officer shall have due regard to the amount of gain of unfair advantage and the amount of loss caused to any person as well as the respective nature of the default.

Cyber Regulations Appellate Tribunal

The "Cyber Regulations Appellate Tribunal" has appellate powers in respect of orders passed by any adjudicating officer. Civil courts have been barred from entertaining any suit or proceedings in respect of any matter which an adjudicating officer or Tribunal is empowered to handle.

Section 48 provides for establishment of one or more appellate Tribunals to be known as Cyber Regulations Appellate Tribunals. It shall consist of one person only (called the Presiding Officer of the Tribunal) who shall be appointed by notification by the Central Government. Such a person must be qualified to be a judge of a High Court or is or has been a member of the Indian legal service in the post in Grade I of that service for at least three years. The presiding officer shall hold office for a term of five years or up to a maximum age limit of 65 years, whichever is earlier.

Section 52 provides for the salary and allowances and other terms and conditions of service of the presiding officer.

Section 53 provides that in the situation of any vacancy occurring in the office of the Presiding Officer of Cyber Regulations Tribunal. The Cental Government shall appoint another person in accordance with the provisions of this Act.

Resignation and removal of the presiding officer (Section 54)

The Presiding Officer shall, unless he is permitted by the Central Government to relinquish his office sooner, continue to hold office until the expiry of three months from the date of receipt of such notice or until a person duly appointed as his successor enters upon his office or until the expiry of his term of office, whichever is the earliest.

No order appointing any presiding officers shall be called in question merely on the ground of any defect in the Constitution of the Tribunal.

The Central Government shall provide such officer for the functioning of the Cyber Regulations Appellate Tribunal. It empowers the Central Government to frame rules relating to salaries, allowances and other conditions of service of such officers and employees.

Appeal to Cyber Regulations Appellate Tribunal

An appeal may be made by an aggrieved person against an order made by a adjudicating officer to the Cyber Appellate Tribunal. The appeal must be within forty-five days from the date on which the order is received. The Cyber Appellate Tribunal may entertain an appeal after the expiry of the said period of forty-five days if it is satisfied that there was sufficient cause for not filing it within that period. However, no appeal shall be entertained if the original order was passed with the consent of both parties. The Tribunal after giving both the parties an opportunity of being heard, shall pass the order as it thinks fit.

Powers and Procedure of the Appellate Tribunal

Section 58 provides for the procedure and powers of the Cyber Appellate Tribunal. The Tribunal shall also have the powers of the Civil Court under the Code of Civil Procedure 1908. Some of the powers specified are in respect of the following matters:

(a) summoning and enforcing the attendance of any person and examining him on oath
(b) requiring production of documents and other electronic records
(c) receiving evidence on affidavits
(d) reviewing its decisions
(e) issuing commissions for examination of witness, etc.

The appellant may either appear in person or may be represented by a legal practitioner to present his case before the Tribunal.

Section 60 provides for period of limitation for admission of appeals from the aggrieved persons to the Cyber Appellate Tribunal.

Section 61 provides that no court shall have jurisdiction to entertain any suit or proceeding in respect of any matter which an adjudicating officer has jurisdiction to determine.

Appeal to High Court (Section 62)

This section provides for an appeal to the High Court by an aggrieved person from the decision of the Cyber Appellate Tribunal. The appeal shall be made within sixty days from the date on which the tribunal's decision is communicated. The appeal shall be on any question of law or fact arising out of the order.

Compounding of Contravention

Section 63 provides that any contravention under the Act may be compounded by the controller or adjudication officer, either before or after the institution of the adjudication proceedings subject to such conditions as he may impose. It is also provided that such sum shall not, in any case, exceed the maximum amount of the penalty which may be imposed under this Act for the contravention so compounded. However, these provisions shall not apply to a person who commits the same or similar contravention within a period of three years from the date on which the first contravention, committed by him, was compounded.

Recovery of Penalty

Section 64 provides for recovery of penalty as arrears of land revenue and for suspension of the licence or Digital Signature Certificate till the penalty is paid.

7.11 OFFENCES

Tampering with computer source documents (Section 65): This section provides for punishment with imprisonment up to three years or with a fine which may extend to ₹2 lakh or with imprisonment up to 3 years, or with both.

Hacking with computer system (Section 66): 'Hacking' is a term used to describe the act of destroying or deleting or altering any information residing in a computer resource or diminishing its value or utility, or affecting it injuriously in spite of knowing that such action is likely to cause wrongful loss or damage to the public or that person. Section 66 provides that a person who commits hacking shall be punished with a fine up to ₹2 lakh or with imprisonment up to 3 years, or with both.

Publishing of information which is obscene in electronic form: Section 67 provides for punishment to whoever transmits or publishes or causes to be published or transmitted, any material which is obscene in electronic form with imprisonment for a term which may extended to five years and with fine which may extended to ₹1 lakh on the first conviction. In the event of second or subsequent conviction the imprisonment would be for a term which may extend to ten years and fine which may extend to ₹2 lakh.

Power of the Controller

1. **Section 68** provides the controller may give directions to certifying Authority or an employee of such authority to take such measures or cease carrying on such activities as specified in the order, so as to ensure compliance with this law. If any person fails to comply, he shall be liable to imprisonment up to 3 years or five up to ₹2 lakh, or both.
2. **Section 69** empowers the controller, if he is satisfied that it is necessary or expedient so to do in the interest of sovereignty and integrity of India. Security of the state, friendly relation with foreign states or public order, to intercept any information transmitted through any computer system or computer network.
3. **Section 70** empowers the appropriate Government to declare by notification any

computer, computer system or computer network to be protected system. Any unauthorised access of such systems will be punishable with imprisonment which may extended to ten years or with fine.

Penalty for Misrepresentation (Section 71)

This section provides that any person found misrepresenting or suppressing any material fact from the controller or the certifying authority shall be punished with imprisonment for a term which may extend to two years or with fine which may extend to ₹1 lakh or with both.

Penalty for Publishing False Digital Signature Certificate

Section 73 provides punishment for publishing a Digital Signature Certificate false in material particulars or otherwise making it available to any person with imprisonment for a term which may extend to two years or with fine which may extend to ₹1 lakh or with both.

Penalty for Fraudulent Publication (Section 74)

This Section provides for punishment with imprisonment for a term which may extend to two years or with fine which may extend to ₹1 lakh or with both to a person whoever knowingly publishes for fraudulent purpose any Digital Signature Certificate.

Act to Apply for Offence Committed Outside India

Section 75 provides for punishment for commission of any offence or contravention by a person outside India irrespective of his nationality if the act or conduct constituting the offence or contravention involves a computer, computer system or computer network located in India.

Confiscation (Section 76)

This section provides for confiscation of any computer, computer system. floppies, compact disks, tape drives or any other accessories related thereto in respect of contravention of any provision the Act, rules, regulations or orders made there under.

It is also provided that where it is established to the satisfaction of the court adjudicating the confiscation that the person in whose possession, power or control of any such computer system, floppies, compact disks, tape drives or any other accessories relating thereto is found is not responsible for the contravention of the provisions of this Act, rule, orders or regulation, made thereunder, the court may instead of making an order for confiscation of such computer, computer system, floppies, compact disks, tape drives or any other accessories related there to, make such other order authorised by this Act against the person contravening the provisions of this Act, rule, orders or regulations made thereunder as it may think fit.

Section 77 further provides that penalty and confiscation provided under this act shall not interfere with other punishment provided under any other law for the time being in force.

Section 78 provides for power to investigate the officers under the Act by a police officer not below the rank of Deputy Superintendent of Police.

7.12 NETWORK SERVICE PROVIDERS NOT TO BE LIABLE IN CERTAIN CASES

Section 79 provides that the network service providers shall be liable for any third party information or data made available by him if he proves that the offence, was committed without his knowledge or consent.

Explanation - For the purpose of this selection

(a) "network service provider" means an intermediary; and
(b) "third party information" means any information dealt with by a network service provider in his capacity as an intermediary.

Power of Central Government to Make Rules

Section 87 of the Act confers on the Central Government the power to make rules by notifying in the Official Gazette and the Electronic Gazette, in respect of certain matters, some of which are:

- the manner in which any matter may be authenticated by a digital signature;
- the manner and format in which electronic records shall be filed or issued;
- the type of digital signature, manner and format in which it may be affixed;
- the security procedure for the purpose of creating same electronic record and secure digital signature;
- the qualifications, experience and terms and conditions of service of Controller, Deputy Controllers and Assistant Controllers;
- the requirements, manner and form in which application is to be made for a licence to issue Digital Signature Certificates;
- the period of validity of the licence;

- the qualification, experience of an adjudicating officer, as well as other officers; and
- the salary, allowances and terms and conditions of service of the presiding officer, etc.

Every notification made by the Central Government shall be laid, as soon as possible after it is made, before each House of Parliament, while it is in session, for a total period of thirty days. This period may be comprised in one session or in two or more successive sessions. If before the expiry of the session immediately following the above period, both the Houses agree in making any modification, the rule will thereafter have effect only in the modified form. Similarly if both the Houses agree that the rule should not be made, the notification shall have no effect, thereafter.

Power of State Government to Make Rules

The State Government may by notification in the Official Gazette, make rules to carry out the provisions of this Act. Such rules may provide for all or any of the following matters:

- the electronic form in which filing, issue, grant receipt or payment shall be effected in respect of use of electronic records and digital signatures in Government and its agencies;
- the manner and format in which such electronic records shall be filed or issued and the fee or charges in connection of the same; and
- any other matter required to be provided by rules by the State Government. Every such rule shall be laid before each House of the State Legislature.

Cyber Revelations Advisory Committee

The Cyber Regulations Advisory Committee shall be constituted by the Cental Government. It shall consist of a chairperson and such member of official and non-official members as the Central Government shall deem fit. Such members shall have special knowledge of the subject matter or the interest principally affected. The committee shall advise the Central Government on any rules or any other purpose connected with the Act, and the Controller in framing regulations under this Act.

Power of Controller to Make Regulations

The Controller has been given powers under Section 89 to make regulations consistent with the Act and the related rules to carry out the purpose of this Act. However, he may do so after consultation with the Cyber Regulations Advisory Committee and with the previous approval of the Central Government on any rules or any other purpose connected with the Act, and the Controller in framing regulations under this Act.

1. the particulars relating to maintenance subject to which the controller may recognise any of every Certifying Authority;
2. the conditions and restrictions subject to which the controller may recognise any foreign Certifying Authority;
3. the terms and conditions subject to which a licence may be granted ;
4. other standard to be observed by the Certifying Authority;
5. the manner in which the Certifying Authority may make the disclosure under Section 34;
6. the particulars of statement to be submitted along with an application for the issue of a Digital Signature Certificate; and
7. the manner in which the subscriber should communicate the compromise of private key to the Certifying Authority.

The procedure for passing the resolution is the same as given in section 87 in respect of notifying rules by the Central Government.

Power of Police Officer and Other Officers to Enter, Search etc.

Section 80 provides that notwithstanding anything contained in the code of Criminal Procedure, 1973, any police officer, not below the rank of a Deputy Superintendent of Police, or any other officer of the Central or State Government, if so authorised by the Central Government, may either any public place and search and arrest without warrant any person found therein who is reasonably suspected of having committed or of committing or is about to commit any offence under this Act. For this, purpose, 'public place' would include a public conveyance, any hotel, any shop or any other place accessible to the public.

The section further provides that where any person is arrested by an officer other than a police officer, such officer shall immediately send the arrested person to a magistrate having jurisdiction or to the officer in charge of a police station.

Liability of Companies (Section 85)

Where a company commits any offence under this Act or any rule thereunder, every person who, at the time of the contravention, was in change of and was responsible for the conduct of the business of the company shall be guilty of the contravention. However, he shall not be liable to punishment if he proves that the contravention took place without his knowledge or that he exercised all due diligence to prevent the contravention.

Further, where a contravention has been committed by a company, and it is proved that the contravention took place with the connivance or consent of or due to any negligence on the part of any director, manager, secretary or other officer of the company, such officer shall be deemed to be guilty and shall be liable to be proceeded against and punished accordingly. For the purpose of this section, 'company' includes a firm or other association of persons and 'director' in relation to a firm means a partner in the firm.

An Appraisal of the I.T. Act 2000

The Information Technology Act will go a long way in facilitating and regulating electronic commerce. It has provided a legal framework for smooth conduct of e-commerce. It has tackled the following legal issues associated with e-commerce.

(a) requirement of a writing; (b) requirement of a document; (c) requirement of a signature; and Cd) requirement of legal recognition for electronic messages, records and documents to be admitted in evidence in a court of law.

However, the Act, has not addressed the following grey areas:

(i) protection for domain names;
(ii) infringement of copyright laws;
(iii) jurisdiction aspect of electronic contracts (*viz.* jurisdiction of courts and tax authorities);
(iv) taxation of goods and services trades through e-commerce; and
(v) stamp duty aspect of electronic contracts.

The Central Government introduced in the winter session of Parliament a Bill styled "Digital Copy Right Bill, 2000" with a view to protecting the copyright of subscribers who have obtained Digital Signature Certificates from the certifying authorities.

QUESTIONS FOR PRACTICE

Section - A (Two Marks Questions)

1. What is hacking?

2. What is digital signature?

3. What is computer virus?

4. What do you mean by e-governance?

5. State the objectives of Information Technology Act.

6. Distinguish between private key and public key.

Section - B (Five Marks Questions)

1. Explain cyber crime.
2. What is Information Technology Act? What are its objectives?

Section - C (Fifteen Marks Questions)

1. What are the penalties imposed on the defaulting party under the Information Technology Act, 2000?
2. Explain the salient features of Information Technology Act, 2000.
3. Explain in detail the various offences under the Information Technology Act, 2000.
4. Explain in detail the provisions pertaining to piracy of copyrights and trademarks.

CHAPTER 8

THE COMPETITION ACT, 2002

8.1 INTRODUCTION

Competition makes any business live and it is the most challenging attempt on the part of the business to take competition in its varied from India, being an agrarian economy had never given a serious though for the most essential aspect of marketing the goods i.e., competition. It was during the opening up for global endeavour even economies like India resorted to its basic concepts, not only our country, even all most all countries which wanted to market its products across the boundaries started on the lines of the other counterparts and stood in the race of competition.

One of the major hurdles in the way of success for Indian corporate sector was the 'unorganised nature' of business units, non-uniformity in product manufacturing for international market, value based business attitude and so on, thus to overcome all these and to achieve success at par with other countries it was very much necessary for Indian markets to prepare for unassuming challenge in the form of global competition. In a way the policy of liberalisation, privatisation and globalisation paved the much needed way for global competition. Almost all the developing economies started encouraging the private participation in most all hitherto controlled business ventures. No unit of business was left untouched by the global competition. The very attitude of authorities was changed and many entrepreneurial ventures were not only encouraged but even funded during their gestation periods.

It was ultimately the emergence of free economy at global standard and every independent country tried to support the cause and benefits of globalisation, privatisation and liberalisation. Restrictions which were so common earlier to this Act, in the from of MRTP Act, 1969 were totally deferred and in the place a new approach of being more liberal, industry-friendly attitude was started gearing up. Even the global changes made the other countries to fall in line with the latest changes by these economies and India too had shown the same spirit and interest to change from dogmatic attitude to liberal and practical attitude of business activities. Thus, on 22nd May 2000, in its recommendations the high level committee on policies, rules, regulation and ultimately the law making body, clearly stated that there is need to have new law titled "The competition Act 2002" replacing completely the present MRTP Act 1969.

Title: *This Act shall be called 'The Competition Act 2002'.*

Scope: *The Act shall apply to the entire Union of India except, the states of Jammu and Kashmir.*

Objectives: *The main objectives of the Competition Act, 2002 are:*

(a) To encourage fair trade practices and protect the interest of consumers.
(b) To prevent all such trade practices which may contribute negatively in Indian Markets.
(c) Establishment of Competition Commission of India (CCI), thereby controlling the negative aspect of competition.
(d) To provide a fair and free atmosphere for trade activities carried on by other participants in markets in India.
(e) To stop all unfair trade practices followed by markets in India.

8.2 DEFINITIONS

The Competition Act of 2002, contains many terms which have their unique meaning and application as per the law. It is beneficial to have the understanding of these special terms used in the Act. All the terms are placed in section 2 of the Act, some important terms are as follows:

1. **Acquisition: [Section 2(a)]** means directly or indirectly, acquiring or agreeing to acquire

   (a) shares, voting rights or assets of any enterprise; or
   (b) control over management or Control over any enterprise.

2. **Agreement: [Sec 2(b)]** refers to an agreement which includes any arrangement or understanding or action in concern:

   (a) whether or not, such arrangements, understanding or action is formal or in writing; or
   (b) whether or not such arrangement, understanding or action is intended to be enforceable by legal proceedings.

3. **Cartel [Section 2(c)]** Cartel refers and includes an association of producers, sellers, distributors, traders or service providers who, by agreement amongst themselves, limit,

control or attempt to control the production, distribution, sale or price of or trade in goods or provision of services.

4. **Consumers [Section 2(f)]** means any person who:

   (a) buys any goods for a consideration which has been paid or promised or partly paid and partly promised, or under any system of deferred payment and includes any user of such goods other than the person who buys such goods for consideration paid or promised or partly paid or partly promised, or under any system of deferred payment when such use is made with the approval of such person, whether such purchase of goods is for resale or for any commercial purpose or for personal use;

   (b) hires or avails of any services for a consideration which has been paid or promised or partly paid and partly promised, or under any system of deferred payment and includes any beneficiary of such services other than the person who hires or avails of the services for consideration paid or promised, or partly paid and partly promised, or under any system of deferred payment, when such services are availed of with the approval of the first-mentioned person whether such hiring or availing of services is for any commercial purpose or for personal use.

5. **Enterprise [Section 2(h)]** means a person or a department of the Government, who or which is, or has been, engaged in any activity, relating to the production, storage, supply, distribution, acquisition or control of articles or goods, or the provisions of services, of any kind, or in investment, or in the business of acquiring, holding, underwriting or dealing with shares, debentures or other securities of any other body corporate, either directly or through one or more of its units or divisions or subsidiaries, whether such unit or division or subsidiary is located at the same place where the enterprise is located or at a different place or at different places, but does not include any activity of the Government relatable to the sovereign functions of the Government including all activities carried on by the departments of the Central Government dealing with atomic energy, currency, defence and space.

   Explanation: For the purposes of this clause:

   (a) "activity" includes profession or occupation;

   (b) "article" includes a new article and "service" includes a new service;

   (c) "unit" or "division", in relation to an enterprise, includes:

      i. a plant or factory established for the production, storage, supply, distribution, acquisition or control of any article or goods;

      ii. any branch or office established for the provision of any service;

6. **Goods** means goods as defined in the Sale of Goods Act, 1930 and includes:

(a) products manufactured, processed or mined;
(b) debentures, stocks and shares after allotment; and
(c) in relation to goods supplied, distributed or controlled in India, goods imported into India.

7. **Person [Section 2(l)]** includes
   (a) an individual;
   (b) a Hindu undivided family;
   (c) a company;
   (d) a firm;
   (e) an association of person or body of individual, whether incorporated or not, in India or outside India;
   (f) any corporation established by or under any central, state or provincial act or a Government company as defined in Section 617 of the Companies Act, 1956;
   (g) Any body corporate incorporated by or under the law of a country outside India;
   (h) a co-operative society registered under any law relating to co-operative societies;
   (i) a local authority; and
   (j) every artificial juridical person not falling within any of the preceding sub-clauses.
8. **Practice [Section 2(m)]** means and includes any practice relating to the carrying on of any trade by a person or an enterprise.
9. **Price [Section 2(o)]** means price in relation to the sale of any goods or to the performance of any services, includes every valuable consideration, whether direct or indirect, or deferred and includes any consideration which in effect relates to the sale of any goods or to the performance of any services although ostensibly relating to any other matter or things.
10. **Relevant market [Section 2(r)]** means, the market which may be determined by the Competition Commission with reference to the relevant product market or the relevant geographic market or with reference to both the markets.
11. **Relevant geographic [Section 2(s)]** means, a market comprising the area in which the conditions of competition for supply of goods or provision of services or demand of goods or services are distinctly homogeneous and can be distinguished from the conditions prevailing in the neighbouring areas.
12. **Relevant product market [Section 2(t)]** means, a market comprising all those products or services which are regarded as interchangeable or substitutable by the

consumer, by reason of characteristics of the products or services, their prices and intended use.

13. **Public Financial Institution [Section 2(p)]** means, a public financial institution specified u/s 4A of the Companies Act, 1956 and includes a state financial, Industrial or Investment Corporation.

14. **Trade [Section 2(x)]** means any trade, business, industry profession or occupation relating to the production, supply, distribution, storage or control of goods and includes the provision of any services.

15. **Service [Section 2(u)]** means, service of any description which is made available to the potential users. It includes the provisions of services in connection with business of any industrial or commercial matters, such as accounting, banking, communication, education, financing, insurance, chit-funds, real estate, transport, storage, material treatment processing, supply of electrical or other energy, boarding, lodging, entertainment, amusement, construction, repair, conveying of news or information and advertising.

16. **Shares [Section 2(v)]** means, shares in the share capital of a company carrying voting rights and includes

    (a) any security which entitles the holder to receive shares with voting right.
    (a) stock expect where a distinction between stock and share is expressed or implied.

17. **Statutory Authority [Section 2(w)]** means, any authority, board, corporation, council, institute, university or any other body corporate, established by or under any central, State or provincial Act for the purpose of regulating product or supply of goods or provision of any services or market there for of any mater connected therewith or incidental thereto.

18. **Turnover [Section 2(y)]** means and includes value of sale of goods or services.

8.3 PROHIBITION OF CERTAIN AGREEMENTS

Anti-competitive Agreements (Section 3)

No enterprise or association of enterprises or person or association of persons shall enter into any agreement in respect of production, supply. distribution, storage, acquisition or control of goods or provision of services, which causes or is likely to cause an appreciable adverse effect on competition within India.

Any agreement entered into in contravention of the provisions shall be void.

Any agreement entered into between enterprises or associations of enterprises of persons or associations of persons or between any person and enterprise or practice carried on, or decision taken by, any association of enterprises or association of persons, including cartels, engaged in identical or similar trade of goods or provision of services, which:

(a) directly or indirectly determines purchase or sale prices;
(b) shares the market of source of production or provision of services way of allocation or geographical area of market, or type of goods or services. or number of customers in the market or any other similar way; or
(c) directly or indirectly results in bid rigging or collusive bidding, shall be presumed to have an appreciable adverse effect on competition.

8.3.1 Analysis

Competition means striking against each other for settling something desired or doing something desired or doing something in the best manner possible a trial of ability. It is a contest between two rivals, or the answering all requirements; having sufficient capacity, ability or authority; possessing the requisite physical, mental, natural or legal qualifications.

Section 3 of the Competition Act, 2002, provides for prohibition of entering into anti-competitive agreements. It shall not be lawful for any enterprise or association of enterprises or person or association of persons to enter into an agreement in respect of production, supply, storage, distribution, acquisition or control of goods or provision of service which causes or is likely to cause an appreciable adverse effects on competition within India. All such agreements entered into in contravention of the aforesaid prohibition shall be void. This clause also specifies certain activities which shall be presumed to have an appreciable adverse effect on competition and also specifies certain agreements which shall be in contravention if such agreoment causes appreciable adverse effects on competition.

Agreement or understanding between two or more persons, in the form of a contract trust, holding company, or other form of association, for the purpose of unduly restricting competition, monopolising trade and commerce in a certain commodity, controlling its production, distribution, and or otherwise interfering with freedom of trade without statutory authority.

Combination in restraint of trade is an effort of two or more parties, acting independently, to secure the business of a third party by the offer of the most favourable terms; also the relations between different buyers or different sellers which result from this effort. It is the struggle between rivals for the same trade at the same time; the act of seeking or endeavouring to gain what another is endeavouring to gain at the same time. The term implies the idea of endeavouring by two or more to obtain the same object or result.

A combination formed for the purpose of and with the effect of raising, depressing, fixing, pegging, or stabilising the price of a commodity is called "price-fixing". It is a co-operative setting of price levels or range by competing firms, which would otherwise be set by natural market forces. Such agreements are prohibited in the US by the Sherman Anti-trust Act. Price-fixing within intent of Sherman Act is either horizontal (dealing with arrangements among competitors, as between competing retailers) or vertical (attempting to control resale price, as agreements between manufacturer and retailer).

8.4 PROHIBITION OF ABUSE OF DOMINANT POSITION (SECTION 4)

No enterprise shall abuse its dominant position. There shall be an abuse of dominant position under sub-section (1), if an enterprise:

(a) directly or indirectly, imposes unfair or discriminatory:
   (i) condition in purchase or sale of goods or services; or
   (ii) price in purchase or sale (including predatory price) of goods or service; or

   Explanation: the unfair or discriminatory condition in purchase or sale of goods or services and unfair or discriminatory price in purchase or sale of goods (including predatory price) or service shall not include such discriminatory conditions or prices which may be adopted to meet the competition; or

(b) limits or restricts:
   (i) production of goods or provision of services or market there for; or
   (ii) technical or scientific development relating to goods or services to the prejudice of consumers; or

(c) indulges in practice or practices resulting in denial of market access; or

(d) makes conclusion of contracts subject to acceptance by other parties of supplementary obligations which, by their nature or according to commercial usage, have no connection with the subject of such contracts; or

(e) uses its dominant position in one relevant market to enter into, or protect, other relevant market.

8.4.1 Analysis

"**Dominant position**" means a position of strength, enjoyed by an enterprise, in the relevant market, in India, which enables it to

(i) operate independently of competitive forces prevailing in the relevant market; or
(ii) affect its competitors or consumers or the relevant market in its favour.

"**Predatory price**" means the sale of goods or provision of services, at a price which is below the cost, as may be determined by regulations, of production of the goods or provision of services, with a view to reduce competition or eliminate the competitors.

8.4.2 Comments

Section 4, prohibits abuse of dominant position by any enterprise. Such abuse of dominant position, *inter alia*, includes imposition, either directly or indirectly, of unfair or discriminatory purchase or selling prices or conditions, including predatory prices of goods or service, limiting production or restricting of goods or provision of service, indulging in practices resulting in denial of market access, making the conclusion of contracts subject to acceptance by other parties of supplementary obligations and using dominant position in one market to enter into or protect other market.

Amalgamation-Absorption [Section 5]

The acquisition of one or more enterprises by one or more persons or merger or amalgamation of enterprises shall be a combination of such enterprises and persons or enterprises, if:

(a) any acquisition where:

 (i) the parties to the acquisition, being the acquirer and the enterprise, whose control, shares, voting rights or assets have been acquired or are being acquired jointly have,

  - either, in India, the assets of title value of more than rupees one thousand crore or turnover more than rupees three thousand crore; or
  - in India or outside India, in aggregate, the assets of the value of more than five hundred million US dollars or turnover more than fifteen hundred million US dollars; or

 (ii) the group, to which the enterprise whose control, shares, assets or voting rights have been acquired or are being acquired, would belong after the acquisition jointly have or would jointly have,

  - either in India, the assets of the value of more than rupees four thousand crore or turnover more than rupees twelve thousand crore; or
  - in India or outside India, in aggregate, the assets of the value of more than two billion US dollars or turnover more than six billion US dollars; or

(b) acquiring of control by a person over an enterprise when such person has already direct or indirect control over another enterprise engaged in production, distribution or trading of a similar or identical or substitutable goods or provision of a similar or identical or substitutable service, if:

 (i) the enterprise over which control has been acquired along with the enterprise over which the acquirer already has direct or indirect control jointly have,

  - either in India, the assets of the value of more than rupees one thousand crore or turnover more than rupees three thousand crore; or

- in India or outside India, in aggregate, the assets of the value of more than five hundred million US dollars or turnover more than fifteen hundred million US dollars; or

(ii) the group, to which enterprise whose control has been acquired, or is being acquired would belong after the acquisition, jointly have or would jointly have,

- either in India, the assets of the value of more than rupees four thousand crore or turnover more than rupees twelve thousand crore; or
- in India or outside India, in aggregate, the assets of the value of more than two billion US dollars or turnover more than six billion US dollars; or

(c) any merger or amalgamation in which

(i) the enterprise remaining after merger or the enterprise created as a result of the amalgamation, as the case may be, have,

- either in India, the assets of the value of more than rupees one thousand crore or turnover more than rupees three thousand crore; or
- in India or outside India, in aggregate, the assets of the value of more than five hundred million US dollars or turnover more than fifteen hundred million US dollars; or

(ii) the group, or its constituent enterprise remaining after the merger or the enterprise created as a result of the amalgamation, would belong after the merger or the amalgamation, as the case may be, have or would have,

- either in India, the assets of the value of more than rupees four thousand crore or turnover more than rupees twelve thousand crore; or
- in India or outside India, the assets of the value of more than two billion US dollars or turnover more than six billion US dollars.

Explanation: For the purposes of this section,

(a) "control" includes controlling the affairs or management by

(i) one or more enterprises, either jointly or singly, over another enterprise or group;

(ii) one or more groups, either jointly or singly, over another group or enterprise;

(b) "group" means two or more enterprises which, directly or indirectly, are in a position to

(i) exercise twenty-six per cent or more of the voting rights in the other enterprise; or

(ii) appoint more than fifty per cent of the members of the Board of Directors in the other enterprise; or

(iii) control the management or affairs of the other enterprise;

(c) the value of assets shall be determined by taking the book value of the assets as shown, in the audited books of account of the enterprise, in the financial year immediately preceding the financial year in which the date of proposed merger falls, as reduced by any depreciation, and the value of assets shall include the brand value, value of goodwill, or value of copyright, patent, permitted use, collective mark, registered proprietor, registered trademark, registered user, homonymous geographical indication, geographical indications, design or layout-design or similar other commercial rights, if any.

Comments: Sec. 5 of the Act, deals with combination of enterprises and persons. The acquisition of one or more enterprises by one or more persons or acquiring of control or merger or amalgamation of enterprises under certain circumstances specified in the said clause shall be construed as combination.

Regulation of Combinations (Section 6)

No person or enterprise shall enter into a combination which causes or is likely to cause an appreciable adverse effect on competition within the relevant market and such a combination shall be void. Any person or enterprise, who or which proposes to enter into a combination, may, at his or its option, give notice to the Commission, in the form as may be specified, and the fee which may be determined, by regulations, disclosing the details of the proposed combination, within seven days of:

(a) approval of the proposal relating to merger or amalgamation, referred to in clause (c) of Section 5, by the Board of Directors of the enterprises concerned with such merger or amalgamation, as the case may be;

(b) execution of any agreement or other document for acquisition referred to in clause (a) of Section 5 or acquiring of control referred to in clause (b) of that Section.

The Commission shall, after receipt of notice deal with such notice in accordance with the provisions contained in Sections 29, 30 and 31.

The provisions of this Section shall not apply to share subscription or financing facility or any acquisition, by a public financial institution, foreign institutional investor, bank or venture capital fund, pursuant to any covenant of a loan agreement or investment agreement.

The public financial institution, foreign institutional investor, bank or venture capital fund, shall, within seven days from the date of the acquisition, file, in the form as may be specified by regulations, with the Commission the details of the acquisition including the details of control, the circumstances for exercise of such control and the consequences of default arising out of such loan agreement or investment agreement, as the case may be.

Comments: Under Section 6, no person or enterprise shall enter into a combination which is likely to cause or causes an appreciable adverse effects on competition within the relevant market in India. It further provides exemption from the provisions of this clause to certain institutions.

8.5 COMPETITION COMMISSION OF INDIA (CCI)

Section 7 to 17 of the Act deals with establishment, process and other concepts of CCI. The Act empowers the establishment of CCI, in the form of a body corporate with all the characteristics of a legal company with perpetual succession, having a common seal, can sue, be sued, can hold property, dispose of the property. The place of operation of Commission shall be decided by the Central Government and it has also further empowered it to have branches throughout India.

Composition of Commission

The Commission shall consist of a Chairperson and not less than two and not more than ten other Members to be appointed by the Central Government. The Central Government shall appoint the Chairperson and a Member during the first year of the establishment of the Commission. A person who is or has been or is qualified to be a judge of a High Court or is having special knowledge of, and professional experience in, not less than fifteen years in International trade, economics, business, commerce, law, finance, accountancy, management, industry, public affairs, administration or in any other matter which, in the opinion of the Central Government, be useful to the Commission shall be eligible for appointment as the Chairperson or as a Member.

Selection of Chairperson and other Members

The Chairperson and other Members shall be selected in the manner as may be prescribed.

Term of office of Chairperson and other Members

The Chairperson and every other Member shall hold office as such for a term of five years from the date on which he enters upon his office and shall be eligible for reappointment:

No Chairperson shall hold office after he attains the age of seventy years and no other member shall hold office after he attains the age of sixty-five years. This section also provides for discharge of functions of the Chairperson by the senior most member in case the Chairperson is unable to discharge his functions.

Resignation, removal and suspension of Chairperson and other Members

Resignation: The Chairperson or any other Member may, by notice in writing under his hand addressed to the Central Government, resign his office: The Chairperson or a Member shall, unless he is permitted by the Central Government to relinquish his office sooner, continue to hold office until the expiry of three months from the date of receipt of such notice or until a person duly appointed as his successor enters upon his office or until the expiry of his term of office whichever is the earliest.

Removal: The Central Government may, by order, remove the Chairperson or any other Member from his office if such Chairperson or Member, as the case may be:

(a) is, or at any time has been, adjudged as an insolvent; or
(b) has engaged at any time, during his term of office, in any paid employment; or
(c) has been convicted of an offence which, in the opinion of the Central Government involves moral turpitude; or
(d) has acquired such financial or other interest as is likely to affect prejudicially his functions as a Member; or
(e) has so abused his position as to render his continuance in office prejudicial to the public interest; or
(f) has become physically or mentally incapable of acting as a Member.

No Member shall be removed from his office on the ground specified unless the Supreme Court, on a reference being made to it in this behalf by the Central Government, has, on an inquiry, held by it in accordance with such procedure as may be prescribed in this behalf by the Supreme Court, reported that the member, ought on such ground or grounds to be romoved.

Restriction on employment of Chairperson and other Members in certain cases

The Chairperson and other Members shall not, for a period of one year from the date on which they cease to hold office, accept any employment in, or connected with the management or administration of, any enterprise which has been a party to a proceeding before the Commission under this Act:

Financial and administrative powers of Member Administration

The Central Government shall designate any Member as Member Administration who shall exercise such financial administrative powers as may be vested in him under the rules made by the Central Government. The Member Administration shall have authority to delegate such of his financial and administrative powers as he may think fit to any other officer of the commission subject to the condition, that, such officer shall, while exercising such delegated powers continue to act under the direction, superintendence and control of the Member Administration. The salary, and the other terms and conditions of service of the Chairperson and other Members including travelling expenses shall not be varied to his disadvantage after appointment.

Vacancy, etc., not to invalidate proceedings of Commission

No act or proceeding of the Commission shall be invalid merely by reason of

(a) any vacancy in, or any defect in the constitution of, the Commission; or

(b) any defect in the appointment of a person acting as a Chairperson or as a Member

(c) any irregularity in the procedure of the Commission not affecting the merits of the case.

Appointment of Director General, etc.

The Central Government may, by notification, appoint a Director General and as many Additional, Joint, Deputy or Assistant Directors General or such other advisers, consultants or officer as it may think fit, for the purposes of assisting the Commission in conducting inquiry into contravention of any of the provisions of this Act and for the conduct of cases before the Commission and for performing such other functions as are, or may be, provided by or under this Act.

Every Additional, Joint, Deputy and Assistant Directors General or such other advisers, consultants or officers, shall exercise his powers, and discharge his functions, subject to the general control, supervision and direction of the Director General.

The salary, allowances and other terms and conditions of service of the Director General and Additional, Joint, Deputy and Assistant Directors General or such other advisers, consultants or officers, shall be such as may be prescribed.

The Director General, and Additional, Joint, Deputy and Assistant Directors General or such other advisers, consultants or officers, shall be appointed from amongst persons of integrity and outstanding ability and who have experience in investigation; and knowledge of accountancy management, business, public administration, international trade, law or economics and such other qualifications as may be prescribed.

Registrar and officers and other employees of Commission

The Commission may appoint a Registrar and such officers and other employees, as it considers necessary for the efficient performance of its functions under this Act. The salaries and allowances payable to and other terms and conditions of service of the Registrar and officers and other employees of the Commission and the number of such officers and employees shall be such as may be prescribed.

8.6 DUTIES, POWERS AND FUNCTIONS OF COMMISSION (SECTIONS 18 TO 40)

Duties of Commission

Subject to the provisions of this Act, it shall be the duty of the Commission to eliminate practices having adverse effect on competition, promote and sustain competition, protect the interests of consumers, and ensure freedom of trade carried on by other participants, in markets in India: The Commission may, for the purpose of discharging its duties or performing its functions under this Act, enter into any memorandum or arrangement, with the prior approval of the Central Government, with any agency of any foreign country.

Inquiry into certain agreements and dominant position of enterprise

The Commission may inquire into any alleged contravention of the provisions either on its own notion or on:

(a) receipt of a complaint, accompanied by such fee as may be determined by regulations, from any person, consumer or their association or trade association; or
(b) a reference made to it by the Central Government or a State Government or a statutory authority.

The Commission shall, while determining whether an agreement has an appreciable adverse effect on competition, have due regard to all or any of the following factors, namely:

(a) certain of barriers to new entrants in the market;
(b) driving existing competitors out of the market;
(c) foreclosure of competition by hindering entry into the market;
(d) accrual of benefits of consumers;
(e) improvements in production or distribution of goods or provision of services; or
(f) promotion of technical, scientific and economic development by means, of production or distribution of goods or provision of services.

The Commission shall, while inquiring whether an enterprise enjoys a dominant position or not have due regard to all or any of the following factors, namely:

(a) market share of the enterprise;
(b) size and resources of the enterprise;
(c) size and importance of the competitors;
(d) economic power of the enterprise including commercial advantages over competitors;
(e) vertical integration of the enterprises or sale or service network of such enterprises;
(f) dependence of consumers on the enterprise;
(g) monopoly or dominant position whether acquired as a result of any statute or by virtue of being a government company or a public sector undertaking or otherwise;
(h) entry barriers including barriers such as regulatory barriers, financial risk, high capital cost of entry, marketing entry barriers, technical entry barriers, economies of scale, high cost of substitutable goods or service for consumers;
(i) countervailing buying power;
(j) market structure and size of market;
(k) social obligations and social costs;
(l) relative advantage, by way of the contribution to the economic development, by the enterprise enjoying a dominant position having or likely to have appreciable adverse effect on competition;
(m) any other factor which the Commission may consider relevant for the inquiry.

For determining whether a market constitutes a "relevant market" for the purposes of this Act, the Commission shall have due regard to the "relevant geographic market" or "relevant product market". The Commission shall, while determining the "relevant geographic market", have due regard to any of the following factors:

(a) regulatory trade barriers;
(b) local specification requirements;
(c) national procurement policies;
(d) adequate distribution facilities;
(e) transport costs;
(f) language;
(g) consumer preferences; and
(h) need for secure or regular supplies or rapid after-services.

The Commission shall, while determining the "relevant product market", have due regard to all or any of the following factors, namely:

(a) physical characteristics or end-use of goods;
(b) price of goods or services;
(c) consumer preference;

(d) exclusion of in-house production;
(e) existence of specialised production; and
(f) classification of specialised producers.

Inquiry into Combination by Commission

The Commission may, upon its own knowledge or information relating to acquisition referred to or acquiring of control referred to or merger or amalgamation referred to inquire into whether such a combination has caused or is likely to cause an appreciable adverse effect on competition in India.

The Commission shall not initiate any inquiry after the expiry of one year from the date on which such combination has taken effect.

The Commission shall, on receipt of a notice or upon receipt of a reference, inquire whether a combination referred to in that notice or reference has caused or is likely to cause an appreciable adverse effect on competition in India.

The Central Government shall, on the expiry of a period of two years from the date of commencement of this Act and thereafter every two years, in consultation with the Commission, by notification, enhance or reduce, on the basis of the wholesale price index or fluctuations in exchange rate of rupee or foreign currencies, the value of assets or the value of turnover, for the purposes of that section.

For the purposes of determining whether a combination would have the effect of or is likely to have an appreciable adverse effect on competition in the relevant market, the Commission shall have due regard to all or any of the following factors, namely:

(a) actual and potential level of competition through imports in the market;
(b) extent of barriers to entry to the market;
(c) level of combination in the market;
(d) degree of countervailing power in the market;
(e) likelihood that the combination would result in the parties to the combination being able to significantly and sustainably increase prices or profit margins;
(f) extent of effective competition likely to sustain in a market;
(g) extent to which substitutes are available or are likely to be available in the market;
(h) market share, in the relevant market, of the persons or enterprise in a combination, individually and as a combination;
(i) likelihood that the combination would result in the removal of a vigorous and effective competitor or competitors in the market;
(j) nature and extent of vertical integration in the market;
(k) possibility of a failing business;
(l) nature and extent of innovation;

(m) relative advantage, by way of the contribution to the economic development, by any combination having or likely to have appreciable adverse effect on competition; and

(n) whether the benefits of the combination outweigh the adverse impact of the combination, if any.

Reference by Statutory Authority

If in the course of a proceeding before any statutory authority, entrusted with the responsibility of regulating any goods or service or market there for, a party has raised an issue that the decision taken by the statutory authority would be contrary to the provision of the Act, then the statutory authority shall be bound to make a reference to the Commission, The Commission will, after hearing parties to the proceedings shall, give to the statutory authority its opinion and the statutory authority shall thereafter pass its orders.

Benches of Commission

The jurisdiction, powers and authority of the Commission may be exercised by Benches thereof, the Benches shall be constituted by the Chairperson and each Bench shall consist of not less than two Members. Every Bench shall consist of at least one Judicial Member.

Explanation: For the purposes of this sub-section, "Judicial Member" means a Member who is, or has been, or is qualified to be, a Judge of a High Court.

The Bench over which the Chairperson presides shall be the Principal Bench and the other Benches shall be known as the Additional Benches. There shall be constituted by the Chairperson one or more Benches to be called the Mergers Bench or Mergers Benches, as the case may be, exclusively to deal with matters referred to in sections 5 and 6. The places as which the Principal Bench, other Additional Bench or Mergers Bench shall ordinarily sit shall be such as the Central Government may, by notification, specify.

Distribution of business amongst Commission Benches (Section 23)

Where any Benches are constituted, the Chairperson may, from time to time, by order, make provisions as to the distribution of the business of the Commission amongst the Benches and specify the matters, which may be dealt with by each Bench.

If any question arises as to whether any matter falls within the purview of the business allocated to a Bench, the decision of the Chairperson thereon shall be final.

The Chairperson, may transfer a Member from one Bench to another Bench; or authorise the Members of one Bench to discharge also the functions of the Members of other Bench:

The Chairperson shall transfer, with the prior approval of the Central Government, a Member from one Bench situated in one city to another Bench situated in another city.

The Chairperson may, for the purpose of securing that any case or matter which having regard to the nature of the questions involved, requires or is required in his opinion or under the rules made by the Central Government in this behalf, to be decided by a Bench composed of more than two Members, issue such general or special orders as he may deem fit.

Procedure for deciding a case where Members of Bench differ in opinion

If the Members of a Bench differ in opinion on any point, they shall state the point or points on which they differ, and make a reference to the Chairperson who shall either near the point or points himself or refer the case for hearing on such point or points by one or more of the other Members and such point or points shall be decided according the opinion of the majority of the Members who have heard the case, including those who first heard it.

Jurisdiction of Bench

An inquiry shall be initiated or a complaint be instituted or a reference be made under this Act before a Bench within the local limits of whose jurisdiction:

(a) the respondent, or each of the respondents, where there are more than one, at the time of the initiation of inquiry or institution of the complaint or making of reference, as the case may be, actually and voluntarily resides, or carries on business, or personally works for gain; or

(b) any of the respondents, where there are more than one, at the time of the initiation of the inquiry or institution of complaint or making of reference, as the case may be, actually and voluntarily resides or carries on business or personally works for gain provided that in such case either the leave of the Bench is given, or the respondents who do not reside, or carry on business, or personally works for gain, as aforesaid, acquiesce, in such institution; or

(c) the cause of action, wholly or in part, arises.

Procedure for inquiry on complaints

On receipt of a complaint or a reference from the Central Government or a State Government or a statutory authority or on its own knowledge or information, under Section 19, if the Commission is of the opinion that there exists a *prima facie* case, it shall direct the Director General to cause an investigation to be made into the matter. The Director General shall, submit a report on his findings within such period as may be specified by the Commission. Where on receipt of a complaint the Commission is of the opinion that there exists no *prima facie* case, it shall dismiss the complaint and may pass such orders as it deems fit, including imposition of costs, if necessary.

The Commission shall forward a copy of the report to the parties concerned or to the Central Government or the State Government or the statutory authority, as the case maybe.

If the report of the Director General relates on a complaint and such report recommends that there is no contravention of any of the provisions of this Act, the complainant shall be given an opportunity to rebut the findings of the Director General. If, after hearing the complainant, the Commission agrees with the recommendation of the Director General, it shall dismiss the complaint. If, after hearing the complainant, the Commission is of the opinion that further inquiry is called for, it shall direct the complainant to proceed with the complaint. If the report of the Director General relates on a reference made and such report recommends that there is no contravention of the provisions of this Act, the Commission shall invite comments of the Central Government or the State Government or the statutory authority, as the case may be, on such report and on receipt of such comments, the Commission shall return the reference if there is no *prima facie* case or proceed with the reference as a complaint if there is a *prima facie* case.

If the report of the Director General recommends that there is contravention of any of the provisions or this Act, and the Commission is of the opinion that further inquiry is called for, it shall inquire into such contravention in accordance with the provisions or this Act.

Comments: In case, the report of the Director General recommends that there is no contravention of the provisions of the Act, the complainant shall be an opportunity to rebut the findings of the Director General. If, after hearing the complainant, the Commission agrees with the recommendations of the Director General, the Commission shall dismiss the complaint. In case, the Commission, after hearing the complainant is of the opinion that further inquiry is required to be conducted, it shall direct the complainant to proceed with the complaint, if the report of the Director General relates to a reference and such report recommends that there is contravention of any of the provisions of the Act; the Commission shall invite the comments from the Central Government or the State Government or the statutory authority, as the case may be, and it shall return the reference if there is no *prima-facie case* or the Commission may proceed with the reference as a complaint if there is a *prima-facie case.*

Orders by Commission after inquiry into agreements or abuse of dominant position

Where after the inquiry the Commission finds that any agreement or action of an enterprise in a dominant position, is in contravention, as the case may be, it may pass all or any of the following orders, namely:

(a) **direct any enterprise** or association of enterprises or person or association of persons, as the case may be, involved in such agreement, or abuse of dominant position, to discontinue and not to re-enter such agreement or discontinue such abuse or dominant position, as the case may be;

(b) **impose such penalty**, as it may deem fit which shall be not more than ten per cent, of the average of the turnover for the last three preceding financial years, upon each of such person or enterprises which are parties to such agreements or abuse.

Any agreement has been entered into by any cartel, the Commission shall impose upon each producer, seller, distributor, trader or service provider included in that cartel, a penalty equivalent to three times of the amount of profits made out of such agreement by the cartel or ten per cent of the average of the turnover of the cartel for the last preceding three financial years, whichever is higher;

(c) **award compensation** to parties in accordance with the provisions contained in section 34;

(d) **direct that the agreements shall stand modified** to the extent and in the manner as may be specified in the order by the Commission;

(e) **direct the enterprises concerned** to abide by such other orders as the Commission may pass and comply with the directions, including payment of costs, if any;

(f) **recommend, to the Central Government** for the division of an enterprise enjoying dominant position;

(g) **pass such other** order as it may deem fit.

Division of enterprise enjoying dominant position

The Central Government, on recommendation may, not withstanding anything contained in any other law for the time being in force, order in writing, direct division of an enterprise enjoying dominant position to ensure that such enterprise does not abuse its dominant position.

In particular, and without prejudice to the generality of the foregoing powers, may order for all or any of the following matters, namely:

(a) the transfer or vesting of property, rights, liabilities or obligations;

(b) the adjustment of contracts either by discharge or reduction of any liability or obligation or otherwise;

(c) the creation, allotment, surrender or cancellation of any shares, stocks or securities;

(d) the payment of compensation to any person who suffered any loss due to dominant position of such enterprise;

(e) the formation or winding up of an enterprise or the amendment of the Memorandum of Association or Articles of Association or any other instruments regulating the business of any enterprise;

(f) the extent to which and the circumstances in which, provisions of the order affecting an enterprise may be altered by the enterprise and the registration thereof; and

(g) any other matter which may be necessary to give effect to the division of the enterprise.

Notwithstanding anything contained in any other law for the time being in force or in any contract or in any Memorandum or Articles of Association, an officer of a company who ceases to hold office as such in consequence of the division of an enterprise shall not be entitled to claim any compensation for such cesser.

Procedure for investigation of combinations

Where the Commission is of the opinion that a combination is likely to cause, or has caused an appreciable adverse effect on competition within the relevant market in India, it shall issue to notice to show cause to the parties to combination calling upon them to respond within thirty days of the receipt of the notice, as to why investigation in respect of such combination should not be conducted.

The Commission, if it is *prima facie* of the opinion that the combination has, or is likely to have, an appreciable adverse effect on competition, it shall, within seven working days from the date of receipt of the response of the parties to the combination, direct the parties to the said combination to publish details of the combination within ten working days of such direction, in such manner, as it thinks appropriate, the combination to the knowledge or information of the public and persons affected or likely to be affected by such combination, The Commission may invite any person or member of the public, affected or likely to be affected by the said combination, to file his written objections, if any, before the Commission within fifteen working days from the date on which the details of the combination were published.

The Commission may, within fifteen working days from the expiry of the period specified, call for such additional or other information as it may deem fit from the parties to the said combination. The additional or other information called for by the Commission shall be furnished by the parties within fifteen days from the expiry of the period specified.

After receipt of all information and within a period of forty-five working days from the expiry of the period specified as above, the Commission shall proceed to deal with the case in accordance with the provisions contained in this Act.

Comments: This section lays down the detailed procedure for investigation of Combinations if the Commission is of the opinion that any combination is likely to cause or has caused an appreciable adverse effect on competition within the relevant market in India.

Orders of Commission on certain combinations

Where the Commission is of the opinion that any combination does not, or is not likely to, have an appreciable adverse effect on competition, it shall by order, approve that combination including the combination in respect of which a notice has been given. Where the Commission is of the opinion that the combination has, or is likely to have, an appreciable adverse effect on competition, it shall direct that the combination shall not take effect.

Where the Commission is of the opinion that the combination has, or is likely to have, an appreciable adverse effect on competition but such adverse effect can be dominated by suitable modification to such combination, it may propose appropriate modification to the combination, to the parties to such combination. The parties, who accept the modification proposed by the Commission, shall carry out such modification within the period specified by the Commission.

If the parties to the combination, who have accepted the modification, fail to carry out the modification within the period specified by the commission, such combination shall be deemed to have an appreciable adverse effect on competition and the Commission shall deal with such combination in accordance with the provisions of this Act. If the parties to the combination do not accept the modification proposed by the Commission, such parties may, within thirty working days of the modification proposed by the Commission, submit amendment to the modification proposed by the Commission.

If the Commission agrees with the amendment submitted by the parties, it shall, by order, approve the combination.

If the Commission does not accept the amendment submitted then, the parties shall be allowed a further period of thirty working days within which such parties shall accept the modification proposed by the Commission.

If the parties fail to accept the modification proposed by the Commission within thirty working days or within a further period of thirty working days the combination shall be deemed to have an appreciable adverse effect on competition and will be dealt with in accordance with the provisions of this Act.

Where the Commission has directed that the combination shall not take effect or the combination is deemed to have an appreciable adverse effect on competition, then, without prejudice to any penalty which may be imposed or any prosecution which may be initiated under this Act, the Commission may order that

(a) the acquisition; or
(b) the acquiring of control; or
(c) the merger or amalgamation shall not be given effect to.

The Commission may, if it considers appropriate, frame a scheme to implement its order.

If the Commission does not, on the expiry of a period of ninety working days from the date of publication pass an order or issue direction the combination shall be deemed to have been approved by the Commission.

Explanation: For the purposes of determining the period of ninety working days specified, the period of thirty working days and a further period of thirty working days specified shall be excluded. Where any extension of time is sought by the parties to the combination, the period of ninety working days shall be reckoned after deducting the extended time granted at the request of the parties.

Where the Commission has ordered a combination to be void, the acquisition or acquiring of control or merger or amalgamation shall be dealt with by the authorities under any other law for the time being in force as if such acquisition or acquiring of control or merger or amalgamation had not taken place and the parties to the combination shall be dealt with accordingly.

Duties of Director General to investigate contravention

The Director General shall, when so directed by the Commission, assist the Commission in investigating into any contravention of the provisions of this Act or any rules or regulations made thereunder, the Director General shall have all the powers as are conferred upon the Commission.

Without prejudice to the provisions of sub-section (2), sections 240 and 240A of the Companies Act, 1956, so far as maybe, shall apply to an investigation made by the Director General or any other person investigating under his authority, as they apply in inspector appointed under that Act.

8.7 COMPETITION ADVOCACY

In formating policy, the Central Government may make a reference to the Commission for its opinion on possible effects of such policy on competition. The Commission is required to give its opinion to the Central Government within sixty days from the date of such reference. Such opinion shall not be binding upon the Central Government, the Commission is also required to take suitable measures for the promotion of competition advocacy creating awareness and imparting training about the competition issues as may be prescribed.

QUESTIONS FOR PRACTICE

Section - A (Two Marks Questions)

1. What is anti-competitive agreement?
2. What is Competition Act?
3. What is 'Combination' under the Competition Act?

Section - B (Five Marks Questions)

1. What are the offences and penalties under the Competition Act?
2. State the duties and functions of the Competition Commission of India.
3. State the objectives of the Competition Act?

Section - C (Fifteen Marks Questions)

1. Explain the salient features of the Competition Act, 2002.
2. Explain the composition, duties, functions, and powers of the Competition Commission of India.

B.Com. (VI Semester)

Model Questions and Answers of Business Law

PART - A

1. Define Business Laws.

Business Law or Mercantile Law of Commercial Law is that branch of general law which regulates the business activities, concerned with the trade, commerce and Industry and regulates the transaction between the traders.

2. What is CONSENSUS-AD-IDEM?

It means, both parties agreeing to do the same thing in the same manner. The parties will have to decide the sequence of performance to avoid inconvenience due to premature performance or delayed performance.

3. What is Obligation?

Obligation is defined as "A legal tie imposing a duty upon the person to the agreement to do or abstain for doing something". Thus an obligation creates a legal tie or legally binds the persons who enter into a contract. It impose a duty to perform.

4. What is free consent?

This consent is said to be free when it is not affected by conditions laid down in section 14. So as per section 14 "consent is said to be free when it is not caused by coercion (section 15), under influence (section16), fraud (section 17), misrepresentation (section 18) and mistake (section 20,21,22)".

5. What is Novation?

Section 62 of the Act deals with novation. Novation means insertion of a new contract in the place of an old contract, before the performance of the contract commences. The new contract can be between the same parties or different parties.

6. Who is a consumer as per the Consumer Protection Act of 1986?

(a) A consumer is a person who buys goods or services for his use.
(b) Any person who buys goods or avails services for commercial purpose is not a consumer.
(c) A consumer should pay the price or agree to pay as per the agreement.
(d) A person who is permitted to use the goods and services by a person who has agreed to pay for it, is a consumer.

7. What is "QUID-PRO-QUO"?

Consideration based on 'QUID-PRO-QUO' i.e., something in return. It is the responsibilities of the parties to get adequate consideration for their sacrifice. If they accept lesser consideration it is nothing but giving an opportunity to be exploited by others, which in other words known as a BAD BARGAIN, for which Law will not come to your rescue.

8. Define "Goods" under Competition Act, 2003.

'Goods' means goods as defined in the Sale of Goods Act, 1930 and includes:

- Products manufactured, processed or mined;
- Debentures stocks and shares after allotment;
- In relation to goods supplied, distributed or controlled in India, goods imported in India [section 2(i)].

According to section 2(7), 'goods' means every kind of movable property other then actionable claims and money; and includes stocks and shares, growing crops, grass and things attached to or forming part of the land which are agreed to be severed before sale or under the contract of sale. Trademarks, copyrights, patent rights, goodwill, electricity, water, gas are all goods.

9. What constitutes an Environment?

Environment section 2(a) 'environment includes water, air, land and their interrelationship which exists among and between water, air, land and human beings, other living beings plants, microorganisms and property'.

10. Who is a Patent Agent?

Patent agent who shall be entitled to practice before the controller and prepare all documents, transact all business and discharge such other function as may be required in the proceedings before the controller.

11. What is an intellectual property right?

Intellectual property means the legal rights which result from intellectual activity in the industrial, scientific, literary and artistic fields.

12. What is foreign exchange?

"Foreign exchange" means foreign currency and includes:

(a) Deposits, credits and balances payable in any foreign currency.
(b) Drafts, travellers' cheque, letters of credit or bills of exchange, expressed or drawn in Indian currency but payable in any foreign currency.
(c) Drafts, travellers' cheque, letters of credit or bills of exchange drawn by banks, institution or persons outside India, but payable in Indian currency [section 2(n)].

PART - B

13. Briefly explain the sources Of Business Law.

Various sources of law can be classified as ancient sources and resent sources. Ancient sources (prior to 16th century) and recent sources (16th century onwards).

Ancient Sources:

(a) **Common Law of England**: Under Common Law of England, king/monarch was supreme authority, his decision were binding on the people, the maxim at that time was **KING DOES NO WRONG**. This was even known as natural of justice as it aims at creating fear complex so that people would not repeat the act. There was not any scope for revising a decision.

(b) **Equity**: Equity is a branch of law developed by learned people who were of , the opinion "every one is innocent till he is proved otherwise", and decisions to be taken only on hearing both parties as there was inconsistency in the decisions of the king in similar situations.

(c) **Statute**: Statute is a branch of law based on "ACTS" passed in various houses of legislature or parliament under the seal of the Government which was authorised to make any alterations, deletions by amendments.

Recent Sources: These are developed by European merchants when they felt that there was a need to protect their trade.

(a) **Lex Mercatoria:** The term Lex Mercatoria means law merchant, it is a branch of law framed and developed by merchants of European Countries in 15th and 16th century. It was a 'code of conduct' for mercantile persons.

(b) **Local Laws:** Any business cannot survive without depending on the society and its customs. As people are abide by local laws. In India the major local laws are,

i. Hindu Law,
ii. Mohammeden Law,
iii. Parsi Law.

(c) **Case Laws:** Case laws are the decisions given by various courts they set guidelines in deciding similar cases and there is scope for improvement when suitable solution is provided for earlier flaws.

14. Write an three differences between coercion and undue influence.

Coercion	Undue Influence
1. Defined under section 15.	1. Defined under section 16(1)(2).
2. Consent given under a threat of an offence (committing of threatening to commit an act forbidden by Indian penal code) or detaining or threatening or detain property unlawfully.	2. Consent given by a person who has a relation with another, the other person is in a position to dominate the will i.e., consent is given under moral influence (mental).
3. There must be an intention of causing any person to enter into an agreement (causing means to give consent).	3. Here the influencing party uses his superior position in the relation to get the unfair advantage over another.
4. It can be committed by party on another or by a stranger on a party or another stranger; it may be either in India or outside India.	4. Strangers have no place in undue influence.
5. Coercion is a criminal offence the person is punished under criminal procedure code when aggrieved party approaches court as per section 19 of the act.	5. Undue influencing is a civil offence and the aggrieved party has to approach the court of law and prove the act, then only he gets the relief under section 19A of the act.

15. State the details of MOHARIBIBI vs DARMADAS case regarding minor

In this case a minor mortgaged his house in favour of a moneylender to secure a loan of ₹20,000/- out of which ₹8,000/- was paid as part payment. Subsequently the minor sued for setting aside the mortgage stating that he was underaged when he signed the mortgage deed. While giving the judgment in this case in 1903, by privy council, **Sir LORD NORTH**, observed contracting parties should be competent to contact and expressedly provide that a person who by reason of infancy is incompetent to contract, cannot make within the meaning of the act, the question whether a contract is void or voidable, presupposes the existence of the contract, within the meaning of the act, and cannot arise in case of an infant.

Ever since this decision there is no doubt regarding to the fact "agreement with a minor is void."

A minor's entry into any type of transaction cannot be denied. When it is entered by him for his benefit. He should be given an opportunity to protect himself.

16. Explain the rights of a consumer under consumer protection Act of 1986.

The following are the rights of the consumer under consumer protection Act of 1986.

(a) Right to be informed about quality, quantity, purity, potency, price, standard of goods or services, so that they are protected from unfair trade practice.
(b) Right to be protected against use of hazardous goods.
(c) Right to have the access to the authority of the goods.
(d) Right to be heard about their grievances.
(e) Right to stop exploitation of consumers.
(f) Right to be educated.
(g) Right of speedy, simple redressal to their disputes.

17. Write a short note on each of the following:

(a) Pollution **(b) Hazardous substance**

Pollution:

Section 2(c) pollution means the presence in the environment of any environment pollutant. Pollution normally takes place in the form of **influx** (allowing the pollutants to mix with the environment) of **extraneous materials** (waste materials in a concentrated state) i.e. without reducing the level of concentration. Pollution has created havoc in the environment.

Hazardous substance:

Section 2(E). It means any substance or preparation which by reason of its chemical or physicochemical properties or handling is liable to cause harm to human beings, other living creatures, plants, microorganisms, property or the environment.

18. Why are the patents lapsed and how they are restored?

(a) The patent may have ceased to have effect by reason of failure to pay any renewal fee within the prescribed period.

(b) The patentee or his legal representative may within one year from the date on which the patent ceased to have effect make an application for the restoration of the patent.

(c) The application can also be made for the patent granted before the commencement of this Act, and lapsed subsequently.

(d) The application shall contain a statement fully setting out the circumstance which led to the failure to pay the prescribed fee.

Restoration of lapsed patent (section 60)

(a) Application for restoration:

A patent may have ceased to have effect by reason of failure to pay any renewal fee within the prescribed period or with in the extended period. In such a case, the patentee or his legal representative may, within one year from the date on which the patent ceased to have effect, make an application for the restoration of the patent.

(b) Application to set out circumstances:

An application for renewal of the patent shall contain a statement fully setting out the circumstance which led to the failure to pay the prescribed fees.

Procedures for disposal of application for restoration of lapsed patent (section 61)

After hearing to the applicant if the controller is satisfied that the failure to pay the renewal fee was unintentional that there has been no under delay in the making of application. In such case he can advertise the application for the renewal of the lapsed patent in the prescribed manner.

Any person interested may give a notice of opposition to the controller within the prescribed period, on the following grounds.

(a) The failure to pay renewal fee was not unintentional.

(b) That there has been under delay in the making of the application.

If no notices of the opposition is given within the period or in the case of opposition, the decision of the controller is in favour of the applicant, the controller can renew the patent.

The restoration shall be made upon payment of any unpaid renewal fee.

19. What is cyber law? State its objectives.

Cyber law is the field of law dealing with computer and the Internet including such issues as intellectual property right, freedom of expression and free accession formation.

Objectives:

(a) To grant legal recognition to transaction carried out by means of electronic data interchange and other means of communication commonly referred to as "Electronic communication" in the place of paper based methods of communication.
(b) To facilitate electronic storage of data.

20. What are the objectives of FEMA?

(a) To regulate certain payments.
(b) To regulate dealings in foreign exchange and securities
(c) To regulate the transaction indirectly affecting foreign exchange.
(d) To regulate import and export of currency and buillion.
(e) For promoting the orderly development and maintenance of foreign exchange market in India.

PART - C

21. Define consideration. Explain the essentials of a valid consideration.

According to Section 2(d) of the act, "when at the desire of the promisor, the promissee or any other person has done or abstained from doing or does or abstains from doing or a promise to do or to abstain from doing, such act or abstinence or promise is called as consideration".

Essentials of a valid consideration:

(a) Consideration will have to move at the instance of promissor:

Any person will have to act only on the basis of instruction of the promissor; The promissor will not be bound by the contract if a person acts at the instance of a 3rd party.

Ref: DURGAPRASAD vs BAL DEO (1880)

Durga Prasad was requested by the collector to effect some repair to the market yard. On the basis of a decision in the meeting of traders with the collector. Who agreed to pay towards expenditure, out of commission earned by them. But when the work was executed, the defendant refused to pay as the work was done not at the instance of promissor. Court upheld the argument of the defendant.

(b) Consideration can also move at the instant of promissor:

As per English law, consideration should move at the instance of promissor.

Ref: TWEEDLE vs ATKINSON

As per Indian law consideration can move even from promisee or a third party also. Indian law aims at consideration, but it is immaterial from whom it is given.

(c) Consideration may be past, present and future:

As per the text of section 2(d) considerations may be past, present or future. But as per English law it can be only present and past consideration is no consideration.

(d) Consideration may be an act or abstinence or forbearance or in return for a promise:

Example: A is indebted to B for ₹10,000/- A fails to pay on the due date. C acts as a surety to A, if B's promise regarding forbearance is an adequate consideration.

(e) Consideration must be real and illusionary:

The object of any consideration is to derive benefit which can be in the form of goods, money, service, which should be tangible. Anything based on imagination is not valid.

(f) Any consideration should not be illegal, immoral, or against public policy:

A contract is an agreement of enforceable under law. In a contract anything which is achieved by the parties should be within the purview of law. So that both parties get mutual benefit. Any act which is detrimental to the interest of any person, or society, is termed illegal, immoral, or any act against the public policy. Such acts do not form valid consideration.

22. What is Public Policy? Explain any four agreements opposed to Public Policy.

Public policy is that principle of law which holds that no subject can lawfully do that which has a mischievous tendency to be injurious to the interests of the public, or which is against the public good or public welfare.

Some of the agreements which are or which have been held to be opposed to public policy and are unlawful are as follows:

(a) Agreements of trading with enemy:

An agreement made with an alien enemy in time of war is illegal on the ground of public policy.

(b) Agreement to commit a crime.

Where the consideration in an agreement is to commit a crime, the agreement is opposed to public policy. The court will not enforce such an agreement.

(c) Agreements which interfere with administration of justice.

An agreement the object of which is to interfere with the administration of Justice is unlawful, being opposed to public policy. It may take any of the following forms:

i. Interference with the course of justice.
ii. Stifling prosecution.
iii. Maintenance and champerty.

(d) Agreements in restraint of legal proceedings.

Section 28 which deals with these agreements renders void two kinds of agreements, viz.,

i. Agreements restricting enforcement of rights.
ii. Agreements curtailing period of limitation.

(e) Trafficking in public offices and titles.

Agreements for the sale or transfer of public offices and titles or for the procurement of a public recognition like Padma Vibhushan or Param Veer Chakra for monetary consideration are unlawful, being opposed to public policy.

(f) Agreements tending to create interest opposed to duty.

If a person enters into an agreement whereby he is bound to do something which is against his public or professional duty, the agreement is void on the ground of public policy.

(g) Agreements in restraint of parental rights.

A father, and in his absence the mother, is the legal guardian of his/her minor child. This right of guardianship cannot be bartered away by any agreement.

(h) Agreements restricting personal liberty.

Agreements which unduly restrict the personal freedom of the parties to it are void as being against public policy.

(i) Agreements in restraint of marriage.

Every agreement in restraint of the marriage of any person, other than a minor, is void (section 26). This is because the law regards marriage and married status as the right of every individual.

(j) Marriage brokerage or brocage agreements.

An agreement by which a person, for a monetary consideration, promises in return to procure the marriage of another is void, being opposed to public policy.

(k) **Agreements interfering with marital duties.**

(l) **Agreements to defraud creditors or revenue authorities.**

(m) **Agreements in restraint of trade.**

23. What is consumer dispute? Briefly explain the composition and working of the various redressal agencies.

As per section 2(1)(e) consumer dispute means a dispute where the person against whom a complaint has been made, denies or disputes the allegations contained in the complaint.

Consumer Disputes Redressal Forum, The District Forum (Section 10 to 15)

Composition: Each district forum shall consist of:

(a) A person who is, or has been, or is qualified to be a district judge, who shall be its president.

(b) Two other members who shall be persons of ability, integrity and standing, and have adequate knowledge or experience of, or have shown capacity in dealing with, problem relating to economics, law, commerce, accountancy, industry, public affair or administration, one of whom shall be a woman.

Manner of complaint (Section 12):

A complaint in relation to any goods sold or delivered or agreed to be sold or delivered or any service provided or agreed to be provided, may be filed with a District Forum.

Procedure on receipt of complaint (Section 13):

Complaint relating to goods. Reference of complaint to opposite party.

The district forum shall, on receipt of a complaint, if it relates to any goods, refer a copy of the complaint to the opposite party mentioned in the complaint. Further it shall direct the opposite party to give his version of the case within a period of 30 days. This period may be extended by a further period not exceeding 15 days as may be granted by the District Forum.

Denial of allegation

Where the opposite party on receipt of a complaint referred to him denies or disputes the allegations contained in the complaint, or omits or fails to take any action to represent his case within the time given by the District Forum, the District Forum shall proceed to settle the consumer dispute in the following manner:

(a) **Reference of sample to laboratory where the complaint alleges a defect in the goods which cannot be determined without proper analysis or test of the goods.** In such case the district forum shall obtain a sample of the goods from the complainant, seal it and authenticate it and refer the samples so sealed to the appropriate laboratory for an analysis or test which ever may be necessary.

The direction for such analysis or test shall be made with a view to finding out whether such goods suffer from any defect alleged in the complaint or suffer from any other defect. The laboratory shall report its findings to the District Forum within a period of 45 days of the receipt of the reference or within such extended period as may be granted by the District Forum.

(b) **Deposit of fees.** Before any sample of the goods is referred to any appropriate laboratory for analysis or test, the District Forum may require the complainant to deposit to the credit of the Forum such fees as may be specified.

Such fees are meant for payment to the appropriate laboratory for carrying out the necessary analysis or test in relation to the goods in question.

(c) **Remission of fees to laboratory and forwarding of report to opposite party.** The District Forum shall remit the amount of fee deposited to its credit to the appropriate laboratory to enable it to carry out the analysis or test. On receipt of the report from the appropriate laboratory. The District Forum shall forward a copy of the report along with such remarks as the District Forum may feel appropriate to the opposite party.

(d) **Objections by any of the parties.** If any of the parties disputes the correctness of the findings of the appropriate laboratory, or disputes the correctness of the methods of analysis or test adopted by the appropriate laboratory, the District Forum shall require the opposite party or the complainant to submit in writing his objections in regard to the report made by the appropriate laboratory.

(e) **Reasonable opportunity to parties of being heard and issue of order.** The District Forum shall give a reasonable opportunity to the complaint as well as the opposite party of being heard as to the correctness or otherwise of the report made by the appropriate laboratory and also as to the objection made in relation thereto. Thereafter, it shall issue an appropriate order under section 14.

Complaint relating services. Reference of claim to opposite party.

If the complaint received by the District Forum relates to any services (or to goods in respect of which the procedure specified above cannot be followed), the District Forum shall refer a copy of such complaint to the opposite party directing him to give his version of the case within a period of 30 days or such extended period not exceeding 15 days as may be granted by the District Forum.

Denial etc. of allegation by the opposite party.

The opposite party may, on receipt of a copy of the complaint, deny or dispute the allegations contained in the complaint or omit or fail to take any action to represent his case within the time given by the district forum. Proceedings of the District Forum final. The proceedings complying with the procedure laid down above cannot be called in question in any court on the ground that the principles of natural justice have not been complied with.

The State Commission - Section 16 To 19:

(a) **Composition** (Sec. 16) Each state commission shall consist of

i. A person who is or has been a judge of a high court, appointed the State Government, who shall be its president. However, no appointment under this clause shall be made except after consultation with Chief Justice of the High Court;

ii. Two other members, who shall be persons of ability, integrity and standing and have adequate knowledge or experience of, or have shown capacity in dealing with, problems relating to economics, law, commerce, accountancy, industry, public affairs or administration. One of these members shall be a woman.

(b) **Jurisdiction** (Sec. 17) the State Commission shall have jurisdiction,

i. To entertain -

A. Complaints where the value of the goods or services and compensation, if any, claimed exceeds ₹Five lakh but does not exceed ₹20 lakhs; and

B. appeals against the orders of any District "Forum within the State" and

ii. to call for the records and pass appropriate orders in any consumer dispute which is ponding before or has been decided by any district forum within the State where it appears to the State Commission that such District Forum

A. has exercised a jurisdiction not vested in it by law,

B. has failed to exercise a jurisdiction so vested, or

C. has acted in exercise of its jurisdiction illegally or with material irregularity.

National Consumer Disputes Redressal Commission

(a) **Composition** (Sec. 20). The National Commission shall consists of

i. A person who is or has been a judge of the Supreme Court, to be appointed by the government, who shall be its president.

However, no appointment under this clause shall be made except after consultation with the chief justice of India.

ii. Four other members who shall be persons of ability, integrity and standing and have adequate knowledge or experience of, or have shown capacity in dealing with problems relating to economics, law, commerce, accountancy, industry, public affairs or administration. One of these members shall be a woman.

(b) **Jurisdiction** (Sec.21). Subject to the other provision of this Act, the National Commission shall have jurisdiction

i. To entertain

A. Complaints where the value of the goods or services and compensation, if any, claimed exceeds ₹20 lakh, and

B. appeals against the orders of any State Commission; and

ii. to call for the records and pass appropriate orders in any consumer dispute which is pending before or has been decided by any State Commission where it appears to the National Commission that such State Commission.

24. Explain the role of the Central Government in protecting the environment.

Powers of the Central Government:

The Central Government is empowered as per this Act to take such measures as are necessary too. Protect and improve the quality of the environment prevent control and obtaining, environmental pollution. Section 3 to 6 of the act specify to measures to protect and improve the quality of environment.

Measures to protect and improve environment (Sec.3)

Central Government ensures co-ordination of actions by the State governments, officers and other authorities in respect of the objects of the act.

(a) Planning and execution of a nationwide programme for the prevention, control and abatement of environmental pollution;

(b) laying down standards for the quality of environment in its various aspects;

(c) Laying down standards for emission or discharge of environmental pollutants from various sources whatsoever. Different standards for emission or discharge from different sources may be laid down having regard to the quality or composition of the emission or discharge of environmental pollutants from such sources;

(d) restriction of areas in which any industries, operations or processes or class of industries, operation, or processes shall not be carried out or shall be carried out subject to certain safeguards;

(e) laying down

i. procedures and safeguards for the prevention of accidents which may cause environmental pollution; and

ii. remedial measures for such accidents;

(f) laying down procedures and safeguards for the handling of hazardous substances;

(g) examination of such manufacturing processes, materials and substances as are likely to cause environmental pollution;

(h) Carrying out and sponsoring investigations and research relating to problems of environmental pollution;

(i) Inspection of any premises, plant, equipment, machinery, manufacturing or other processes, materials or substances. The inspection is to be done with a view to giving directions to authorities and officers to take steps for the prevention, control and abatement of environmental pollution;

(j) Establishment or recognition of environmental laboratories and institutes to carry out the functions entrusted to such environmental laboratories and institutes under this Act;

(k) Collection and dissemination of information in respect of matters relating to environmental pollution;

(l) Preparation of manuals, codes or guides relating to the prevention, control and abatement of environmental pollution;

(m) Such other matters as the central government deems necessary or expedient for the purpose of securing the effective implementation of the provisions of this Act.

Mention the objectives of Environment Protection Act 1986.

Environment Protection Act, 1986 came into effect on 9th November 1988 with the following objectives.

(a) To co-ordinate the activities other various regulatory agencies already in existence.

(b) Creating an authority or authorities with adequate power for environmental protection.

(c) Regulation of discharge of environmental pollutions and handling of hazardous substances.

(d) Speedy response in the event of accidents threatening environmental equilibrium and different punishment to those who endanger human and environmental safety health.

25. Explain the duties, power and functions of competition Commission of India.

Section 3(1) of 4(1) either on its own motion or on receipt of a complaint from any person, consumer or their association or trade association or on a reference made to it by the central government or a state government or a statutory authority alleging violation of any of those provisions. In future lays down the factors which shall be considered by the Commission for the purpose of determining whether an agreement has an appreciable adverse effect on competition whether an enterprise enjoys the dominant position, or whether a market constitutes a relevant market for the purpose of the Act.

The Commission shall, while determining whether an agreement has an appreciable adverse effect on competition under section 3, have due regard to all or any of the alloying factors, namely.

(a) Certain barriers to new entrants in the market,
(b) Driving existing competitors out of the market,
(c) Foreclosure by competition by hindering entry into the market,
(d) Accrual of benefits of consumers,
(e) Improvements on production or distribution of goods or provision of services; or
(f) Promotion of technical, scientific and economic development by means of production or distribution of goods or provision of services [Section 19(3)].

The Commission shall, while inquiring whether an enterprise enjoys a dominant position or not under section 4, have due regards to or any of the following factors, namely;

(a) Market share of the enterprise;
(b) Size and resources of the enterprise;
(c) Size and importance of the competitors;
(d) Economic power of the enterprise including commercial advantage over competitors;
(e) Vertical integrations of the enterprise or sale or service network of such enterprise;
(f) Dependers on consumers on the enterprise;
(g) Monopoly or dominated position whether acquired as a result of any statute or by virtue of being a government company or a public sector undertaking or otherwise;
(h) Entry barriers such as regulatory barriers, financial risk, high capital, cost of entry, marketing entry barriers, technical entry barriers, economies in scale, high cost of substitutable goods or services for customers.
(i) Countervailing buying power;
(j) Market structure and size of market;

(k) Social obligations and social costs;

(l) Relative advantage, by way of the contribution to the economic development, by the enterprise enjoying a dominant position having or likely to have appreciable adverse effect on competition;

(m) Any other factor which the Commission may consider relevant for the inquiry [Section 19(4)]

For determining whether a market constitutes a "relevant market" for the purposes of this Act, the Commission shall have due regard to the "Relevant geographic market" or "Relevant product market".

The Commission shall, while determining the "Relevant geographic market", have due regard to all or any of the following factors namely.

(a) Regulatory trade barriers;

(b) Local specification requirements;

(c) National procurement policies;

(d) Adequate distribution facilities;

(e) Transport costs;

(f) Language;

(g) Consumer preferences;

(h) Need for secure or regular supplies or rapid after sales services [section 19(6)]

The commission shall, while determining the "Relevant product Market", have due regard to all or any of the following factors, namely;

(a) Physical characteristics or end-use of goods;

(b) Price of goods or services;

(c) Consumer preferences;

(d) Exclusion of in-house production;

(e) Existence of specialised producers;

(f) Classification of industrial products. [Section 19(7)]

Index

A
Acceptance,
  communication of, 23
  definition of, 19
  meaning of, 19
Adjudication, 188
Admission of complaint,
  procedure on, 131
Alien, 39
Appellate Tribunal,
  powers & procedure of, 191

B
Business law,
  definitions of, 2
  essentials of, 3
  meaning of, 2
  scope of, 2, 4

C
Central Consumer Protection Council, 123
  objects of, 125
  procedure for, 125
Certain agreements,
  prohibition of, 203
Certifying authorities,
  duties of, 187
  regulation of, 185
Coercion, 41
  essentials of, 42
Companies Act, 1956, 122
Competition Act, 2002, 199,
  definitions of, 200
Competition advocacy, 221
Competition Commission of India (CCI), 209
  duties of, 212
  functions of, 212
  powers of, 212
Consensus ad idem, 9
Consideration,
  definition of, 25
  meaning of, 25
  need for, 26
  legal rules of, 26
Consumer Disputes Redressal Agencies,
  119, 127
  establishment of, 127
Consumer Protection Act, 1986,
  background of, 117
  definitions of, 120
  objectives of, 119
Consumer Protection Council, 123
Consumer rights,
  emergency of, 117
Contingent contracts, 82
  essential characteristics of, 83
  rules of, 83
Contracts,
  capacity to, 34
  classification of, 11
  definition of, 8
  discharge of, 69

meaning of, 8
performance of, 62
remedies for, 75
specific performance of, 81
stranger to, 30
Convict, 39
Corporation, 39
Counter offers, 19
Cross offers, 19
Cyber law,
definition of, 171
meaning of, 171
need of, 172
scope of, 172
Cyber Laws and Information Technology Act, 2000,
introduction & background of, 171
Cyber Regulations Appellate Tribunal, 190
appeal to, 191
Cyber Revelations Advisory Committee, 195

D

Damages,
rules of, 78
suit for, 77
Dealings in foreign exchange,
restrictions of, 158
Digital Copy Right Bill, 2000, 197
Digital signature certification, 187
Digital signature,
suspension of, 188
Discharge,
types of, 70
District Consumer Protection Council, 126
objects of, 127
District Forum,
composition of, 128
findings of, 134
jurisdiction of, 129
limitation period of, 130
powers of, 134
Duress, 43

E

Electronic governance, 180
Electronic records,
dispatch of, 184
English business law, 4
Environment pollution,
entry of, 112
inspection of, 112
prevention of, 112, 114
protection of, 112
Environment Protection Act, 1986,
background of, 109
definitions of, 109
objectives of, 110

F

Fact,
mistake of, 52
Foreign Exchange Management Act, 1999 (FEMA),
introduction & background of, 151
enactment of, 152
regulation & management of, 154
salient features of, 152
Fraud, 46
essentials of, 47
Free consent,
definition of, 40
meaning of, 40

G

Guardians and Wards Act 1980, 34

H

Hazardous substance, 113
Human Development Report, 1998, 118

I

Indian business law,
source of, 4
Indian Contract Act, 1872, 7
Indian Majority Act, 1875, 34
Indian Panel Code 1860, 41
Information and Technology Act, 2000, 181
Infringement, 105
Injunction, 82
Insolvent, 39

Intellectual property legislations,
background of, 99
meaning of, 99
Intellectual Property Rights, 106
International Organization of Consumers Union, 117
Internet frauds, 173

J

Justice,
administration of, 1

L

Law,
mistake of, 51
persons disqualified by, 38
Legal rules, 16, 20
Licence,
conditions of, 165

M

Mastermind web frauds, 175
Minors, 34
liability for necessaries, 37
Misrepresentation, 49
essentials of, 50
Mistake, 51

N

National Commission,
composition of, 141
jurisdiction of, 144
power and procedure of, 144
term of, 143
Network services, 194

O

Object,
legality of, 54
Offences, 192
Offer,
communication of, 22
definition of, 14
meaning of, 14
types of, 15

P

Partnership Act, 1932, 61
Patent Act, 1970, 99
application of, 102
objectives of, 100
definitions of, 100
salient features of, 100
specifications of, 101
Patents (section 53),
lapse of, 104
opposition to grant of, 103
revocation of, 105
surrender of, 104
term of, 103
Penalties, 188
Performance,
rules relating to, 62
Presiding officer,
resignation and removal of, 190
Public policy,
agreements opposed to, 57

Q

Quantum meruit, 80
Quasi contracts, 89
types of, 89

R

Reciprocal promises, 66
Rescission, 76
Revocation, 23
communication of, 24
notice of, 24

S

Sale of Goods Act, 1930, 123
Secure digital signatures, 185
Secure electronic records, 185
State Commission,
composition of, 136
jurisdiction of, 139
process of appointment, 137
State Consumer Protection Council, 125
objects of, 126

Subscribers,
duties of, 188

T

Tenders, 18

U

Undue influence, 43
essentials of, 44
United Nations Charter of Human Rights, 118
Unsound mind,
persons of, 37

V

Valid contract,
essential elements of, 9

W

Wagering agreements, 85
essentials of, 86
exceptions of, 88
Water Pollution Act, 1974, 114
World Consumer Rights Day, 117